"Rick Bensignor has gathered together twelve of the top individuals in the field of technical analysis. Their methods and vast experience **will open your mind to new opportunities**."
EDWARD J. SOLARI
Vice President and Senior Foreign Exchange Advisor
BMO Nesbitt Burns

"A compendium of methodologies from recognized practitioners in technical analysis, *New Thinking* **presents precise strategy platforms for today's traders**."
LOUISE YAMADA
Managing Director and head of Technical Research
Salomon Smith Barney

"The increasing importance of technical analysis in the contemporary marketplace is dramatically highlighted by this new compendium from a dozen top technical analysts. Traditional techniques are presented side-by-side with current innovations, giving the reader **a broad view of technical analysis**."
JOHN BOLLINGER, CFA, CMT
President and founder, Bollinger Capital

"*New Thinking in Technical Analysis* **will someday be viewed as a classic** because it opens the eyes of veteran traders to new methods. Rick deserves a lot of credit for having the foresight to put this book together."
BILL ABRAMS
Former Specialist on the New York Stock Exchange

"Rick Bensignor has put together a significant new book filled with methodologies from **some of the best names in the trading business**."
BENNETT MOSTEL
Senior Vice President
Prudential Securities

"Baseball legend Yogi Berra once commented, 'You can observe a lot by just looking.' With *New Thinking,* Rick Bensignor has scored **a home run** in that the collaborative wisdom of the assembled team offers a valuable insight for new entrants and market veterans alike."
JASON PERL
Associate Director and Technical Analyst
UBS Warburg (London)

New Thinking
in
Technical
Analysis

Also available from
BLOOMBERG PRESS

Thriving as a Broker in the 21st Century
by Thomas J. Dorsey

Tom Dorsey's Trading Tips:
A Playbook for Stock Market Success
by Thomas J. Dorsey and the DWA Analysts

Investing in Hedge Funds:
Strategies for the New Marketplace
by Joseph G. Nicholas

Market-Neutral Investing:
Long/Short Hedge Fund Strategies
by Joseph G. Nicholas

Small-Cap Dynamics:
Insights, Analysis, and Models
by Satya Dev Pradhuman

—■—

A complete list of our titles is available at
www.bloomberg.com/books

ATTENTION CORPORATIONS

Bloomberg Press books are available at quantity discounts with bulk purchase for sales promotional use and for corporate education or other business uses. Special editions or book excerpts can also be created. For information, please call 609-279-4670 or write to: Special Sales Dept., Bloomberg Press, P.O. Box 888, Princeton, NJ 08542.

BLOOMBERG ® WEALTH MANAGER magazine is the premiere
professional information resource for independent financial planners and
investment advisers who are serving clients of high net worth.
See wealth.bloomberg.com or call 1-800-681-7727.

BLOOMBERG PROFESSIONAL LIBRARY

New Thinking
in
Technical
Analysis

∎

TRADING MODELS FROM
THE MASTERS

Edited by
RICK BENSIGNOR

BLOOMBERG PRESS
PRINCETON

First edition published 2000
5 7 9 10 8 6 4

Bensignor, Rick, editor
New thinking in technical analysis: trading models from the masters /edited by Rick Bensignor;
contributing authors, Linda Bradford Raschke . . . [et al.].
p. cm. — (Bloomberg professional library)
Includes index.
ISBN 1-57660-049-1 (alk. paper)
1. Investment analysis. I. Bensignor, Rick. II. Bradford Raschke, Linda. III. Series
HG4529.N49   2000
332.6—dc21   00-057179
                                                              CIP

Book Design by Laurie Lohne / Design It Communications

Fifty years ago most investors suffered from a lack of useful information and approached the stock market with a certain fear because of it. Today the investment environment is overloaded with information, and a major problem facing investors is sifting the useful from the useless. Another issue is that good companies aren't always good stocks and bad companies sometimes are profitable investments. Time is limited and we are all searching for a way to understand complex material quickly and draw conclusions from it.

Over the years I have found technical analysis helpful to me both as an investor and as a strategist. It enables me to grasp the psychological factors that are so important in determining the market's or a stock's performance. Rick Bensignor has assembled an impressive group of expert practitioners whose chapters will help both the layman and the professional understand the origins, development, and current applications for technical analysis. It is not sorcery; it is a valuable craft. If you apply the lessons well, technical tools will help you make more money in the stock market in good times and limit your losses when times get rough.

BYRON R. WIEN
Chief U.S. Investment Strategist
Morgan Stanley

Contents

3 APPLYING MOVING AVERAGES TO POINT AND FIGURE CHARTS 47

Kenneth G. Tower

4 SPOTTING EARLY REVERSAL SIGNALS USING CANDLE CHARTS 63

Steve Nison

About the Contributors

Editor **Rick Bensignor** is a vice president and senior technical strategist at Morgan Stanley. He is also an adjunct professor at New York University's School of Continuing and Professional Studies, where he teaches technical analysis. Formerly he was Bloomberg LP's senior product specialist for technical analysis, futures, and commodities, following a fourteen-year career as a floor trader on several New York futures exchanges. The author of a chapter contribution to *Investor's Business Daily Guide to the Markets,* Mr. Bensignor has written extensively for *BLOOMBERG® MARKETS* magazine and is a popular speaker at industry conferences.

Linda Bradford Raschke, the president of LBRGroup, began her career trading equity options as a member of the Pacific Coast Stock Exchange. In 1984, she became a member of the Philadelphia Stock Exchange, where she continued to be a self-employed trader of equities, options, and futures. In the early 1990s, she started LBRGroup and later became a registered Commodity Trading Advisor. Currently the director and principal trader for the Watermark Fund Ltd., she manages a commercial hedging program in the metals markets. She was featured in Jack Schwager's *New Market Wizards,* and also in Sue Herera's *Women of the Street: Making it on Wall Street—The World's Toughest Business.* Ms. Bradford Raschke also runs an online education trading site where she shows trades real time made for her own account and provides market commentary. A sought-after speaker at investment conferences across the nation, she serves on the Board of Directors of the Market Technician's Association and is a coauthor of *Street Smarts—High Probability Short Term Trading Strategies.*

Tom DeMark is president of Market Studies Inc., a supplier of proprietary market timing indicators to various electronic data networks and vendors. On the institutional level, the indicators are available on Bloomberg as well as through other major networks. Mr. DeMark also serves as a consultant to large hedge funds. Currently he is a consultant to SAC Capital Funds. Previously, Mr. DeMark was executive vice president of Tudor, a multi-million dollar hedge fund, and CPO partner with Van Hosington, a multibillion dollar bond fund manager. He was also a special adviser to Leon Cooperman, a four billion dollar hedge fund manager; former partner of Charlie DiFrancesca, one of the largest individual traders on the Chicago Board of Trade; and chairman of Logical Information Machines, Inc., an institutional software provider. He has been a consultant to large financial institutions including Soros, Morgan Bank, Citibank, Goldman Sachs, IBM, and Union Carbide. Mr. DeMark is the author of *DeMark on Day Trading Options, New Market Timing Techniques: Innovative Studies in Market Rhythm & Price Exhaustion,* and *The New Science of Technical Analysis.* The subject of numerous feature and cover story articles in many widely read financial magazines, he appears regularly on television and radio as well as at seminars both domestically and internationally.

Peter Eliades, who began his financial career as a stock broker, appeared as a market analyst for several years on Los Angeles television station KWHY, the nation's first financial TV station, beginning in 1973. Several times in the fall of 1974, in a market that had seen the average share of stock drop for almost six years since December 1968, he predicted on KWHY that a major market bottom would occur during the week of December 9–13, 1974. The exact Dow low of 570.01 occurred on December 9, 1974. As a result of that spectacular and well-noted forecast, he began publishing *Stockmarket Cycles* in 1975. In 1985, the first year he was rated by the independent rating services, Mr. Eliades earned *Timer Digest's* Timer of the Year award, and he placed second in 1986 in a close race not decided until the final trading day of the year. In 1989 *Hulbert Financial Digest* named Mr. Eliades as the "Most Consistent Mutual Fund Switcher" based on Eliades' timing signals for the years 1985, 1986, 1987, and 1988. From January 1985 through August 1990, *Stockmarket Cycles* had the number one market timing record in the country, with a timing gain of 174.3 percent versus a comparable gain in the Wilshire 5000 Total Return Index of 119 percent. Mr. Eliades repeated that winning performance again from June 1986 through June 1996. Over that ten-year period, Stockmarket Cycles' Fidelity Select mutual fund portfolio was the winner by a very substantial margin over all the other rated mutual fund portfolios in the country, as recorded in the September 1996 *AAII* (American Association of Individual Investors) *Journal.* Mr. Eliades has been a regular panelist on ABC's *Business World* and has made frequent guest appearances on FNN, CNBC, *Wall Street Week, Larry King Live,* and *Nightly Business Report.* He has been featured in numerous publications including *Barron's, The Wall Street Journal, Forbes,* and *Futures* magazine. In recent years, Mr. Eliades has directed his attention to the development of trading systems, but has remained deeply involved with studying and developing technical indicators for analyzing the stock market.

Lawrence McMillan is recognized as an options trading industry expert, and serious investors have relied on his insights, observations, and recommendations for years. As president of McMillan Analysis Corporation, he authors the *Daily Volume Alerts*, a unique daily fax service that selects short-term stock trades by looking for unusual increases in equity option volume, and edits and publishes *The Option Strategist,* a derivative products newsletter covering equity, index, and futures options. He serves as editor of *The Daily Strategist* newsletter. Mr. McMillan has a short term stock and option trading Web site at www.option-strategist.com and is a popular speaker on option strategies at numerous traders conferences, seminars, and colloquiums in the United States, Canada, and Europe. He is the author of two best-selling books, *Options as a Strategic Investment* and *McMillan on Options* and coauthor of *The Conservative Investor's Guide to Trading Options.* From 1982 to 1989 Mr. McMillan was senior vice president in charge of equity arbitrage at Thomson McKinnon Securities, Inc., and from 1989 to 1990 was in charge of the Proprietary Option Trading Department at Prudential Bache Securities.

Robin Mesch of Robin Mesch Associates works with traders worldwide instructing them in the art of reading and comprehending the language of the markets through her market commentary and her customized on-line educational programs. Her unique approach combines Market Profile and Drummond Geometry as the cornerstone of her trading methodology. She is recognized as a leading authority on the fixed-income markets. She is regularly featured on CNBC and has been profiled in such books as *Bulls, Bears, and Millionaires, The Outer Game of Trading, The Day Trader's Advantage, The Tao of Trading,* and *Women of the Pits.* Ms. Mesch is one of a few recognized experts on Market Profile and Drummond Geometry and has had extensive personal study with their founders. Her work with Pete Steidlmayer, creator of Market Profile, includes serving as the editor of his recent book *141 West Jackson, A Journey Through Market Discovery.* With Charles Drummond, she facilitated the formulation of his ideas into a software product now available through Omega Trade Station. To find out more about Robin Mesch, her market commentary, and her instructional services, readers may log onto her Web site at robinmesch.com.

John Murphy, the technical analyst for CNBC-TV for seven years, has been a professional market analyst for over twenty-five years. He is the author of the best-sellers *Technical Analysis of the Financial Markets: A Comprehensive Guide to Trading Methods and Applications, The Visual Investor: How to Spot Market Trends,* and *Intermarket Technical Analysis: Trading Strategies for the Global Stock, Bond, Commodity and Currency Markets.* Mr. Murphy heads his own consulting firm based in New Jersey and is also president of MURPHYMORRIS.COM, which was created to produce educational software products and online services for investors. A speaker at financial conferences around the world, he is also frequently quoted in the financial media. In addition to CNBC-TV appearances, he has been interviewed on *Wall Street Week with Louis Rukeyser, Nightly Business Report,* and CNN's *Moneyline.* Mr. Murphy has served on the Board of Directors of the Market Technicians Association and has taught on the faculty of the New York Institute of Finance. Considered to be the world's leading expert on intermarket analysis, he was given the first award for contribution to global technical analysis at the Fifth World Congress of the International Federation of Technical Analysts in 1992.

Steve Nison, CMT, is president of Nison Research International, Inc. (NRI) and is acknowledged as the first to reveal the method of Japanese technical analysis known as "candle charts" to the West. He is the internationally recognized authority on the subject and is credited with revolutionizing technical analysis through his introduction of these methods in the United States and throughout Europe. He is the author of two internationally acclaimed books, *Japanese Candlestick Charting Techniques* and *Beyond Candlesticks,* which have been translated into eight languages. Mr. Nison has been featured in the *Wall Street Journal, Barron's, Institutional Investor, Euroweek,* and many other financial publications. He has addressed audiences throughout the world, including the Federal Reserve and the World Bank. Through NRI, Mr. Nison specializes in Web-based and on-site seminars and advisory services to institutions. Readers may visit his Web site at www.candlecharts.com or e-mail him at nison@candlesharts.com.

Steven Poser is president of Poser Global Market Strategies, Inc., an international markets advisory firm. Prior to forming Poser Global Market Strategies Inc., Mr. Poser worked for more than a decade at Deutsche Bank Securities in New York City as a technical strategist, following earlier experiences as a computer analyst in the fixed income research department and then as coordinator of quantitative research. Well known for his ability to combine fundamental and technical information to weave a cohesive world markets outlook, he has achieved numerous kudos for his prescient calls on the U.S. bond, currency, and stock markets. A regular guest on CNBC, CNNfn, and Reuters Financial Television, he is frequently quoted by the wire services. Mr. Poser's writings have appeared widely in the financial press, including *Forbes, Barrons, Futures* magazine, and *The International Financing Review.* During 1996, Mr. Poser took highest honors in Bridge Financial's trading game. He teaches general markets and technical analysis courses for the New York Institute of Finance and was a featured speaker at the TAG 21 technical analysis conference, the largest and oldest technical analysis conference in the United States.

Bernie Schaeffer began publishing *The Option Advisor* monthly newsletter in 1981. As senior editor, he aspired to show traders how they could use options to discover profit opportunities in both stable and volatile markets. Today, as chairman and CEO of Schaeffer's Investment Research, Mr. Schaeffer has guided the monthly publication to growth and success as the nation's largest circulation options newsletter. Along with developing the newsletter, several recommendation services, and SchaeffersResearch.com, he has authored *The Option Advisor: Wealth-Building Techniques Using Equity & Index Options.* Mr. Schaeffer's thriving approach to market timing has earned him a "Best of the Best" award in the field of Sentiment Analysis from the Market Technician's Association, as well as a number-five market timing ranking from *Timer Digest* over the past decade. The *Dick Davis Digest's* Hall of Fame inducted Mr. Schaeffer as a member for his bearish posture ahead of the 1987 crash. Many also know him for maintaining a bullish market posture throughout the 1990s. Widely recognized as an expert on equity and index options and investor sentiment, he writes monthly options columns for *BLOOMBERG PERSONAL FINANCE*™ magazine and CNBC.com. The financial news media, including *Nightly Business Report, Business Week, Investor's Business Daily,* and *USA Today,* frequently seek his views on the stock market and the economy. Additionally, Mr. Schaeffer is a three-time winner of *The Wall Street Journal's* stock picking contest and is a CNBC Market Maven.

Courtney Smith is currently president and chief investment officer of Courtney Smith & Co. (courtneysmithco.com), a company that has been providing investment management services for individuals and institutions since 1990. He is also president and chief investment officer of Pinnacle Capital Strategies,

Inc., which manages hedge funds. The flagship fund is the Macro Fund, which has built a compound return of over 23 percent per year for almost five years with virtually no correlation with the stock market or other hedge funds. He is the editor of *Courtney Smith's Hotlist* as well as *Courtney Smith's Wall Street Winners* newsletter. Mr. Smith is the owner and editor-in-chief of *Commodity Traders Consumer Reports* (CTCR) (ctcr.investors.net). CTCR is considered the premier tracking service for the futures industry as well as the most prestigious publication for futures trading insights, and has been providing insights to the futures community since 1983. He also was the chief investment strategist and officer of Orbitex Management, Inc., which manages and administers over $5 billion in mutual funds and portfolios for institutions and individuals. Mr. Smith is the author of a number of books, including *Option Strategies, Profits Through Seasonal Trading; Commodity Spreads, How To Make Money In Stock Index Futures;* and *Seasonal Charts for Futures Traders.* He has been a featured speaker at investment conferences throughout North America and Europe, and has appeared many times on such national television shows as *Wall Street Journal Report* and *Moneyline* as well as other shows on CBS, Fox News, BLOOMBERG TELEVISION®, CNN, and CNNfn.

Kenneth G. Tower, CMT, is vice president and chief market strategist at UST Securities Corporation and a member and former president of the Market Technicians Association (MTA). He has been a contributor to the *MTA Journal,* as well as speaker at the 11th Annual MTA Seminar. Mr. Tower has also been a guest lecturer on technical analysis at the College of New Jersey, Pace University, and Rutgers University as well as at various regional chapters of the MTA and the American Association for Investment Management and Research (AIMR). He has been widely acknowledged for his contribution to Dr. Martin Zweig's best-selling book, *Winning On Wall Street,* and contributed to the point and figure section of John Murphy's *Technical Analysis of the Financial Markets.* Mr. Tower appears frequently as a guest speaker on CNBC, CNNfn, Reuters TV, BLOOM-BERG TELEVISION®, BLOOMBERG RADIO™, and AP Radio financial programs and is often quoted in the financial press.

Larry Williams has thirty-five years of trading experience, during which he has set several trading records, including winning the World Cup Trading Championship by taking $10,000 to $1.1 million in real-time trades. Ten years later, his sixteen-year-old daughter won the same contest with the second highest gain ever recorded. Mr. Williams was the first recipient of the Omega Research Lifetime Achievement award as well as *Futures* magazine's Doctor of Futures accolade. He also has served on the Board of Directors of the National Futures Exchanges. He is perhaps best known for his short-term trading seminars, where he trades $1 million in real time, then giving 20 percent of the profits to attendees. He publishes several newsletters and is the author of seven books, including *Long-Term Secrets to Short-Term Trading, Day Trade Futures Online,* and *The Definitive Guide to Futures Trading.*

Acknowledgments

I take this opportunity to express gratitude to all the authors for their contributed chapters. In particular, I want to thank my mentor, Tom DeMark, for his guidance, patience, willingness to share market knowledge, and most of all, his very valued friendship. I would also like to extend my appreciation to the students who have taken my course at NYU, for continually inspiring me with their enthusiasm.

A creative project of this scope and magnitude inevitably involves the participation of a number of key behind-the-scenes operators as well, and this book is no exception. Special thanks to Andy Bekoff, who was hugely instrumental and supportive in the early stage of the book development process. Much credit is due the incredibly talented and dedicated production team of JoAnne Kanaval and Laurie Lohne for their skilled chart work and book design. Thanks also to John Kreuter and James Rolle for technical assistance. On the editorial side, recognition is due the versatile talents of editors Heather Ogilvie and Tracy Tait. Finally, thanks to senior acquisitions editor Kathleen Peterson, who conceived this project and initially offered me the role as editor, and who took so much organizational work off my shoulders.

Preface

My love of financial markets, and more specifically, my love for teaching about them, is one of the greatest joys of my life. Those who have taken my course at New York University or who have attended the Bloomberg Technical Analysis seminars I have conducted know that teaching people how to make money in the markets is a passion. Teaching is natural to me, but moreover, I see the opportunity to teach as a special gift I have been given. Students allow me to come into their lives, we share who we are and what we know, and both I and my students come away from the experience with the immense satisfaction of newly learned knowledge. Although I may be the one in front of the room teaching, my horizons are being expanded as well.

Teaching people to successfully apply technical analysis in their investment decision-making process is my way of giving back to the investor community some of the knowledge I have acquired and prospered from over the past two decades. I continually receive cards, letters, and e-mail from former students, saying that after hearing me speak, reading an article I wrote, or taking my class they have a significantly deeper understanding of financial markets as well as of how to successfully implement profitable trading techniques. The commitment I make teaching Monday nights at NYU, or when traveling to spread the technical analysis message, is time away from my beloved wife and three young children. It is particularly hard for my daughters to understand why I am not home every night as they want me to be, yet I hope that as they grow older they will learn to understand and appreciate how important it is to me to make a difference in helping others to achieve financial success.

So, when Bloomberg Press approached me to write a book on technical analysis, I thought that this too was, perhaps, one of those rare chances in life, an opportunity to make a difference, but this time on a much grander scale, reaching more people. I initially hesitated, as the work involved in this project and the additional time I would have to spend away from my family would be far too great. However, the solution came to me: why not go to some of the most respected people in the business, and ask them to write about their favorite technique, model, or study? My solution was to create a book about expert methods by expert trading technicians. And so began the concept for

New Thinking in Technical Analysis: Trading Models from the Masters.

As I rounded out the list of the dozen authors, I realized the importance of this book and the impact it could have on the investing world. To my knowledge, no one else had tackled a project like this, one that would encompass in one volume the work of so many different and proven practitioners. Jack Schwager's *Market Wizards* was a terrific insight into the minds of some of the best traders, but it lacked definitive "how to" information from empiricists. Schwager made readers realize the importance of psychological aspects of successful trading, but the book did not describe or convey an understanding of how these experts actually do what they do. The goal of *New Thinking in Technical Analysis: Trading Models from the Masters* is to answer that much-asked question.

Each of the twelve authors in this book is a recognized master in the particular model or approach to technical analysis that is described. The book starts out with an introductory chapter covering swing trading and underlying principles of technical analysis from Linda Bradford Raschke, one of the most recognized names in successful technical trading. Chapter 1 is followed by the preeminent thinking on intermarket analysis of John J. Murphy, author of *the* reference book that most all of us studied to learn technical analysis.

The book then moves on to three consecutive chapters on using different types of technical charts. CNBC regular guest Ken Tower describes how moving averages can better define market dynamics on point and figure charts. Japanese Candlestick authority Steve Nison then explains how to combine candle charts with standard technical analysis tools to better define risk/reward parameters. Third, in an incredibly insightful chapter on the use of one of my favorite models but one that is lesser known, Robin Mesch, a master at anticipating the moves of the U.S. bond market, provides a compelling argument for using the tool of Market Profile.

The middle part of the book delves into models that define market turns, cycles, and projections. My friend and mentor, Tom DeMark, elaborates two revolutionary oscillators that redefine the concept of overbought/oversold parameters. Readers will be convinced to discard old favorites like Relative Strength Index and stochastics. Tom is followed by one of the biggest names in cycle work, Peter Eliades, who deftly explains the concept and uses of market cycle definition to help predict timing, price movement, and projection points. This section of the book concludes with the work of Steve Poser, one of the very few people I know who can actually make money using Elliott Wave analysis—in real time. This methodology has always been a mystery to me as I have rarely found anyone who knew which wave count the market was in *while it was in it*. Steve has a very good grasp of the concept and practice, and has written a terrific chapter for both the newcomer and the long-time wave surfer.

The book then broadens its depth and focus by including some very robust work in the field of options and market sentiment. This penultimate section starts with the truest of masters in the options world, Larry McMillan. More people have learned options from Larry's textbook, *Options as a Strategic Investment,* than from any other. His contribution here on volatility trading is a classic. Larry is followed by another giant in option analysis, Bernie Schaeffer. Bernie's powerful chapter on options, technical analysis, and investor sentiment provides the tools readers will need to learn how to combine the three topics to make more profitable trading decisions. The section concludes with an exciting new area— sentiment for individual stocks—written by the single greatest name in the futures markets, Larry Williams. Larry describes how market decision makers can gain access to the underlying sentiment for individual stocks, a largely unexplored area, yet one that can aid tremendously in judging extreme optimism or pessimism prevalent regarding a stock at any time.

The book concludes with weather-tested money management techniques from one of the best in the business, Courtney Smith. Courtney's insights into the market are constantly sought, making him a frequent guest on Bloomberg Television, CNBC, and CNNfn, as well as a speaker at countless industry seminars. Take special note of Courtney's lessons in money management to develop a well-rounded and rigorous investment discipline, which will save you heartache, headache, and most of all, money.

New Thinking in Technical Analysis: Trading Models from the Masters, with its wealth of illustrative charts and examples, is specifically designed to guide you through each master's technique and models in a logical and progressive way. I have purposely tried to make each chapter independent rather than force the reader to string chapters together to absorb a cohesive theme. The authors followed basic structural guidelines, but the content was uniquely theirs. The theme that runs true throughout the book is each contributor's desire to share carefully developed and easily applied thinking that can make a difference in your investing success. Truly, these twelve men and women are deservedly called masters of technical analysis.

RICK BENSIGNOR

CHAPTER 1

Swing Trading and Underlying Principles of Technical Analysis

LINDA BRADFORD RASCHKE

Traditionally, there have been two major methods of forecasting market movements—the fundamental method and the technical method. Fundamental factors include analyzing long-term business cycles and identifying extremes in security prices and public sentiment. An investor looking to establish a line of securities after a long-term business cycle low is said to be playing for the "long swing." Short-swing trading (also referred to as "swing trading") seeks to capitalize on the short and intermediate waves or price fluctuations that occur inside the longer major trends.

The market's short-term swings are caused by temporary imbalances in supply and demand. This causes the price action to move in "waves." A combination of up waves and down waves forms a trend. Once you understand the technical aspects of these imbalances in supply and demand you can apply the principles of swing trading to any time frame in any market.

Swing charts have been used for the past one hundred years as a way to analyze the overall market's price structure, follow a market's trend, and monitor changes in the trend. Swing trading has come to refer to trading on the smaller fluctuations within a longer-term trend, but historically, swing charts were used to stay with a trade and follow the market's trend, as opposed to "scalping" for quick in and out profits. Whether analyzing the market's swings for short-term trade opportunities or monitoring them for trade management purposes, it is important to understand the enduring principles of price behavior that forecast the most probable outcome for a market. All these principles are deeply entrenched in the foundation of classical technical analysis. The first part of this chapter places swing trading within a historical perspective. The second part examines the principles of price behavior that set up the highest probability trades, and the last part examines the three main types of trade strategies that fall into a swing trading category.

Swing trading is based on the technical study of price behavior, including the price's strength or weakness relative to the individual market's technical position. In other words, the length and amplitude of the current swing is compared to those of the prior swings to assess whether the market is showing signs of weakness or signs of strength. A trader attempts to forecast only the next most immediate swing in terms of the probabilities of reasonable risk/reward ratios for the next leg up or down. A swing trading strategy should show more winners than losers. Swing traders make frequent trades but spend limited time in those trades. Short-term swing trading involves more work in exchange for more control and less risk.

Influential Thinkers in Technical Analysis

The earliest fathers of traditional technical analysis as well as many great traders in the first half of the past century examined both the longer-term cycles and short-term price fluctuations. Most of them practiced swing trading to some degree. By studying their work, you will understand the origins of the principles of price behavior that are responsible for the three basic types of swing trading patterns today.

Charles Dow

Perhaps the best-known individual who contributed to the foundation of technical analysis was Charles Dow (1851–1902). From 1900 to 1902, he wrote a series of editorials that set forth his ideas on the markets. His original theories were actually intended to serve as a barometer of general business activity. It was later that his principles were developed into forecasting methods.

Sam Nelson, another writer and market technician, had tried unsuccessfully to persuade Dow to set forth his ideas in a book. Nelson ultimately collected Dow's editorials and developed his ideas into principles of market behavior. Nelson was the one who coined the phrase "Dow Theory," which became the cornerstone for technical analysis. Two other technicians also deserve to be noted as developing Dow's ideas into a more formal structure. The first was William Hamilton, who became the editor of the *Wall Street Journal* after Dow died, and the second was Robert Rhea.

Dow set forth that there are three different market movements going on simultaneously. They are called the primary, secondary, and minor or day-to-day trends. Although Dow Theory concentrates on forecasting the primary trend, which can last three to six years, the theorems and observations as to the nature of the secondary trends, which can last anywhere from three weeks to a few months, form the basis for swing trading.

The first principle that Dow pointed out is that of action/reaction. It states that the market moves in waves, or up legs and down legs. In a bull market the swings upward are called primary swings and the downswings are called secondary reactions. The greater the swing in one direction, the greater the eventual reaction in the other. It is important to note that each market movement represents a different time frame, and different time frames can be in opposite trends at the same time. For example, the primary, or longer term, trend could be up, yet the minor trend, or intermediate-term time frame, could be down.

Dow gave us the classic definition of a trend based on the movement of the secondary reactions. For an up trend to be established, the price action must display both a higher high and a higher low. For an up trend to reverse, a lower high and lower low must occur. A trend will remain intact until it changes according to the above definitions, and a trend has greater odds of continuation than it does of reversal. In a strongly trending environment, a swing trader looks to trade only in the direction of the trend, for this is the true path of least resistance.

The theorem that Dow is best known for is "the averages discount everything!" The markets represent a composite of all known information and prevailing emotions. This remains today the underlying assumption of technical analysis—all known variables have already been discounted by the current price action. Swing trading is technical and purely price-based. Traders do best having no opinions or preconceived ideas. Ideally, all they have to do is identify the trend and wait for a low-risk entry in the direction of the trend.

Dow also gave us the concept of confirmation/nonconfirmation, which is one of the most widely applied principles of technical analysis today. He stated that a change in the primary trend must be confirmed by two other indices—the Dow Industrials and the Transportation Averages. Today this principle of confirmation/nonconfirmation (also known as divergence) is used in comparing one market to another market or index on both a short- and a long-term basis. It can also be used to compare the price action to a variety of technical indicators. A nonconfirmation is one of the tools used to warn of a "failure test" or potential for a swing reversal. For example, in **Figure 1.1** note that the Dow Industrials make new highs at points B and C, which are not confirmed by the Transports. A downtrend then follows. This is an example of nonconfirmation.

Finally, Dow looked at the importance of volume in confirming the movement of the secondary reactions. For example, a market that is oversold will dis-

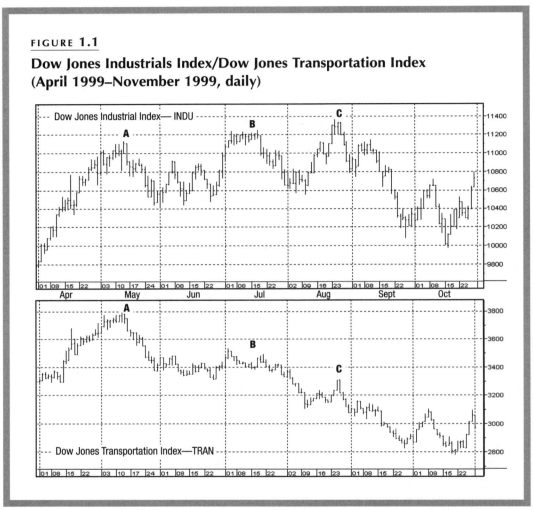

FIGURE 1.1

Dow Jones Industrials Index/Dow Jones Transportation Index (April 1999–November 1999, daily)

play light volume during sell-offs and increasing volume during rallies. Upswings can often start on light volume and end with excessive activity. (Analysis of volume can be used in conjunction with swing trading, but is not essential.) More important, volume can also be used to confirm a breakout from a "line" or consolidation area. Breakouts are the third type of swing trading pattern. (The first types are retracements and the second types are "tests" or failure swings, to be discussed later.)

This last concept, that of a *sideways line*, was originally defined as a sideways movement extending for a few weeks within a 5 percent price fluctuation. This represents a period of accumulation or distribution. Lines often occur in the middle of secondary swings. However, small "lines" or periods of consolidation occur in just about any chart in any market on any time frame. Differentiating a breakout from a line, however, requires analyzing more factors than just price direction. It also involves consideration of cycles in volatility, or the principle that contraction in range is followed by range expansion.

Robert Rhea

Robert Rhea studied Dow's work and spent much time compiling market statistics and adding to Dow's observations. He noted that indices are more inclined than is an individual stock to form horizontal lines or extended chart formations. He was also one of the first technicians to specify that a leg must have a minimum amplitude to be considered a legitimate secondary swing. The second half of this chapter (starting with General Principles of Price Behavior) examines different criteria that can be used to categorize a market's swing, including percentage filters for the amplitude of a wave. This is particularly important when it comes to building your own swing charts.

Analyzing the market's swings is much easier when the market has good volatility and range. It is much trickier when the price starts trading sideways and the range narrows. The amplitude (height or depth) of a swing, in addition to its duration, are two of the main criteria used to assess the relative strength or weakness of the market's technical position. The third criteria is the volume on each swing. In a trending environment, the amplitudes of the market's reactions tend to be similar in nature. A swing trader can look for equal-length swings as a measuring method for a market's expected move.

Richard Schabacker

While Dow set forth some basic principles of price behavior, including the theory that market movements are comprised of a series of swings and reactions, Richard Schabacker (1902–1938) could be called the father of the "science" of technical analysis. Schabacker categorized concrete tools that help the technician not only to forecast a move, but also to recognize signs that a swing might end. He was the first to classify common chart formations, to develop "gap" theory, to formalize the use of trend lines, and to emphasize the importance of support and resistance levels. Few people are aware that Schabacker was R. D. Edwards's uncle, and much of Edwards and Magee's *Technical Analysis of Stock Trends* (New York: AMACOM, 1997) is essentially an exposition of Schabacker's work.

Richard Schabacker, the youngest-ever financial editor of *Forbes* magazine, was a prolific writer and managed to pen three huge volumes before his untimely death at age thirty-six. The bulk of his writings were published in the early 1930s. In addition to being a consummate technician, he was also a renowned forecaster and an astute trader. No one has written with more insight than Schabacker about the differences between short-term swing trading and long-swing investing. He said, in general, that a long-swing investor has less worry, fewer chances of making mistakes, smaller commissions, and most likely, smaller profits. Trading for the short-swing movements, a person has more work, more worry, higher commissions, but chances for much larger profit.

Some of Schabacker's greatest insights are on the psychological aspects of trading. Regarding the difficulty in holding positions for the long run, he stated, "You'll start out with the best of intentions, but you probably won't be able to buck human nature. And even if you do succeed in holding conscientiously to your long-swing basis all the way through, it will be so difficult that you won't have much fun in doing it." Short-term swing trading is more in line with human nature, with a desire for fairly rapid action.

Schabacker's most popular tool was bar charts, which record the market's price action. When studying the market's technical position, the practice of chart reading is devoted to studying certain patterns to forecast future price move-

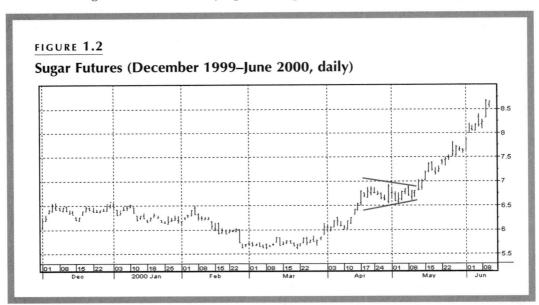

FIGURE 1.2

Sugar Futures (December 1999–June 2000, daily)

ment. Schabacker grouped these patterns into two classes—continuation patterns and reversal formations. He noted that the chart patterns with the most forecasting significance do not occur very frequently, but they are quite important when they do show up. It is important for swing traders to remember that they do not need to be in the market all the time, and that it requires a great deal of patience to wait for the high-probability trades to set up.

Continuation patterns include triangles, small rectangles, pennants, and flags. Usually, these formations occur because the preceding movement has been too rapid. Aggressive swing traders understand that continuation patterns are one of the best methods for isolating the most favorable risk/reward setups. The more time a trader spends in the market, the more risk exposure there is. The object of trading on the short-term swings is to try to capture the most amount of gain in the least amount of time. Note, for example, the so-called bull flag continuation pattern illustrated in **Figure 1.2**. The upswing preceding the consolidation was so strong that it formed a "pole" for the flag.

Reversal formations take a much longer time to form and are prone to more false breakouts. As a general rule, the longer the duration of the particular chart pattern, the greater the odds that it will be a reversal pattern.

Schabacker pioneered work with price gaps and categorized them into common gaps, breakaway gaps, continuation gaps, and exhaustion gaps. He considered gap phenomena to have great forecasting value regarding the potential for the next immediate price swing. He was also one of the first to write extensively on both trend lines and support and resistance levels. Trend lines, lines drawn to contain the price action, serve two main purposes. They help define the probable limits of intermediate-term declines and recoveries within established trends. When a market finds support or resistance at these levels, it forecasts continuation of the trend. Trend lines can also warn of an impending reversal when they are broken. The more times the price touches the trend line, the more significant that trend line becomes.

The general study of support and resistance levels is one of the most practical tools for both the market student and swing trader. Trend lines forecast future support and resistance levels in a trending market. However, in a trading range environment, key swing highs and lows serve as basic support and resistance. Once the market moves out of its trading range, previous resistance levels become future support levels and old bottoms become future tops.

Much of the study of chart formations, trend lines, gaps, and support and resistance levels seems so basic that the average market student glosses over it.

What is most important, though, is not mere knowledge of these phenomena, but the practical application of them in a trader's nightly analysis. Much forecasting information is revealed by price, and studying price will always be faster than analyzing a derivative of price. Some of the best swing traders in history have been master tape readers.

When studying the charts or price, the market's technical strength or weakness is assessed by its position relative to the previous leg or market action. For example, if the previous up leg was greater than the previous down leg, and the subsequent reaction was shallow, forming a continuation pattern, the odds would favor that only the long side should be traded. This process would continue until there was a failure test and the up leg failed to show continuation. Experienced traders can play this failure test, but the most conservative play would be to wait until the down leg was greater than the previous upswing and then sell the next reaction.

Schabacker understood intimately the importance of tape action. "If the market or individual stock does not act according to one's primary analysis, the market itself is trying to tell the trader to change that analysis, or at least cut losses short and get out until confidence can be resumed in new analysis." Price should always be the primary factor for a swing trader, and the number one rule is: Don't argue with the tape! If a trader is long, expecting an upswing, but the market goes sideways instead, the probabilities are that the trade is not working and the trader should look to exit as quickly as possible.

Richard Wyckoff

While Schabacker's work concentrated on organizing price data and classifying chart patterns, his approach tended to be rather mechanical in its orientation of observing formations. Richard Wyckoff took the process of analyzing market swings one step further. He used volume and tape reading to analyze whether the patterns represented accumulation or distribution, and then organized the market activity into an overall sequence.

Wyckoff started working as a runner on Wall Street in 1888. In the early 1900s, he began to publish an advisory letter as well as his research. He first published his method of technical analysis in 1908, and later, in 1931, published a correspondence course. His technique used a combination of bar, point and figure, and wave charts to analyze the market swings. It is based on the simple approach of monitoring the forces of supply and demand for a directional bias, and learning to select the markets that have the most immediate potential, thus making most effective use of a trader's capital.

The basics of analyzing supply and demand come from studying the individual bar charts and monitoring the market's action in relationship to volume, and using trend lines, or "supply" and "support" lines, to follow the market's movement. Bottoms and tops are formed by a process with which Wyckoff introduced some key concepts used by all swing traders, such as a "selling climax" and a "secondary reaction."

In the case of a downtrending market (the sequence is essentially reversed for a topping process), assume that the market has been moving down and a decline is mature. The first attempt at finding a bottom is called "preliminary support." On this day, there will be a definite increase in volume and the market will find some type of support, or make a short-term low. This point cannot be anticipated, only observed as it is happening or after the fact. The ensuing rally should still be contained within the channels of the downtrend.

After this first swing low is made and the market reacts by moving up a bit, the downtrend resumes and flushes out the last longs with a "selling climax." There is extremely heavy volume on this day and the range should expand. If prices rally toward the end of the day, it indicates that the last longs have been flushed out.

Next, there is an "automatic rally" that is comprised primarily of the shorts

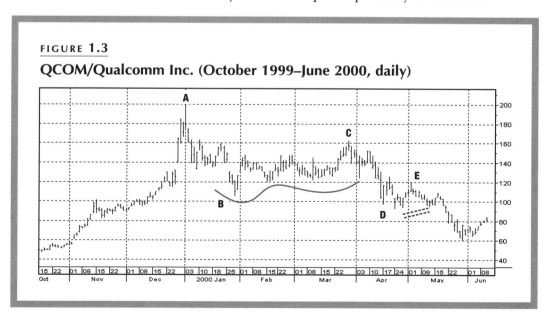

FIGURE 1.3

QCOM/Qualcomm Inc. (October 1999–June 2000, daily)

covering. In general, the volume is much lighter on this rally. No large market participants or institutions have established heavy long commitments yet. A "secondary test" then follows the "automatic rally." This is a retest of the low of the selling climax, which tends to take place on lighter volume. Also, the range will not be as wide as the range on the day of the selling climax. Usually the market will make a higher low on this test.

Once the secondary test takes place, a trading range has been established, and may last quite a while. The market will finally indicate that it is ready to break out from this trading range by showing a "sign of strength." This is a strong thrust up indicating an increase in upside momentum, accompanied by an expansion in the volume. The reaction that follows this "sign of strength" is often just a sideways pause, but it is marked by a contraction in daily range and a drop-off in the volume. This is called the "last point of support" and is the last chance to get on board before a trend begins. **Figure 1.3** shows a "Wyckoff Sequence" at the top, including: A. Buying climax, B. Automatic reaction, C. Retest back up, D. Break below support (which Wyckoff called the ice)—sign of weakness, and E. Rally back up to the ice forming a "bear flag."

"Springs" and "upthrusts," two more patterns that Wyckoff described, also set up key pivot points (swing highs or lows) for a swing trader. Springs and upthrusts describe the tests or false breakouts that can occur in a trading range.

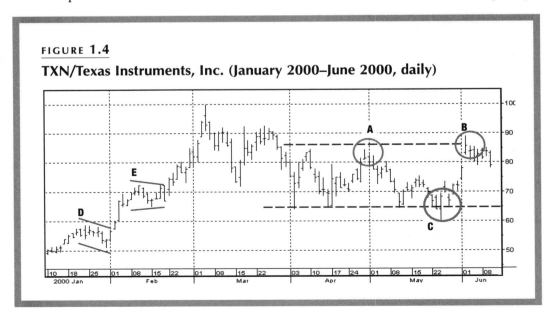

FIGURE 1.4

TXN/Texas Instruments, Inc. (January 2000–June 2000, daily)

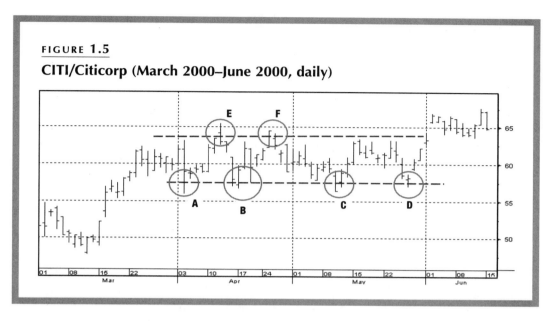

FIGURE 1.5

CITI/Citicorp (March 2000–June 2000, daily)

A *spring* occurs when the market breaks below support and then quickly reverses itself. There is little volume on the breakout and the market manages to shake out weak longs. *Upthrusts* occur when the market tests the upper band of trading range but is quickly met by overhead supply.

Each of these patterns represents "price rejection" and provides a setup for a short-term trade in the opposite direction. The false breakout sets up a well-defined risk point, and, in general, the market should then move to test the other end of the trading range. **Figure 1.4** presents examples of springs and upthrusts, with points A and B representing upthrusts and point C representing a spring. These false breakouts lead to a swing back to the opposite end of the trading range. (Note that points D and E are good examples of bull flags.)

After a market makes a big move, it enters a consolidation period. Numerous springs (points A, B, C, and D) and upthrusts (points E and F) form short-term trading opportunities, as shown in **Figure 1.5**.

Wyckoff developed an index comprised of five leading stocks used to indicate early reversals in the market swings. The stocks can be rotated to include the most active leaders at the time. He used a line chart (also called a wave chart) to detect early reversals at critical swing points. Wave charts help monitor the responsiveness of the market to buying and selling impulses. The theory is that the five leading stocks should be the most sensitive. The length and time of each wave indicates the technical strength of the buyers and the sellers. The principles of confirmation/nonconfirmation are also used when comparing the index of the leaders to the overall market.

Wyckoff also incorporated the use of point and figure charts in his overall methodology to determine probable length of the swing once the market breaks out of its "sideways line" or chart formation. Although it is useful to have a rough expectation of the swing's potential or objective level, a true swing trader knows that the best method is to follow the tape action and wait for the swing charts to indicate signs of reversal instead of "scalping" out too early and playing for small profits only.

Although short-term swing analysis is often used to identify one particular pattern to trade, it is important to understand that Wyckoff's main emphasis was on formulating a comprehensive approach to the whole business of trading. The ultimate goal is to make trades with a minimum of risk, using only the best markets when all conditions are favorable, and being conscientious about when to exit a trade after it is made. Avoidance of a large loss is the guiding principle in swing trading. When in doubt, do nothing. Learn to wait and see.

Wyckoff was the first to seriously study the action within congestion areas, such as buying and selling tests and volume characteristics, and to seek clues about potential reversal points. He also looked to enter on swing reactions instead of entering via a breakout from chart formations, as Schabacker often did. While Schabacker calculated measured move objectives from various chart formations, Wyckoff used point and figure charts to calculate a price objective. However, he strongly advised judging the market by its own action, by following the tape action and taking what it gives you.

Ralph N. Elliott

While Schabacker classified chart patterns that preceded the market swings and Wyckoff looked for signs of accumulation and distribution within these patterns, a third dimension was added to the study of the market's swings through the work of Ralph N. Elliott (1871–1948). He saw patterns in the market's waves or cycles and set forth some basic tenets classifying these waves.

Elliott started out as a devout student of Dow Theory. He believed that market timing was the key to successful investing, and when to buy was far more important than what to buy. When a long illness in the late 1920s and early 1930s kept him bedridden, he began an intensive study of market behavior that ultimately went into much greater detail than Dow's work. He developed his first set of principles in 1934. These were later published as "The Wave Principle," and his work eventually became known as the Elliott Wave Principle (or Elliott Wave Theory).

Elliott concentrated on the cyclical behavior of the market's swings or waves as opposed to chart patterns. He noted that these waves had a tendency to repeat themselves. This price behavior forms a structure that one can predict and use as the forecasting tool.

A full wave or "cycle" consists of five waves up followed by three waves down. The swings that occur in the direction of the trend are called "impulse" waves. Elliott observed that the laws of nature tend to unfold in an upward direction, and thus there is an upward bias to the cycle. Each wave or cycle can be divided into smaller degrees. The larger cycles are subject to the same principles as the smaller cycles. Recognizable swing trading patterns can occur on any time frame.

Waves are defined by measuring both price and time. The market alternates between impulse type waves, or those that occur in the direction of the trend, and corrective waves. Elliott did not use closing prices, but instead looked at ranges. The distance between a swing high and a swing low defines a wave over a given period of time. The range of the impulse wave in relation to the range of the corrective wave is used to forecast the next impulse wave. A technique called channeling is the easiest way to visualize this process. **Figure 1.6** illustrates how Elliott used channeling to show how each impulse wave can forecast the move

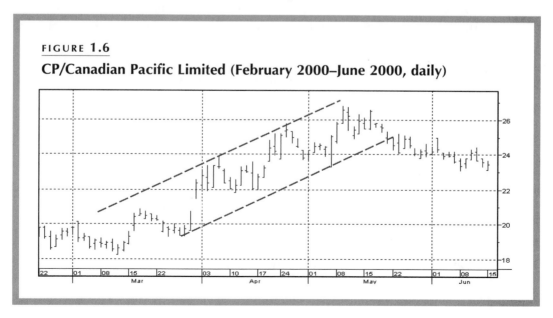

FIGURE 1.6

CP/Canadian Pacific Limited (February 2000–June 2000, daily)

for the next swing. Note how Canadian Pacific moves in a well-defined channel.

In general, the degree of correction in a market swing indicates the strength of the next wave. Although Elliott did not analyze volume to the extent that Wyckoff did, both technicians noted that volume tends to dry up during corrections. Volume also tends to be lighter on fifth waves, which sometimes look similar to Wyckoff's description of a test of a buying or selling climax.

Elliott tried to characterize the personalities of different waves. Each swing is analyzed in terms of volume and volatility. All of Elliott's rules on wave characteristics served to build a generalized model of market behavior that can be used as a forecasting tool. (See Chapter 8 for an in-depth discussion of Elliott Wave Theory.) However, Elliott went to great lengths in his writings, as did Wyckoff and Schabacker, to emphasize that theory varies greatly from actual practice. It took Elliott several years of constant application before he himself felt comfortable in applying the swing principles he had observed.

Human emotions cause waves, and thus cycles are more visible when a market is broad and active with good commercial interest. Volume and liquidity makes swing trading patterns more readily visible to the eye. Don't trade in dead, quiet markets!

W. D. Gann

W. D. Gann (1878–1955) was another famous technician/trader in the first half of the twentieth century who helped contribute to the foundation of technical analysis and swing trading. Born in the same decade as Elliott and Wyckoff, he started trading in 1902 and thus developed his market theories by observing the same markets as Schabacker, Wyckoff, and Elliott. He was an extremely creative technician who also traded and wrote extensively about his work.

Gann was an adept student of the market. He had experience as a runner, a broker, a trader, and an author. He wrote on a variety of market aspects, including market psychology, practical trading tips, and more esoteric ideas touching on astrology and geometry. One of his main contributions to analyzing the market swings was the importance of studying the time element. He felt that time was the most important factor, because time governs when price extremes will occur. His most famous concept is that "price equals time." In other words, so much time must pass before prices reverse direction.

Gann counted the number of days from swing highs and swing lows in order to determine time cycles and time periods. Many technicians use the length of a price swing to determine the trend. For example, when the length of the upswing

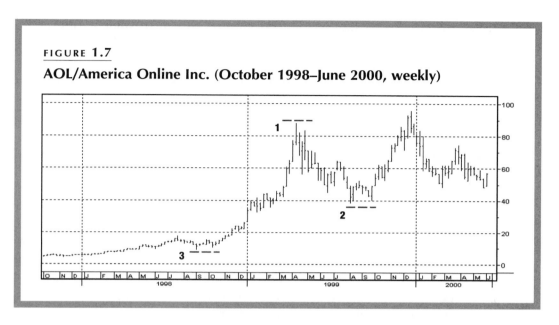

FIGURE **1.7**

AOL/America Online Inc. (October 1998–June 2000, weekly)

exceeds the length of the prior downswing, a trend reversal is imminent. Gann applied the same concept to time. If the number of days a market has been moving higher exceeds the time duration of the last down leg, the trend has reversed.

Although he observed that time cycles govern overall market structure, Gann still used traditional chart patterns and technical studies of price movement for confirmation. He noted the importance of gap and limit days, making the same observations as Schabacker and Wyckoff. He also used the same terminology as Wyckoff for defining market swings, such as "secondary rallies" or "reactions."

Primary levels of support and resistance come in at previous swing highs and lows. Gann also calculated the percentage retracements of swings, and considered the 50 percent reaction to be one of the most important trading points. The wider the swing and longer the time period, the more important the halfway point becomes. If the market has been in an up trend, look to buy around the 50 percent retracement level with a stop just underneath. A market that fails to retrace a full 50 percent in its reaction back down shows a sign of strength. **Figure 1.7** exemplifies this 50 percent swing retracement rule, at point 2, which is 50 percent of the distance between points 1 and 3.

Even though Gann elaborated in his later works about using geometric structures and numerology to determine support and resistance levels, he ultimately let the price action dictate his trading decisions. Swing highs and lows are always the most important points to watch. A swing trading student is always looking for tests of the highs and lows that have been defined in the past. Gaps, limit days, reversal days, and basic support and resistance levels were at the core of his tool-kit for analyzing the market's action.

Swing trading requires that a great deal of time be spent in preparation and study. Much emphasis is always given to the initial trade setup, but the successful traders in the past discussed above all wrote an equal amount about the habits and organization it takes to successfully swing trade. Gann felt that a successful trader must have a plan, and knowledge is key in putting it together. The more time you spend gaining knowledge, the more money you will make later. Gann's extensive use of pivot points, time cycles, seasonal dates, and intricate charting methods were his way of "gaining knowledge." These methods keep a trader intimately involved with the market's price action. Many successful swing traders keep charts and logs by hand, and credit this process in aiding their market "feel."

In addition to technical knowledge, Gann also insisted that separate trading rules were essential for success. Always use stop orders. Never let a profit turn into a loss. When in doubt, get out, and don't get in when in doubt. Trade only in active markets. Never limit your orders—trade at the market. Don't close out trades without a good reason. Follow up with a stop-loss order to protect your profits. Never average a loss. Avoid getting in and out of the market too often. And finally, avoid increasing your trading after a long successful run.

General Principles of Price Behavior

So far, we have looked at swing trading in terms of its historical context. It is a way of approaching market analysis and risk management that is derived from the basic tenets of technical analysis. It is also a very practical and clear-cut method of trading based strictly on odds and percentages. A trade is based on the market's most probable immediate course of action as opposed to a long-term fundamental valuation.

The majority of short-term high probability swing trading patterns that have consistently held up over time are based on one of four enduring principles of price behavior. Each of these principles can be quantified. Almost all mechanical systems are based on one of them. Although these concepts can be tested and are considered to be durable and robust, swing trading in the traditional sense should still be considered a method rather than a system.

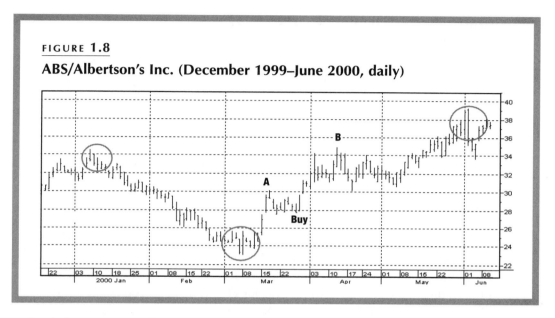

FIGURE 1.8

ABS/Albertson's Inc. (December 1999–June 2000, daily)

Principle 1: A Trend Is More Likely to Continue Than Reverse

This principle is one of the basic tenets of Dow Theory: A trend has a higher probability of continuation than it does of reversal. An up trend is defined as both a higher high and a higher low, and vice versa for a downtrend. If the market is in a well-defined trend, the highest probability trades will occur in the direction of the trend. When the price is moving in a clearly defined trend, there are numerous strategies for entry based on the small retracements that occur along the way. These reactions allow the trader to find a tight risk point while still playing for a new leg in the direction of the trend. A test of the most recent swing high or low is the initial objective level, but ideally the market will make a new leg up (or down).

A swing trader should be aware of certain characteristics of trends. The absence of any clearly defined swing or price pattern implies a continuation of the trend. (This can include a sideways trend, too.) In a steady uptrend, the price action can creep upward in a steady, methodical manner characteristic of low volatility. A slow "oozing" action or steady price deterioration can characterize a downtrend. This type of environment can be frustrating for a swing trader, as there tend to be fewer reactions to enter, but it is important to keep in mind that once a trend is established, it takes considerable power and time to turn it. Never try to make a counter-trend trade in a slowly creeping market.

Principle 2: Momentum Precedes Price

If momentum makes a new high or low, the price high or low is still likely yet to come. Momentum is one of the few "leading" indicators. Elliot used the term *impulse* to refer to an increase in the market's momentum. Impulse occurs in the direction of the trend, so a swing trader should look to enter in the direction of the market's initial impulse. New momentum highs can be made both in a trending environment and on a breakout of a trading range environment. Finally, new momentum highs or lows can also indicate a trend reversal or beginning of a corrective swing up when they follow a buying or selling climax (creating a "V" spike reversal). As seen in **Figure 1.8**, buying and selling climaxes mark the extremes. The first sharp swing in the opposite direction at point A sets up an opportunity to initiate a trade from the long side at point B. The market rallies to a perfect retest of the previous swing high before consolidating further.

A trader should look to establish new positions in the market on the first reaction following a new momentum high or low. Any of the retracement methodologies detailed in the second half of this chapter can be used. The only exception to this rule is that a trader needs to be aware of when the market makes a buying or selling climax. This is not a new momentum high or low, but an

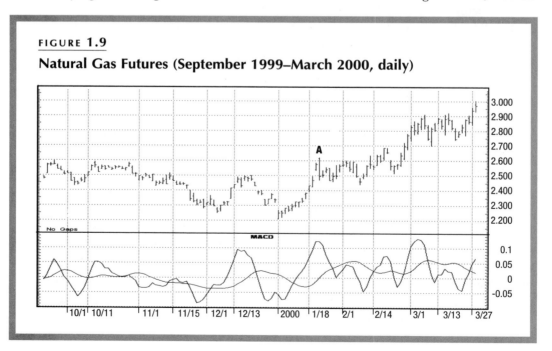

FIGURE 1.9

Natural Gas Futures (September 1999–March 2000, daily)

exhaustion point that creates a vacuum in the opposite direction.

Figure 1.9 shows a moving average oscillator that made new highs at point A. Momentum precedes price. Point A was the first time the length of the upswing exceeded the length of the last down leg. Note the steady trend of higher highs that followed.

Principle 3: Trends End in a Climax

A trend will continue until it reaches a buying or selling climax. This tends to be marked by an increase in volatility and volume. There must be a marked increase in the range that exceeds the previous bars. A buying or selling climax indicates that the last buyer or seller has been satisfied. The market then usually begins a process of backing and filling, testing and retracing. As noted previously, Wyckoff detailed the common sequence of backing and testing that the market makes as the volatility creates good tradable swings. Crowd emotions are high, as few are comfortable with the new price level.

Trading on the crosscurrents *after* a move has exhausted itself sets up an excellent swing-trading environment as setups occur on both the long and the short side of a market. As a broad trading range begins to form, whipsaws and spikes or springs and upthrusts create support and resistance levels. It is a short-term swing trader's job to note these areas of resistance and support, as it is at

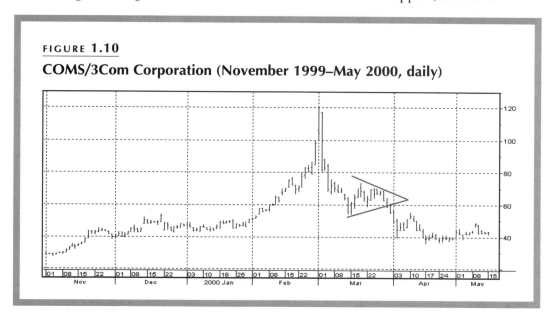

FIGURE **1.10**

COMS/3Com Corporation (November 1999–May 2000, daily)

these points where risk can be minimized. Once support and resistance are defined, the market's range will tend to contract as it begins its drawn-out process of consolidating toward an equilibrium point again.

A market that makes an extremely sharp reversal, following a buying or selling climax, has made a "V" spike reversal, one of the most powerful technical patterns. Essentially, a vacuum is created in the opposite direction, and the market's impulse sharply reverses direction without the normal consolidation period.

Figure 1.10 illustrates an example of Principle 3. This buying climax left a vacuum to the down side. The downside impulse led to the formation of a bear flag. Do not look to buy retracements after a buying climax.

Principle 4: The Market Alternates between Range Expansion and Range Contraction

Price action tends to alternate between two different states. The range is either contracting in a consolidation mode, or it is expanding in a breakout or trending mode. When the range is contracting, the market is reaching an equilibrium level. At this point, it becomes very difficult to read the market swings. The only thing you can predict is that a breakout is increasingly likely. Once a market breaks out from an equilibrium point, there are high odds of continuation in the direction of the initial breakout. It is easier to predict a pending increase in volatility than it is to predict the actual price direction of a breakout. A trader should think of a breakout strategy as another form of swing trading, as the objective is to capture the next most immediate leg with a good risk/reward ratio.

Figure 1.11 illustrates how the market alternates between range contraction and range expansion. Note how the circled periods of consolidation are followed by a jump in volatility at the points marked with an *X*. Also note how cyclical this phenomenon is.

Creating Swing Charts

Swing charts are a trader's road map by which to anticipate the next most probable play. They are similar to point and figure charts in that they eliminate the time axis and can represent a lot of price action in a relatively small amount of space. Thus, it is easy to see multiple support and resistance levels from past price action. A new swing is drawn in only when the last one is completed, so in one sense they might appear to be one step behind. However, they are the best tool for quickly assessing the overall market's trend and highlighting the small reac-

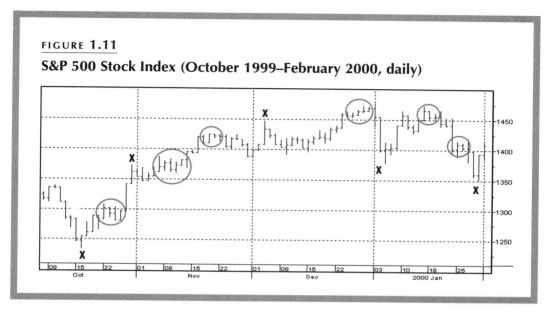

FIGURE **1.11**

S&P 500 Stock Index (October 1999–February 2000, daily)

tions that occur in a trend. Although most software charting packages do not have a swing-charting format, it takes very little time and work to keep them by hand. In fact, a well-trained eye will be able to see the market swings by studying a simple bar chart.

There are several ways to create or calculate swing charts. The easiest way is to mark the significant swing highs and lows, in other words, a high that is surrounded on both sides by a lower high. The first decision to make is what level of detail to include. There are many smaller swings within swings, and the sensitivity of the chart can be adjusted to include the minor swings or only the greater picture. Gann kept two swing charts concurrently. The first recorded reverse moves or reactions that lasted two to three days. A bar that reached a low that was surrounded on either side by a higher low marked the bottom of a downswing, and vice versa for an upswing. He also kept a swing chart of a longer time frame that marked the highs and lows on a weekly chart. Thus, he was always able to see the short swings within the context of a larger trend.

A trader can adjust the threshold for the swings by changing the number of bars and requiring higher lows to follow a key swing low. If the rule states that an upswing will begin only after four higher lows have followed a key swing low, there will be fewer swings but less "noise" than if a trader uses Gann's method of looking at just two- to three-day lows. Of course, Gann kept longer-term charts too, and as a trader will quickly see, there is no right or wrong parameter for creating swing charts. It all depends on one's personal time horizons for making a trade.

A second way to create a swing chart is to add a percentage function to the most recent swing low (or subtract it from the most recent swing high). If the market trades above this level, a new wave has started in the opposite direction. In his book *Filtered Waves* (Analysis Publishing, 1977), Arthur Merrill, one of the great market technicians, used a 5 percent swing function to analyze the swing structure of bull and bear markets.

The third way to create swing charts uses volatility functions popularized by the influential technical analyst Welles Wilder in his book, *New Concepts in Technical Trading Systems* (Greensboro, NC: Trend Research, 1978). A True Range function is added to the most recent swing low or subtracted from the most recent swing high to signal a new wave in the opposite direction. True Range is defined as either the distance between today's high and today's low or the distance between today's extreme price and the previous day's close, whichever is greater. It is best to use a moving average of the True Range to smooth this variable out. The look-back period for the moving average can be one of personal preference. Also, it is best to multiply the moving average of the True Range by a factor of two to three, or else the swings will be too sensitive and include far too much "noise" to be of value.

Let's assume the market is making new lows in a downtrend. When the price can rally above two times a ten-period moving average of the True Range, an up wave will begin. When the price closes below this most recent swing high, less a factor of two times a ten-period moving average of the True Range, a down wave will begin. Again, the length of the moving average used and the multiplier factor can be a range of variables. There is no right or wrong parameter!

Thus, the swing trader is able to quantify a "wave" through one of three different methods. An uptrend is established when two up waves make higher highs and higher lows. The swing trader then looks to enter on all retracements in the uptrend until a new downtrend is signaled by two down waves with lower lows.

This sounds simple enough. But traders really gain an edge when they learn to use two time frames at once, just as Gann did. The longer time frame is used to identify the trend, and the lower time frame is used to look for short-term reversals in the direction of the trend. If the weekly chart is in an uptrend, wait for a down wave on the daily charts to reverse itself and use this as a long entry.

The Three Types of Trades

As mentioned previously, almost all trades fall into one of three categories: retracements, tests, or breakouts. Let's look at a few tools that can be used to isolate each type.

Retracements

Retracement methodologies imply entering on a corrective reaction either in a trending environment or following an initial impulse-type move. Although technically, a trend is defined as a higher high and a higher low (or vice versa), there are a variety of other conditions that indicate the potential of a trend. For an uptrend, you can demand that (1) the price be above a certain moving average, (2) a shorter moving average is greater than a longer period moving average, (3) the market is making new four-week highs or some other channel function, (4) an Average Directional Indicator (ADX) has risen above a certain threshold, or (5) there has been a large standard deviation move. This is just to name a few tools that can be used to highlight what the charts are already indicating.

Once the market has been identified as being in an uptrend or having some initial upside impulse, there are many ways to quantify a pullback in this environment. You can use an oscillator to indicate a pullback. You can subtract an Average True Range function from the last swing high. You can look for the price to retrace below a shorter period moving average, such as a five-period moving average, or you can look for the price to retrace a percentage of the previous swing, such as the 50 percent level.

All of these methods can quantify a retracement setup. This is useful if you want to scan a database of a large number of markets. Let's create a model for identifying a retracement in an uptrend:

- The twenty-period exponential moving average is greater than the forty-period moving average. This will be the trend filter.
- A five-period Relative Strength Index (RSI) pulls back below 40. This identifies an initial retracement.
- Buy above the highest high of the previous two bars. This is the "trigger" indicating that the initial trend is resuming.
- Place a stop below the lowest low of the previous two days.
- Manage the trade by monitoring the price action as it approaches the most recent swing high. Is it picking up momentum, indicating a whole new leg up, or is it losing momentum indicating a potential failure test?

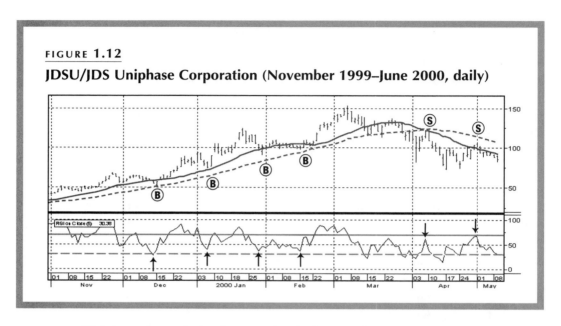

FIGURE **1.12**

JDSU/JDS Uniphase Corporation (November 1999–June 2000, daily)

This is not intended to be a mechanical system by any means. Rather, it is one example of how you can impose an artificial structure on the market in an attempt to organize the data. **Figure 1.12** shows four buy setups and two sell setups over a six-month period based on the above parameters.

Here is a very simple rule: Any time a market makes a new high, look to buy the first pullback. Any time a market makes a new low, look to sell the first reaction up. This same idea can also be applied to the use of oscillators. Any time an oscillator makes a new high over the past one hundred bars, look to buy the first pullback, and vice versa. Look back at Figure 1.9 and note the trade entries that could have been made after the oscillator's new high or new low, where momentum precedes price.

New momentum highs or lows can be made in a trending environment or on a breakout of a trading range environment in which the initial thrust can be the beginning of a whole new leg up or down. New momentum highs or lows can also indicate a trend reversal if there is a countertrend impulse following a long sustained trend.

A trader should look to establish new positions in the market on the first reaction following a new momentum high or low. The only exception to this rule is a momentum extreme that occurs at a buying or selling climax at the end of a long trend.

Moving averages serve as a useful tool in judging how far a market should retrace. The shorter the period used for the moving average, the more potential trade setups there are, but the weaker the signals. In general, markets have a tendency to retrace deeper at the beginning of a trend. As a trend progresses, the retracements become shallower as more people try to get on board.

Oscillators can also serve as useful tools to highlight reactions in a trending market. Once again, the shorter the period used for the oscillator setting, the higher the number of potential trade setups. Cycle lows tend to coincide with a more deeply oversold reading, which an oscillator with a longer period would pick up. Trades established at cycle lows usually can be held for longer periods of time.

Almost any type of traditional oscillator, such as a stochastic, RSI, or moving average oscillator, can be used to indicate a new momentum high or low. A simple "rate of change" indicator works exceptionally well, too.

Tests

There are two types of tests. The first is the test that occurs at the end of a sustained trend. A "failure test" occurs when the market fails to make a new leg up or down in a trending environment. It is a warning of a loss of momentum, but it does not indicate a trend change in and of itself. The second type of test also

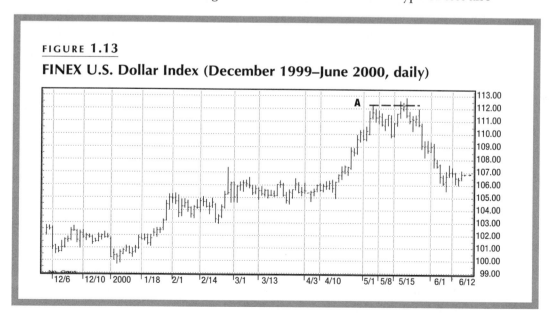

FIGURE **1.13**

FINEX U.S. Dollar Index (December 1999–June 2000, daily)

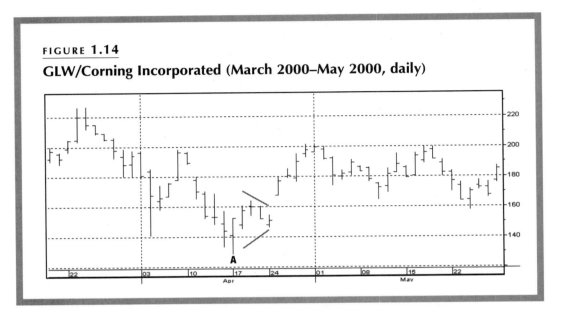

FIGURE 1.14

GLW/Corning Incorporated (March 2000–May 2000, daily)

occurs in a trading range environment in which the market is consolidating following a sustained move. Once initial support and resistance levels are established, the market could be said to have formed a "box." If the market penetrates
one end of this box but then closes back inside the box, the odds are that it will
then test the other side of the box. The best "tests" are the ones that immediately reverse the penetration of a previous swing high or low, indicating "price rejection." A stop should always be placed just beyond the failure point. A trader
should keep in mind that the initial play is always one leg or swing at a time and
not look for the beginning of a whole new trend. **Figure 1.13** illustrates a "failure test" at point A, leading to a large downswing in the opposite direction.

Breakouts

A good tradable swing occurs after a breakout from a contraction in the market's volatility. There are several tools a trader can use to identify when a good
breakout opportunity is approaching. The first is an indicator that highlights a
contraction in the True Range (discussed previously in Creating Swing Charts).
True Range can be measured from a one-bar period to a thirty-bar period. A low
reading on a standard deviation indicator also alerts to the potential of a break-
out-type trade. There is also no substitute for classic chart formations and not-
ing when trend lines start to converge.

There are many ways to enter a breakout trade, but two techniques are best. The first is to use a channel breakout method. This is nothing more than looking back and buying on a breakout of the previous x-number bar's high or selling on the previous x-number bar's low (x equals the chosen number of bars to designate the desired channel width). The second method is to use an average True Range function. This can be added or subtracted from the previous bar's close or the current bar's open. A trader can play many variations on this theme. Simple mechanical volatility breakout systems became popular in the 1980s, and continue to hold up today. **Figure 1.14** has a breakaway gap following the narrowest range day of the previous three weeks. Gaps are a form of impulse and lead to continuation in the direction of the close. Note the perfect "test" at point A.

Trade Management

Technical analysis is not just the application of timing tools to determine a directional bias, particular pattern, or trade setup. It also is a tool to determine when the odds do not favor trading at all. Much of making money is learning not to give it back when conditions are marginal. Analysis of individual swings is a key tool in minimizing risk, as trades are made as close as possible to initial support or resistance levels. Place stops under support and above resistance—logical points where your initial analysis would be considered wrong. As soon as the trade shows enough of a profit, move the initial stop up (or down), ideally to the break-even level if the trade has moved enough in your direction. As the market moves in your favor, move stops to lock in profits. Although this sounds like common sense, if you do not do it you may close out a winning trade too soon for fear of reversal. As long as the market is in a trending mode, you can monitor the swings for signs of continued impulse or higher highs and higher lows (in a long trade). However, you should also look to exit at the first sign of danger or adverse movement against the position. When the position is not working, or there is doubt in your mind, reduce the size of the position. (For additional coverage of money management, see Chapter 12.)

As mentioned previously, short-term swing analysis is a lot more work and involves a larger time commitment than investing for the long swing. The importance of routine and mechanics can be critical to a trader's success. Most successful swing traders find it useful to maintain and study charts on a daily basis. Although this process may seem laborious, it keeps the trader actively involved with the markets.

CHAPTER 2

Forecasting Trends Using
Intermarket Analysis

JOHN MURPHY

For the greater part of the past century, technical analysis was based primarily on single-market analysis. Over the past decade, however, emphasis in the technical world has shifted away from single-market work to a more intermarket approach. It is not unusual for technical analysts to supplement their stock market analysis with consideration of currency trends (to see where global money is flowing), commodity prices (to gauge inflationary trends), bond charts (to see which way interest rates are moving), and overseas markets (to measure the impact of global market trends). Those who fail to do so run the risk of seeing only a small part of the intermarket picture. In an increasingly interrelated financial world, the ability to study all markets gives intermarket technical analysts a huge advantage. With some understanding of how those markets interrelate, chartists should have a decided edge over their economic and fundamental counterparts.

While intermarket principles are invaluable in understanding how bonds, stocks, commodities, and currencies work off each other, it has also proven to be extremely helpful in understanding why certain sectors of the market do well at certain times and badly at others. An understanding of intermarket principles sheds new light on the application of sector rotation, which has become so important in recent years. More and more, it isn't so much a question of whether a trader (or investor) should be in the market as much as *where* to be in the market. Being in the right sector at the right time (and out of the wrong sectors) has become one of the keys to stock market success. Showing how to do that is the main focus of this chapter. But first, let's review the basic principles of intermarket technical analysis.

Basic Principles

The basic premise of intermarket analysis is that all markets are related. In other words, what happens in one market has an effect on another. On a macro level, the four interrelated markets are the commodity, currency, bond, and stock markets. Market analysts have long understood the impact of interest rates on stocks, for example. Rising interest rates have historically been bad for stocks, especially those in certain rate-sensitive market sectors. Interest rates are affected by the direction of commodity prices. Rising commodity prices are usually associated with rising inflation, which puts upward pressure on interest rates.

The direction of commodity prices is affected by the direction of a country's currency. A falling currency, for example, usually gives a boost to commodities priced in that currency. That boost reawakens inflation fears and puts pressure on central bankers to raise interest rates, which has a negative impact on the stock market. Not all stocks, however, are affected equally—some stock groups get hurt in a climate of rising interest rates, while others actually benefit in a climate of rising rates.

Global markets play an important role in intermarket analysis as well. For example, the collapse in Asian currencies during 1997 caused a corresponding collapse in Asian stock markets, which had a ripple effect around the globe. Fears of global deflation pushed commodity prices into a free fall and contributed to a worldwide rotation out of stocks into bonds. What started as a downturn in Asian currencies in the summer of that year eventually caused a serious downturn in the U.S. stock market several months later.

During 1999, the opposite scenario played itself out. A sharp rise in the price of oil at the start of that year pushed interest rates higher around the globe as inflation fears resurfaced. A recovery in Asian stock markets also contributed to global demand for industrial commodities like copper and aluminum. The subsequent rise in commodity prices reawakened inflation fears and prompted the Federal Reserve to embark on a series of rate hikes in the middle of the year. That, in turn, had a negative impact on the sectors of the U.S. stock market that are especially sensitive to interest rate direction.

As further proof of how closely linked global markets really are, the remarkably close correlation between the Japanese stock market and the yield on U.S. Treasury bonds is discussed later. First, let's review the key relationships involved in intermarket analysis as they relate to the four major market groups:

- Commodity prices and bond prices usually trend in the opposite direction. (Commodity prices and bond yields usually trend in the same direction.)
- Bond prices usually trend in the same direction as the stock market.
- Rising bond prices are good for stocks; falling bond prices are bad for stocks. (Falling bond yields are good for stocks; rising bond yields are bad for stocks.)

- The bond market usually changes direction long before stocks do; therefore, the bond market is a leading indicator of potential trend changes in stocks.
- Commodity prices usually trend in the opposite direction of the dollar.
- A rising dollar is bad for commodities; a falling dollar is good for commodities.
- A rising dollar is normally good for U.S. stocks and bonds because it is non-inflationary.
- A strong currency attracts foreign money into a country's stock market.

Commodities versus Bonds

The direction of commodity prices during 1999 played a key role in the direction of U.S. interest rates. It was no coincidence that 1999 saw the biggest upturn in commodity prices in years, and one of the biggest downturns in bond prices (and biggest upturns in bond yields). As a result of rising inflation pressures (that showed up in commodity prices first), the Federal Reserve started raising rates in the middle of the year. That had a subtle negative effect on the U.S. stock market—particularly on "old economy" stocks that have traditionally been more affected by interest rate direction. ("New economy" technology stocks proved relatively immune to rising rates during 1999.) The most dramatic impact on the stock market could be seen in the pattern of sector and industry group rotation, which was dramatically affected by rising rates during 1999.

CRB Index versus Rates

Figure 2.1 is a comparison of the CRB Index (a basket of seventeen commodity markets) and the yield on the 10-year Treasury note (which has become the new benchmark for long-term U.S. interest rates). The left side of the chart shows that the decline in long-term interest rates coincided with a falling commodity index through most of 1997 and 1998 (as global deflation fears pushed money out of commodities and into Treasury bonds and notes). Both markets started changing direction near the end of 1998 and the start of 1999. Although the yield on the 10-year note turned up during the fourth quarter of 1998, it did not break its two-year down trendline until March 1999. It was at precisely that point that the commodity index bottomed out and started to trend higher. The balance of 1999 saw rising commodity prices coinciding with rising long-term rates as inflation fears associated with rising commodity prices contributed to rising interest rates.

Despite its eventual rise, the CRB Index was held back by relatively weak agricultural commodity markets during the first half of 1999, and may have

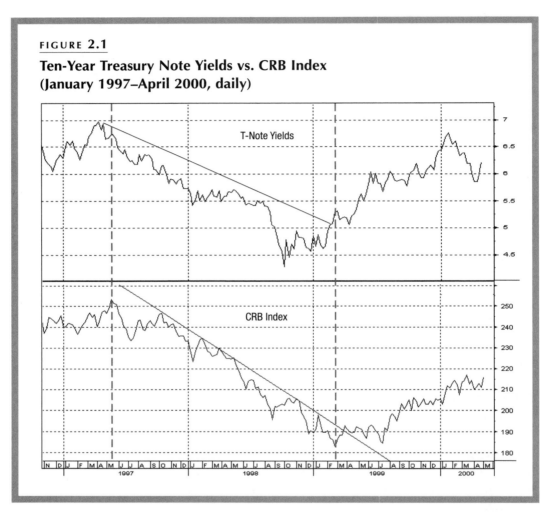

FIGURE **2.1**

**Ten-Year Treasury Note Yields vs. CRB Index
(January 1997–April 2000, daily)**

understated the inflation threat from commodity markets. Other commodity indices, like the Journal of Commerce (JOC) Raw Materials Index and the Goldman Sachs Commodity Index (GSCI), rose much faster than the CRB Index earlier in the year. The JOC Raw Materials Index turned up during the first part of the year, and was primarily influenced by new bull markets in aluminum, copper, and other economically sensitive commodities. The GSCI, which is heavily weighted toward energy prices, also increased sharply as oil prices tripled. The jump in oil prices had a dramatic and unmistakable effect on interest rates.

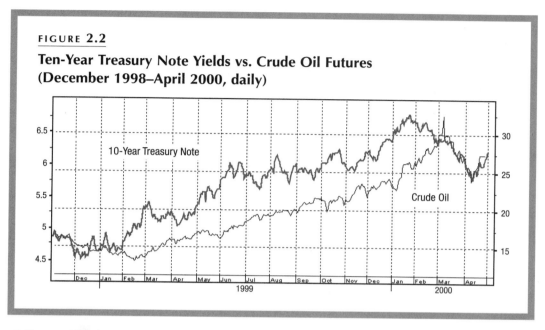

FIGURE **2.2**

**Ten-Year Treasury Note Yields vs. Crude Oil Futures
(December 1998–April 2000, daily)**

Oil versus Rates

Figure 2.2 is a comparison of crude oil futures prices and the yield on the U.S. 10-year Treasury note. In this case, the correlation between the two markets is much more dramatic and striking. For most of 1999, it is hard to tell the two markets apart. There seems little doubt that the dramatic ascent in oil prices (and its inflationary impact) was one of the principal forces driving long-term rates higher during the entire year. (By the middle of the year, the Federal Reserve was concerned enough to start raising short-term interest rates.) To the far right, the chart shows that a correction in oil prices during the first quarter of 2000 coincided with a pullback in long-term rates.

Bonds versus Stocks

Normally, rising rates would be expected to have a negative impact on the stock market. That negative impact on the U.S. stock market was present in 1999, but in a subtle way. Although "new economy" technology stocks rose sharply during the second half of 1999, "old economy" stocks stopped rising right around the time the Fed started tightening in the middle of that year. **Figure 2.3** shows that the New York Stock Exchange (NYSE) Composite Index, for example, peaked in July 1999. Nine months later (in May 2000) the NYSE Composite Index was 5

FIGURE **2.3**

NYSE Composite Index
(May 1999–April 2000, daily)

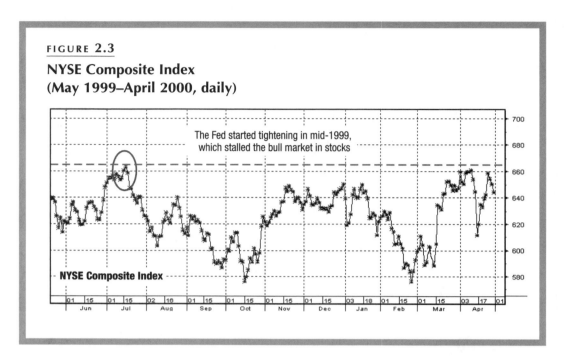

The Fed started tightening in mid-1999, which stalled the bull market in stocks

NYSE Composite Index

FIGURE **2.4**

Treasury Bond Prices vs. NYSE Advance-Decline
(April 1997–April 2000, daily)

New York Advance Decline

Treasury Bond Prices

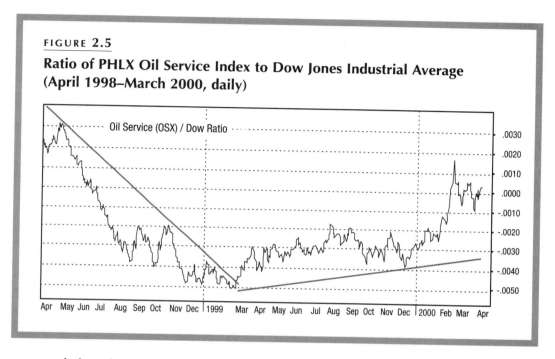

FIGURE 2.5

Ratio of PHLX Oil Service Index to Dow Jones Industrial Average (April 1998–March 2000, daily)

percent below the peak of the previous summer. The Dow Jones Industrial Average lost 8 percent during that nine-month period.

The most dramatic impact of rising rates on the stock market was reflected in its impact on the broader market. For example, **Figure 2.4** compares Treasury bond prices with the NYSE Advance-Decline line and shows a dramatic fall in market breadth during year 1999. The chart suggests that the broader stock market was more adversely affected by rising interest rates than most people realized. It also contradicted the view put forward by some market observers that the stock market was largely unaffected by rising rates (and rising oil prices). But the most telling illustration of the impact on the stock market of rising oil prices and rising rates during 1999 was seen in its effect on sector and industry group rotation that took place within the market during that period of time.

Intermarket Sector Effect

Although intermarket forces say a lot about the direction of inflation and interest rates (and can have an important influence on asset allocation strategies), their most practical day-to-day impact can be seen in the area of sector

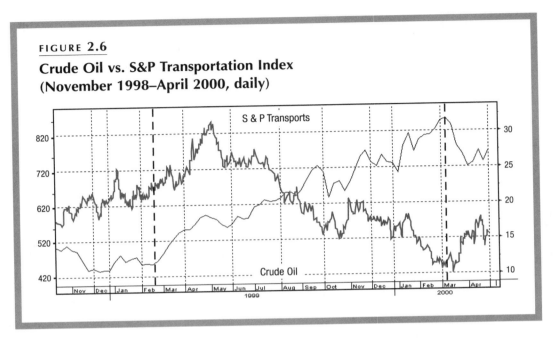

FIGURE **2.6**

**Crude Oil vs. S&P Transportation Index
(November 1998–April 2000, daily)**

and industry group rotation, that is, how money tends to flow from one sector or industry into another. **Figure 2.5** shows, for example, how one segment of the market actually benefited from rising oil prices. The chart plots a ratio of the PHLX Oil Service Index (OSX) divided by the Dow Jones Industrial Average during 1998 and 1999. Ratio (or relative strength) charts are particularly helpful in spotting those sectors that are getting hot and those that are cooling off.

Generally speaking, it is better to focus one's capital on those market groups that are outperforming the rest of the market (which is characterized by a rising relative strength or ratio line). Figure 2.5 shows oil service stocks underperforming during 1998 (as oil prices fell). A dramatic upturn during the first quarter of 1999 (identified by the breaking of the down trendline) signaled to the intermarket chartist that oil stocks were starting to outperform the Dow Jones Industrial average and were a good place to be for the following year. The upturn in energy stocks at the start of 1999 also confirmed the chartist's suspicions that oil prices were indeed headed higher, as there is usually a positive correlation between the direction of oil prices and oil shares. While oil shares benefited from rising oil prices, other groups suffered as a result.

FIGURE 2.7

Ratio of NYSE Financial Index to Dow Jones Industrial Average (March 1998–April 2000, daily)

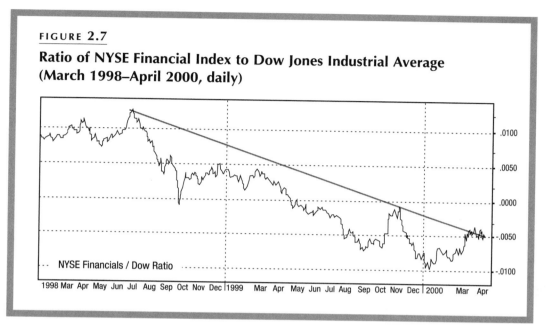

Transports Hurt by Rising Oil

Figure 2.6 shows the negative impact rising oil prices had on transportation stocks (airlines in particular). Within a couple of months of the upturn in oil prices at the start of 1999, transportation stocks started a major decline that lasted into the following spring. During that period, transportation stocks lost a whopping 40 percent of their value.

(On the right side of the chart, you can see how the pullback in oil during the first quarter of 2000 had the opposite effect of giving a boost to transportation stocks.)

Transportation stocks were not the only group hurt by rising oil prices during 1999. As rising oil prices led to rising interest rates, those market groups that are most sensitive to rates began to suffer, especially financial stocks.

Figure 2.7 presents the relative strength ratio of the NYSE Financial Index divided by the Dow Jones Industrial Average. The falling ratio line is a dramatic demonstration of how badly financial stocks did during the second half of 1998 and all of 1999 relative to the rest of the market. The poor performance by rate-sensitive financial stocks during 1999 also confirmed the trend in the futures pits toward higher commodity prices and higher U.S. interest rates.

Figures 2.5, 2.6, and 2.7 show the importance of being in tune with inter-

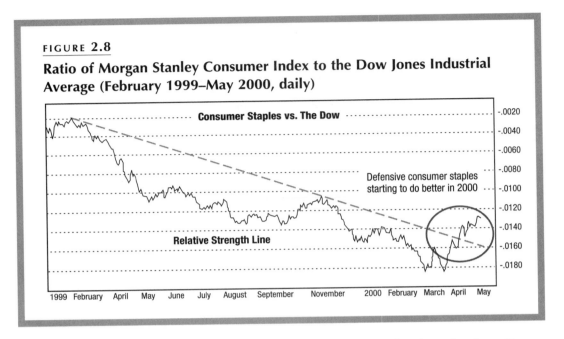

FIGURE 2.8

Ratio of Morgan Stanley Consumer Index to the Dow Jones Industrial Average (February 1999–May 2000, daily)

market forces from a sector rotation standpoint. They also show that in a climate of rising oil prices and rising interest rates (as in 1999), oil stocks are a good place to be while financial and transportation stocks are not.

Other Sector Influences

The preceding examples may seem fairly obvious, but there are more subtle intermarket influences that play on various market groups. During a period of rising industrial commodity prices, for example, basic material stocks (like aluminum and copper) usually do relatively well. At the same time, consumer staples (like drugs) and retail stocks usually do worse. As rising interest rates begin to slow the economy (which the stock market usually spots six to nine months early), economically sensitive cyclical stocks start to weaken (relatively speaking) while consumer-oriented stocks start to take up the slack.

Figure 2.8 is a ratio of the Morgan Stanley Consumer Index (CMR) to the Dow. It shows poor performance by consumer stocks during 1999 (as rates were rising). However, the first quarter of 2000 showed new signs of strength in this defensive sector. The chart shows the ratio line breaking a year-long down trendline and hitting the highest level in six months. To the intermarket chartist, that was a signal that consumer stocks were returning to favor. It was also a signal that the market

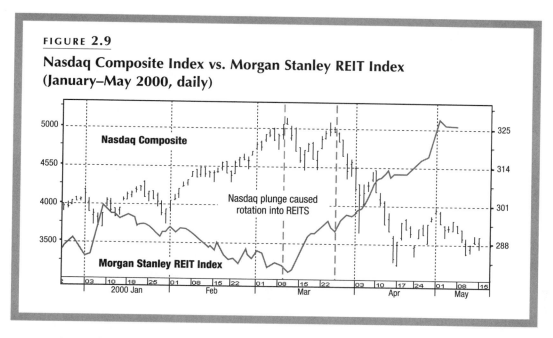

FIGURE 2.9

**Nasdaq Composite Index vs. Morgan Stanley REIT Index
(January–May 2000, daily)**

was starting to favor more defensive issues (that usually do better in the early stages of an economic slowdown). Other defensive groups that started to rise in the spring of 2000 were real estate and utility stocks, two traditional defensive havens.

Sector Rotation and the Economy

Various market sectors do better at different stages of the economic cycle. Near the end of an economic expansion, for example, energy stocks usually take over market leadership. That is due primarily to the buildup of inflation pressures, which are reflected in rising energy prices. Unfortunately, rising oil prices put pressure on the Fed to raise interest rates (which started in the middle of 1999). In time, rising interest rates have the effect of slowing the economy. When the market starts to sense economic slowing, consumer staples start to become market leaders. That being the case, the rising relative strength of energy stocks and consumer staples usually signals that an economic expansion is nearing an end (or is at least starting to slow).

REITS Turn Up As Technology Turns Down

Part of the flow into consumer staples, and defensive stocks in particular, dur-

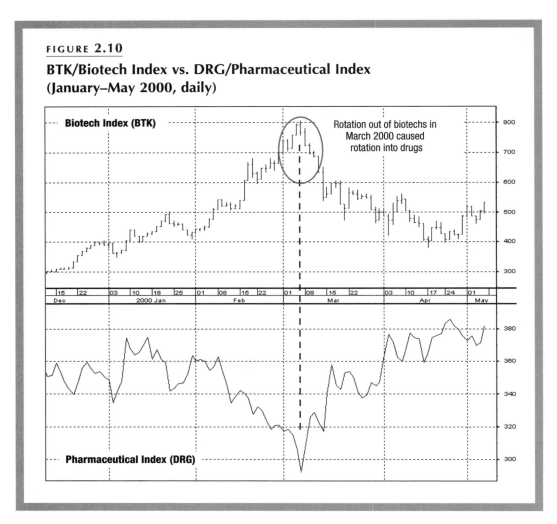

FIGURE 2.10

**BTK/Biotech Index vs. DRG/Pharmaceutical Index
(January–May 2000, daily)**

ing the first half of 2000 was also caused by a sudden downturn in technology
stocks and a more cautious mood in the stock market. In the spring of 2000, the
Nasdaq Composite Index lost over 30 percent in the space of a few weeks.
Although the decline hurt those investors heavily concentrated in technology
stocks, it gave a boost to more defensive shares like real estate stocks (REITs).
Figure 2.9 shows that the sharp downturn in the technology-dominated Nasdaq
Composite Index during March 2000 coincided almost perfectly with a sharp
upturn in the Morgan Stanley REIT Index (RMS). The chart shows that some of
the money fleeing the technology sector found its way into the REIT market.

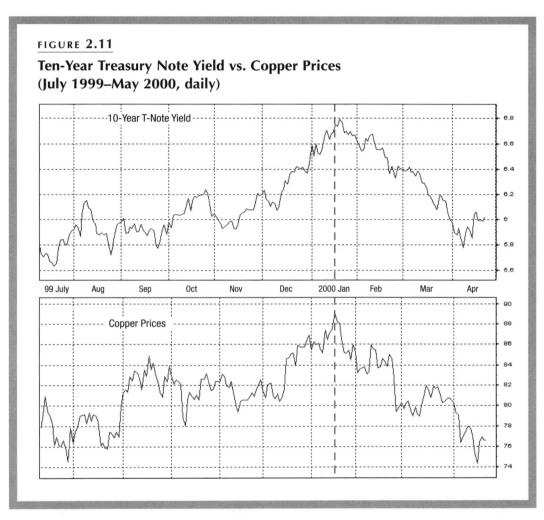

FIGURE **2.11**

**Ten-Year Treasury Note Yield vs. Copper Prices
(July 1999–May 2000, daily)**

REITs have traditionally acted as a defensive haven during times of market weakness because of their low correlation to the rest of the market. Fortunately, the intermarket chartist was easily able to spot these changes in market sentiment and profit from them.

From Biotechs to Drugs

The plunge in the Nasdaq market in the spring of 2000 caused another more subtle rotation that was easily spotted on price charts. This rotation occurred within the health care sector. **Figure 2.10** compares the Biotech Index (BTK)

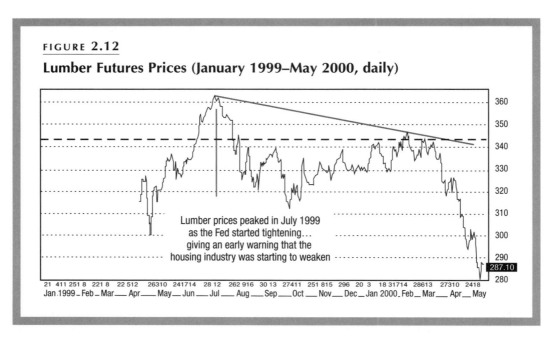

FIGURE **2.12**

Lumber Futures Prices (January 1999–May 2000, daily)

Lumber prices peaked in July 1999
as the Fed started tightening…
giving an early warning that the
housing industry was starting to weaken

with the Pharmaceutical Index (DRG) during the first half of 2000. During the first three months of 2000, a strong biotech group helped lead the Nasdaq market higher. At the same time, traditional drug stocks were out of favor. That all changed at the start of March, however, as the Biotech Index peaked (and pulled the Nasdaq down with it). Figure 2.10 shows a dramatic upturn in drug stocks just as the biotechs peaked. As money tends to stay within a broad market sector, the chart seems to reflect a group rotation within the health care sector—out of riskier biotech stocks into safer and more defensive drug stocks.

Commodities as Economic Indicators

At the beginning of this chapter it was noted how the upturn in commodity prices at the start of 1999 pulled interest rates higher through the balance of that year. Although the primary focus of the earlier discussion was on the oil market, copper was also mentioned. That is because copper is a good barometer of global economic trends. A strong copper market implies economic strength. A weak copper market implies economic weakness. A glance at **Figure 2.11** shows why it is a good idea for traders in Treasury notes (and bonds) to keep an eye on copper as well. The chart shows the remarkably close correlation between copper futures prices and the yield on the 10-year Treasury note dur-

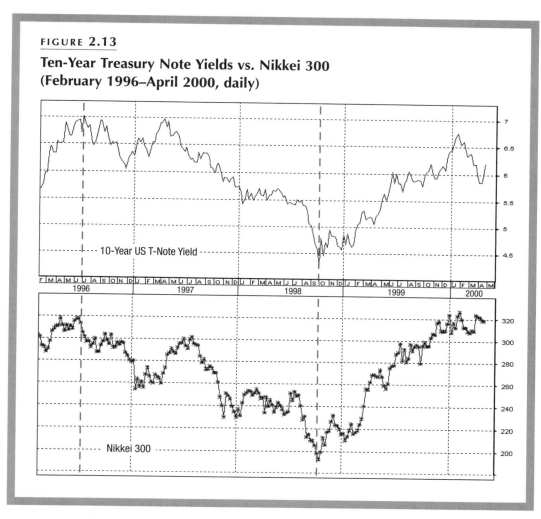

FIGURE 2.13

Ten-Year Treasury Note Yields vs. Nikkei 300 (February 1996–April 2000, daily)

ing the second half of 1999 and the first quarter of 2000. A downside correction in copper starting in January 2000 coincided perfectly with a pullback in Treasury note yields.

Another commodity that may have some predictive value for the economy and the stock market is the lumber market. Lumber is directly tied to the housing market, which itself is considered a leading indicator of economic trends. **Figure 2.12** shows lumber prices peaking in July 1999, just as the Federal Reserve Board started to raise interest rates. Although the conventional wisdom at the start of year 2000 was that the series of Fed rate hikes was having little dampening effect on the U.S. economy, the collapse in lumber prices seemed to be telling a different story. Falling lumber prices might have been viewed as an early warning that the housing sector was starting to feel the impact of rising interest rates, which in time could have a negative impact on the entire economy (and the stock market).

Japan's Effect on U.S. Markets

Global market trends affect those in the United States. To demonstrate that principle, **Figure 2.13** compares the Japanese stock market to the yield on the U.S. 10-year Treasury note market over a four-year span. You can see that the two markets have a striking correlation. Although it may seem strange at first, the chart makes perfect sense. Japan has the second largest economy in the world. For most of the past decade, the Japanese economy has been in a deflationary recession, which in turn has contributed in no small way to the global downtrend in long-term rates. That helps explain the simultaneous drop in Japanese stocks and U.S. rates from 1996 to 1998.

Notice that the bottom in Japanese stocks in the fourth quarter of 1998 coincided exactly with the bottom in U.S. interest rates. Both markets rose together through 1999. The upturn in Japanese stocks at the start of 1999 anticipated recovery in the Japanese economy later that year. New strength in Japan (and Asia in general) also improved global demand for industrial commodities like copper and oil, and both rose.

Rising commodity prices contributed to higher global interest rates. U.S. economists spent most of 1999 questioning the rise in the U.S. interest rates in the face of relatively low U.S. inflation. What they may have failed to recognize is that the upturn in U.S. interest rates may have had more to do with strength in the Japanese economy than the U.S. economy. The intermarket chartist was able to study these global trends and benefit from them accordingly.

The Technical Nature of Intermarket Analysis

It is hard to separate market trends from economic trends. Economists have known for years that bond and stock markets anticipate economic trends. (They may not be as aware of the importance of commodity prices in the intermarket chain.) That is where the technical analyst comes in. The technical analyst is mainly interested in market trends. If those market trends have some application to economic forecasting, so be it. But those trends usually show up in the financial markets first, where the intermarket chartist can easily spot them.

One of the main advantages of technical analysis is the ability to plot several markets at the same time. Chartists can easily track the course of the dollar, oil, bonds, and the stock market. They can also track the relative performance of market groups. In addition, it is a simple task to chart and analyze the trends of major global markets.

The ability to chart so many things at the same time gives the technical analyst a big edge in the area of intermarket analysis. Once the various markets are charted, it is just another logical step to study their interrelationships. Fundamental analysts, by contrast, tend to specialize in small market groups. The nature of fundamental analysis, with its emphasis on economic analysis, virtually demands specialization. That gives the intermarket chartist a unique benefit when it comes to grasping the big picture. And, more and more, some grasp of the big picture is a necessary ingredient in a thorough market view.

Awareness of the financial markets' intermarket condition also sheds light on why certain market sectors do better or worse at certain times. That insight, combined with relative strength (or ratio) charts, is invaluable in the implementation of sector rotation strategies. These sector rotations also shed light on the current state of the economy. Because financial markets act as leading indicators for economic trends, intermarket analysis elevates the usefulness of technical analysis into the realm of economic forecasting.

Technical analysis of any one market class, such as the stock market, is incomplete without some understanding of what is happening in the other three classes (commodities, currencies, and bonds). The events of 1999 (and the early part of 2000) show why it is important for Wall Street (and Main Street) to keep an eye on the futures pits of Chicago and New York and apply intermarket principles to sector and industry group rotation. In real estate, location is the key to success. Location is also crucial to stock market success.

As noted previously, being in the right sectors and industry groups at the right time is more important than being in the market as a whole. During 1999, rising oil prices proved to be bullish for energy stocks, but bearish for financials and transports. Rising interest rates also kept downward pressure on consumer staples and retail stocks for most of that year. That started to change in 2000 because of continued Federal Reserve tightening and a resulting inverted yield curve during the first quarter.

Inverted Yield Curve Implies Weakening

An inverted yield curve, such as occurred during the first quarter of 2000, means that short-term interest rates have risen above long-term rates. That usually occurs after a round of Fed tightening and, in the past, has been an early warning of economic weakness. Its occurrence may explain the rotation out of overbought sectors of the market (like biotech and high tech) during the first quarter of 2000 into more defensive market sectors (like drugs, real estate, and utilities), which usually do better when the economy is slowing. Whether that proves to be the case, the markets themselves usually provide the clues to future price direction and that of the economy.

The Evolving Intermarket Model

When I wrote a book entitled *Intermarket Technical Analysis: Trading Strategies for the Global Stock, Bond, Commodity, and Currency Markets* in 1991, many of these ideas seemed revolutionary. Some in the technical community even questioned whether intermarket work had any place in the world of the technical analyst. I'm happy to report that the Market Technicians Association (MTA) now includes intermarket analysis as an official branch of technical analysis. In 1991 most of the emphasis was put on the macro picture of intermarket interrelationships, with special application in the area of asset allocation between competing asset classes. Fortunately, most of the ideas put forward almost a decade ago have stood the test of time and held up very well during the 1990s.

One of the basic premises of technical analysis is that the markets discount economic and fundamental information. The chartist studies the markets to try to decipher their message about future trends. Nowhere is that more true than in the field of intermarket analysis. Financial markets always carry a message. The trick is knowing how to read it. That can best be done by tracking all the markets—not just one or two—and taking all of their interrelationships into consideration. This model aids in a macro approach to asset allocation strategies, and is even more relevant in the application of sector and industry rotation strategies.

CHAPTER 3

Applying Moving Averages to Point and Figure Charts

KENNETH G. TOWER

Moving averages are a widely accepted means of smoothing data in order to reveal the underlying trend. Although ubiquitous on bar charts, they have not been widely applied to point and figure charts, even though point and figure charts have been around since the late 1800s. Point and figure charts, which measure price changes and the direction of those changes without any consideration for volume or time, differ substantially from bar charts in construction. In bar (and candlestick) charts, the horizontal scale measures time. Thus, for a daily chart, a new entry is made for each day. Point and figure charts recognize that not all days are created equal. On some days a particular stock may undergo a great deal of activity, while on others the specialist market makers are so bored they exchange jokes and take naps.

Point and figure charts reflect the fact that some days' trading is more significant than others. One-box reversal charts, the original method of point and figure charting, best display the days' trading activity. Because this method uses intraday price activity, there may be many chart postings on an active day. Conversely, during periods of inactivity or lackluster trading, a chart may be untouched for a week or more. This means that point and figure moving averages are unaffected by inactive trading days, resulting in fewer whipsaws.

PCs have generally made technical indicators and charts much more accessible. Unfortunately, programmers have designed the software to use fixed width data fields. Accurate point and figure charts require a variable length data field in order to reflect the increased volatility of an active trading day. This has resulted in a lot of inaccurate point and figure charts in software packages. Furthermore, because it is more difficult to accommodate than end-of-day data, the use of intraday data has contributed to something of a drop in the popularity of point and figure charts. The inclusion of intraday data, however, is essential to point and figure charting. In the same way that utilizing the open in a candlestick chart reveals more details of a day's trading than a traditional bar chart, the use of intraday data in point and figure charts reveals much more clearly the workings of the forces of supply and demand. By including the intraday data, the point and figure chart responds quickly to an increase in trading volatility which is then immediately reflected in the moving averages, allowing investors to recognize trading opportunities more quickly.

Background of Point and Figure Charting

Point and figure charts, although invented in the 1880s, did not become popular until the 1920s when some of the most successful pool operators used them to great success. (During the "bad old days" of stock trading in the 1920s, a pool was a group of investors who combined—"pooled"—their money to trade stocks. Nothing wrong with that, but the way they operated led securities regulators to institute the down-tick rule—ending manipulation of stock prices by unscrupulous pools.) It seems hard to believe today as our computer screens display mountains of data, but the ticker tape machine was a revolution for stock traders. Using the technology of the telegraph, the ticker tape allowed traders and investors to keep track of their investments without waiting for the evening papers and without having to be physically present on the floor of the stock exchange. The number of active investors increased greatly with this new source of information.

Many of the investment pools became expert in "painting" the tape—that is, pushing the price of a given stock up in such a way as to induce other investors to believe that the smart money had found a new winner. Of course, this practice occurred near the end of a long bull market, one that had made many investors wealthy, and nothing breeds overconfidence like success. At any rate, investors were trading stocks at a fever pitch (the peak volume in 1929 would stand as a record for nearly forty years), and point and figure charts became popular because investors believed that by using the intraday data they could better track the movements of the pool operators.

Basics of Chart Construction

Let's imagine that Sears closed yesterday at $40. In simplest form, constructing a point and figure chart of this security would involve using a box size of $1 and making a one-box reversal chart. A $1 box size means keeping track of every $1 price move. A one-box reversal chart means making use of all of the price reversals. So to recognize that the stock closed yesterday at $40, place an "X" on the graph paper just above the horizontal line at $40.

$40 | x

Let's examine two examples, a lively day and a dull day. On the dull day, Sears opens at $40.50 and trades up to $40⅞ before falling to, and closing at, $39.50. The chart has a box size of $1 and since the last posting was at $40, we are looking for a move to $41 or $39 before making the next X on the chart. Thus, at the end of the dull day, the chart is entirely unchanged.

On the lively day, Sears also opens at $40.50. By noon it has risen to $41 and continues to rise to $42.125 before falling to $39 in a late day sell-off. Now the chart looks like this:

```
      | x
      | x x
$40  | x x
      |   x
```

The two Xs above the initial one at $40 reflect the stock's move up to $42. At that point the stock begins to fall. Remember, the box size is $1, so once the stock falls to $41 you need to make another X. If you make it immediately under the X at $42, it will not be visible because of the X already placed there. Thus, you need to move one column to the right. Having placed the X in a new column at $41, the stock continues to fall to $40 and finally $39. These Xs can be placed directly below the X just marked at $41. There is no need to move out of the new column that the posting of $41 necessitated, because there is no overlap. If on the next day the stock opened at $40, fell to $39, rose again to $40, fell again to $39, and closed at $41 the chart would look like this:

```
      | x
      | x x        x
$40  | x x x x x
      |   x x x
```

By this time you might be wondering why the chart is full of Xs rather than a combination of Xs and Os. Os are used to represent falling prices in down columns on three-box reversal charts, which were invented as a shortcut to the traditional method. On a one-box reversal chart the first posting in a new column may be the start of a significant price move, or it may not (such as the first move up from the $39 low in the example above). Since one cannot be sure that the new column will be an up or down column, one simply always plots an X.

Consolidation Zones

Why keep track of the smaller price moves? Point and figure chart analysts do so because these moves make up consolidation zones. A *consolidation zone* is an area where the stock moves back and forth between two relatively well-defined areas. In a consolidation zone, the forces of supply and demand are in balance. A move outside the zone is called a *breakout*. A breakout suggests that the previous balance between supply and demand no longer exists and that a new trending phase has begun. The longer the consolidation zone, the more significant the breakout. Thus the breakout from the first chart pattern below is less important than that of the second chart pattern.

Why is this so? Quite simply because the move this pattern represents is assumed to affect more investors. In both examples depicted here, the stock has established a trading range between $42 and $39 with the final X (at $38) indicating a breakdown. However, the second pattern, being longer than the first, indicates that more investors are affected than in the first pattern, and thus indicates a more significant outcome. We all know that owning a stock whose shares are falling provokes a much different emotional response than that of a stock that is rising. Even seasoned fund managers, who one might expect to be impervious to the effects of short-term market swings, are under a great deal of pressure to outperform the market. Because the reaction to losses tends to be more extreme, the breakdown in the second (larger) pattern is assumed to be more significant since it reflects a greater amount of trading and involves more investors. Point and figure moving averages are based on columns, so the second consolidation pattern will greatly affect those moving averages whereas the first (shorter) consolidation will not.

```
        | X                              | X    X  X  X
        | X X    X X                     | X X    X X X X X X X X    X
  $40   | X X X X X X X              $40  | X X X X X X X X X X X X X X X
        |   X X      X X                  |   X X  X   X      X   X   X
        |                 x-breakdown     |                       x-breakdown
        |                    point        |                          point
```

Price Objectives

One of the great advantages of relying on the point and figure chart is the facility with which it enables the trader to calculate price objectives. To illustrate simple point and figure price objectives, the two preceding consolidation patterns are presented again below and on the following page with the columns numbered.

To calculate a target one must first identify a consolidation zone. We know where these consolidation zones end (with a downside breakout at $38), so we need to find what is termed the up-wall at the beginning of the zone to determine its size. In both cases, the chart's first column (a move from $40 to $42) provides that initial up column. In the first example, starting from the up-wall, simply count the columns over to the downside breakout (columns 2 through 7). Those six columns are then subtracted from the middle of the zone. In this example, the middle is at $40. $40 minus $6 gives a price target of $34 for the new downtrend. Stated another way, the breakdown at $38 suggests the stock will drop to $34.

```
        | x     x
        | x x   x x
 $40 | x x x x x x x
        |   x x     x x x
        |               x-breakdown point
        | 1 2 3 4 5 6 7
```

For the second example, you again count from the first up-wall in the consolidation to the column with the breakdown. This includes columns 2–18. These seventeen columns are then subtracted from the middle of the zone ($40), and a target of $23 is derived. In the days of paper charts these objectives were commonly calculated by means of a compass. The analyst would place the point of the compass in the breakout column (the last one on the chart in this example), and the pencil point at the column with the up-wall at the beginning of the consolidation. The analyst would then move the pencil down and to the right, creating an arc that would bottom at the price objective (note that the example shown does not arrive at the precise level because the chart is not presented on graph paper). Note that this ability to provide price objectives depends on the size of the consolidation zone. The consolidation zones will only be accurately depicted if intraday data is used.

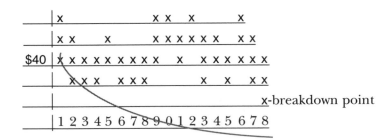

```
      | x                 x  x   x          x
      | x  x      x          x x x x x x      x x
$40   | x x x x x x x x x      x    x x x x x x
      |    x x x    x x x              x    x    x x
      |                                              x-breakdown point
      | 1 2 3 4 5 6 7 8 9 0 1 2 3 4 5 6 7 8
```

Constructing Moving Averages on
Point and Figure Charts

The mechanics of constructing a moving average on a bar chart are simple, but constructing a moving average on a point and figure chart is more complicated. As a result, moving averages have seldom been used in conjunction with point and figure charts. In fact, as computerized charting packages were introduced in the 1980s and proliferated in the 1990s, point and figure charts were little used due to their differing data requirements. UST Securities Corp. brought point and figure charts into the computer age and introduced the use of log scales, individualized box sizes, and moving averages.

Moving averages are useful because they smooth often volatile short-term data and help reveal the underlying trend. Investors have long known, and academic studies confirm, the importance of recognizing the underlying trend. Moving averages can be constructed in a weighted or unweighted (simple) form. The examples in this chapter use the simple form. For the actual calculation of the moving average, the mid-point of each column is the input value. For example, when using a $1 box size and the first column contains postings at $40, $41, and $42, the value used for the calculation of the moving average from that column would be $41. Short-term (10-column) and long-term (20-column) moving averages appear on each chart.

Moving averages can be used in several ways to reveal the trend. The two most common methods are determining the slope of an average and using a crossover system comprised of a short- and long-term average. Combining these techniques illustrates the advantages of adding moving averages to a traditional breakout system.

Recognizing the Long Consolidation Breakout Pattern

Studying the long consolidation breakout pattern (involving sideways price action lasting from one to three years) provides a long-term investment perspective. A sideways price move, or trading range, indicates that supply and demand are in balance. Whenever the stock gets down to the bottom of the range, buyers step in (or perhaps sellers decide to wait) and the price begins to rise. At the top of the trading range the reverse occurs. The buyers disappear or perhaps additional sellers appear. It is not important which of these alternatives occurs, but something happens to keep the stock in its trading range.

At some point the stock trades at a price outside the trading range. Technicians call this a breakout, and it indicates a shift in the supply or demand curve. It implies that the forces that have held the stock to a narrow range have shifted. The trading range is finished and a new trend, in the direction of the breakout, has begun.

The likely extent of this new trend is indicated on a point and figure chart by the size of the previous consolidation zone. These long consolidation breakouts are very clear cut, but there are many occasions when the market trend is not so obvious. It is in these cases that moving averages are invaluable.

Identifying Moving Average Reversals

Figures 3.1–3.4 offer examples of moving average reversals. **Figure 3.1** (Hilfiger Corp.) is a one-box reversal chart with a box size of 3.6 percent. These are log scale charts so the reversal is not really 3.6 percent; rather, it is the logarithmic equivalent of 3.6 percent. This equivalent avoids the problem that occurs when rising and falling percentage changes are not equal numbers. For example, suppose a stock closes on a Monday at $100, then falls 10 percent on Tuesday to close at $90. On Wednesday it rises 10 percent, so it is now at $99, not the $100 it closed at on Monday. The reversals are quoted in percentage terms because many people are not familiar with logarithms. The box sizes are determined by UST Securities Corp. analysts with the goal of accurately reflecting each stock's trading characteristics. More volatile stocks require larger reversal values to accurately display their trading patterns.

After the October 1998 bottom (see point A in Figure 3.1), TOM advances strongly and the moving averages both turn positive at point B. This is helpful because the base that the stock has now broken out of is quite small. The reversal of both moving averages suggests that this is the beginning of a larger rise than might be expected from the small base pattern that formed around the low. At

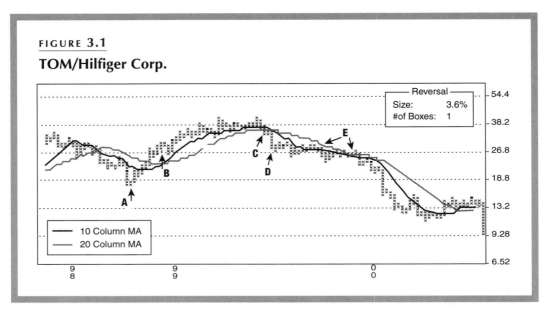

FIGURE 3.1

TOM/Hilfiger Corp.

Reversal	
Size:	3.6%
#of Boxes:	1

10 Column MA
20 Column MA

Source: UST Securities

point C there is a breakdown from a minor top, but not enough to elicit a long-term sell. This pattern changes at point D where both moving averages have turned down. The stock remains in this sell signal for the next year as it falls to $9.

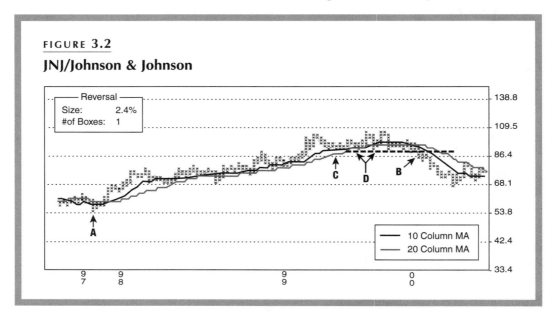

FIGURE 3.2

JNJ/Johnson & Johnson

Reversal	
Size:	2.4%
#of Boxes:	1

10 Column MA
20 Column MA

Source: UST Securities

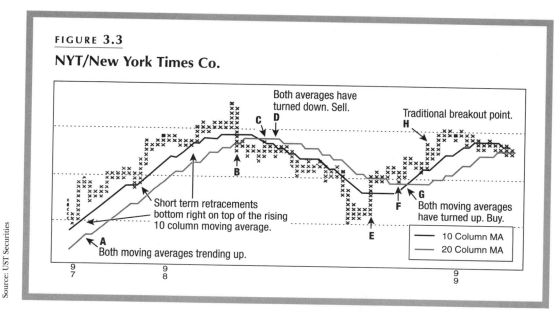

FIGURE 3.3

NYT/New York Times Co.

Both averages have turned down. Sell. C D

Traditional breakout point. H

Short term retracements bottom right on top of the rising 10 column moving average.

B

A
Both moving averages trending up.

E

F G
Both moving averages have turned up. Buy.

10 Column MA
20 Column MA

Source: UST Securities

Points E in Figure 3.1, where the stock rallies up to the declining moving averages, confirm the downtrend and offer additional chances for current holders to sell and opportunities for traders to sell short or buy put options.

The preceding example illustrates perhaps *the* most valuable advantage of using technical analysis: it keeps you from holding losers. There is a natural tendency for investors to hold on to a stock until it rallies back to their purchase price or some recent high. In this example, while the trade from B to D does not make much money, there is no bounce back up after point D. This technique provides a discipline that helps investors get out.

Figure 3.2 (Johnson & Johnson) is a one-box reversal chart with a box size of 2.4 percent. After the October 1997 bottom the stock enters a buy signal (point A) as the stock breaks out of a small consolidation pattern and both moving averages turn up. This buy signal remains in force until early in the year 2000 (point B). At that point the moving averages have turned down, the short-term average has fallen below the long-term average, and the stock has fallen below major support (points C and D). Three strikes and you're out—there is no excuse for continuing to hold this stock. (Remember, there is a big difference between a good company and a good stock.)

Figure 3.3 (New York Times) starts out in a strong uptrend (point A). Early in 1998 the stock falls sharply (point B). The decline penetrates short-term sup-

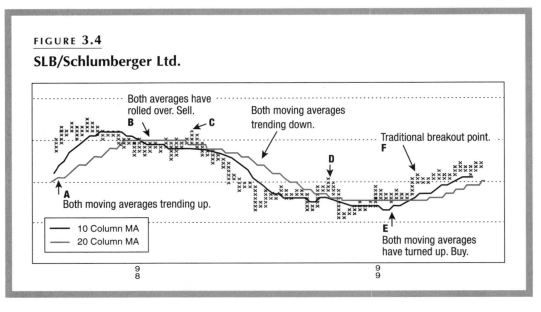

FIGURE 3.4

SLB/Schlumberger Ltd.

port and both up-trending moving averages. Rally attempts fail at the moving averages, which are now rolling over (point C). These are excellent sell points.

At point D, both moving averages have turned down and, shortly thereafter, the stock falls sharply. The process is then reversed when a sharp recovery penetrates both moving averages, followed by declines that bottom at the now flattening moving averages (points E and F). Both moving averages turn up, signaling an early buy point (point G). This moving average buy point is slightly ahead of the traditional breakout buy signal (point H).

Figure 3.4 (Schlumberger) begins at the end of a strong uptrend (point A). The stock then drifts lower and falls below both moving averages. The averages have both turned down at point B. The rally at point C is a bull trap. It signals a short-term breakout and rises above both moving averages.

The secret to avoiding this trap is to watch for confirmation from the long-term moving average. In this case, the 20-column moving average never turns up, and the decline signaled at point B is quickly resumed. This decline continues for most of 1998, with another bull trap at point D. This trap is avoided in the same manner as at point C. Finally, at point E, the stock price has remained above the moving averages long enough to turn them higher. As in Figure 3.3, this moving average buy point is slightly ahead of the traditional breakout buy signal (point F).

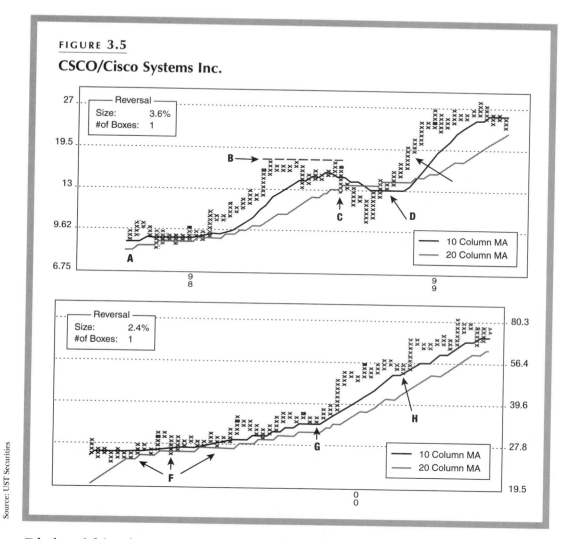

FIGURE 3.5

CSCO/Cisco Systems Inc.

Distinguishing between Temporary Pullbacks and Tops

A common question is "when do I buy a stock that's already in a strong uptrend?" **Figures 3.5** and **3.6** are examples of how to use moving averages to differentiate pullbacks within uptrends from important tops. **Figure 3.5** (Cisco) is a one-box reversal chart with a box size of 3.6 percent. This chart begins in late 1997 when the stock is already in an uptrend (both moving averages are trending higher) that continues into the year 2000.

The stock forms a triple top during the second quarter of 1998 (point B) and breaks down from a small consolidation area at point C. From this point the stock drops a further 30 percent before bottoming around $10. From this low the stock rebounds sharply and moves through short-term resistance (the break-down level at point C) and goes on to signal that all is well by making a new high at D. Throughout this correction, the long-term (20-column) moving average never turns down, therefore it never issues a sell signal. Conservative investors could easily have bought the stock at point D as renewed strength is indicated.

The slope of the uptrend flattens out a bit early in 1999. The lows during this period (point F) coincide with the moving averages and offer excellent buying opportunities. The rate of ascent begins to accelerate again in the third and fourth quarters of 1999. During this period, the lows do not come all the way down to the long-term moving average. Instead they descend only to the short-term moving average (points G and H), which remains higher than the long-term average. In general, this is the best type of uptrend to buy. It is so strong that declines do not even reach the upward sloping long-term moving average.

Figure 3.6 (EMC Corp) is a one-box reversal chart with a box size of 3.4 percent. This chart begins in late 1996 and is in a buy signal for the entire period (the long-term moving average never turns down). During 1997 the stock forms a small double top at point A and breaks down from this small consolidation area at point B. As long as the long-term moving average remains in an uptrend, this weakness must be considered a buying opportunity.

Point C, a display of short-term strength, offers an excellent buy point. Notice how little chart space is taken up by the year 1997. This reflects the fact that there was not much price volatility in EMC that year. From a point and figure basis, this indicates that there was not a great deal of interest in the stock. Thus, the decline from the double top (point A) to the late 1997 low is given much less significance than it would have been on a bar chart. On a bar chart, the stock would have fallen below a falling 200-day moving average by the time that low was reached. On this chart, the 20-column moving average is still trending higher.

The stock then moves sharply higher before entering an irregular consolidation at point D. Once again, all price declines during periods when the long-term moving averages are trending higher are buying opportunities. Although the low at point E is below the 20-column average, that average is still rising, and another excellent buying opportunity presents itself with the short-term strength exhibited at point F.

After another sharp rise, the stock enters a consolidation zone in early 1999.

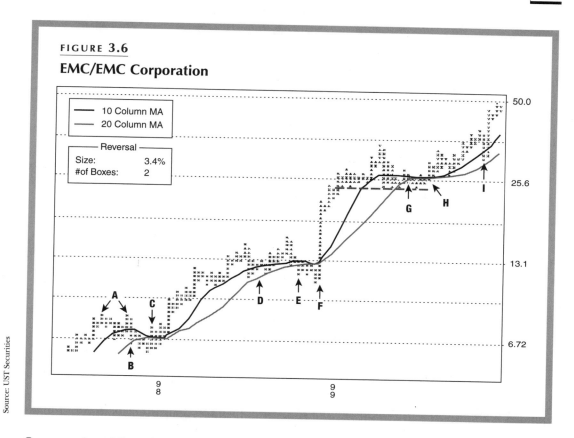

FIGURE 3.6

EMC/EMC Corporation

Source: UST Securities

Once again, although the stock falls below the long-term moving average at point G, that moving average is still rising. Additionally, this consolidation has a very flat floor which provides additional evidence that this is just a consolidation and not a top. Short-term strength at point H provides an excellent buy point as does the pullback at point I.

These techniques work equally well in downtrends. Referring back to the Hilfiger chart in Figure 3.1, notice the excellent sell (or sell short) opportunities at point E, where the price rallies back up to the downward sloping moving averages.

Advantages of Point and Figure Charts over Bar Charts

Figure 3.7 illustrates the difference in presentation between bar charts and point and figure charts. Both panels of Figure 3.7 display Xerox Corp. from November 1996 through March 2000. First, note that on the point and figure

FIGURE **3.7**

Point and Figure vs. Bar Charts, XRX/Xerox Corporation

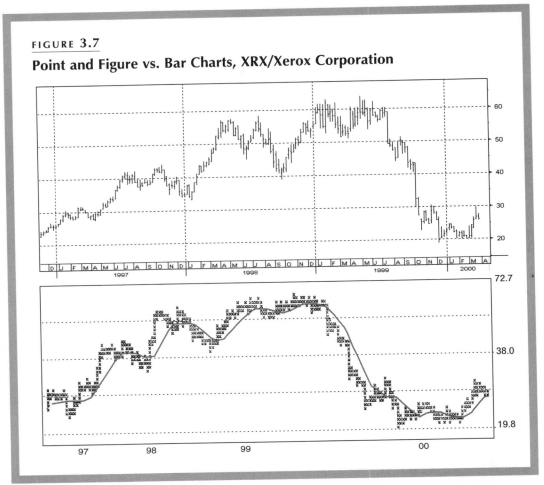

chart the amount of space each year occupies varies. The amount of space between 1997 and 1998 is much smaller than the amount between 1999 and 2000. This indicates that there was much more trading volatility in 1999 than in 1997. Of course, on the weekly bar chart the amount of horizontal space occupied by each year is the same.

The point and figure chart indicates that 1999 was a much more significant period than either of the two previous years. It magnifies the stock's major top in early 1999 and minimizes the uptrend years of 1997 and 1998. Notice also that the late 1999 to early 2000 bottom occupies much more space than it does on the weekly bar chart. Again, this gives a better indication that a significant bottom has been reached. In point and figure charts the horizontal scale reflects price movement—not the earth's rotation.

Remember, what moves a point and figure chart is a change in the direction of the stock's price. In the uptrend years of 1997 and 1998 the buyers are in firm control (demand exceeds supply). What causes the amount of activity to increase in 1999 is the loss of control by the bulls. As the bulls weaken, the stock price changes direction more frequently. Remember also, that every time a stock trades there is a buyer and a seller. The buyer believes the stock will move higher (bullish); the seller believes that there is somewhere better to invest his money (bearish). This increased competition between bullish and bearish investors is what causes 1999 to occupy so much more space on the chart than 1997 or 1998. Finally, in July, the price falls below the March low, and the long term moving average is declining, signaling a major breakdown.

When and How to Use the Technique

Although they display the same data, point and figure charts provide a different view of stock price activity than bar charts. Bar charts are much more widely used than point and figure charts, and, in the battle for investment returns, that in itself is a good reason to check a point and figure chart to see if it gives the same signals. Bar chart mavens try to overcome some of the bar chart's shortcomings by attempting to construct variable-length moving averages. This is an acknowledgment that not all days are of equal significance. Because point and figure charts reflect trading activity, they already possess the quality of a variable-length moving average. This is particularly noticeable in the EMC chart (Figure 3.6), with the compressed activity of 1997. It also reveals itself in the sometimes rapid creation of a topping area.

Any investor knows that pullbacks can occur within even the strongest uptrend. Moving averages provide a framework that helps investors stay in a stock during a short-term decline. They also help investors to distinguish the significant declines from the pullbacks. Investors should always be aware of the status of the moving averages before making a trade. This will help them overcome the greatest obstacle to investment success—their own emotions. Fear and greed threaten investor profits at every turn—point and figure charts with moving averages can help keep them at bay.

Many investors ask why logarithmic scales would be used to display point-and-figure price data. The simple answer is that it is essential when prices vary significantly over time. Pit traders in Chicago do not need log scales because the prices they track are only slightly different over the course of the day. To provide an idea of how a stock will perform over the next six to eighteen months, an investor needs to routinely review the past three years of price history. It is quite common for a stock to have doubled, tripled, or much more over that time period. A log scale is necessary to display the data on a mathematically accurate scale. Think of it this way. In one of the most brutal bear markets in history, the Dow lost about 500 points from the 1973 high to the 1974 low. That 500 point drop represented a 50 percent decline. Today, with the Dow over 10,000, a 500 point drop would not even trigger the first round of circuit breakers.

There are two drawbacks to using log scales. The first is that the scale numbers at the margins of the graph do not result in conveniently round numbers. The second is that it is extremely awkward to post a log scale chart by hand. Yes, we have to agree with the old-timers that posting a chart by hand is superior in many ways to simply looking at a chart on one's computer screen. However, the computer makes it so much easier to follow hundreds of stocks, and the value of using historical data that is accurately displayed far outweighs those drawbacks.

Chaos theory states that similar patterns appear in nature on different scales. This has been found to be true of stock price patterns as well. Keep in mind that a good company does not always mean a good stock. Wal-Mart, for example, has been a good company for many years. Yet it was a bad stock between 1993 and 1997. Four years is a long time to wait for the good fundamentals to reassert themselves. Point and figure charts, by revealing the forces of supply and demand that are at work in the markets, can help an investor distinguish between a good stock and a bad stock. Because they naturally respond to changes in market dynamics, point and figure charts are beautifully suited to moving average trading systems.

By eliminating time, point and figure charts offer a different perspective on stock price action. They clearly illustrate changes in market dynamics as volatile markets lead to greater chart activity than quiet markets. This responsiveness to market conditions gives point and figure charts an advantage over time-based charts. An increase or decrease in volatility is immediately reflected in the chart and moving averages, which leads to fewer false signals than simple bar chart moving averages. While point and figure moving averages do not replace the traditional long consolidation breakouts, they offer a great deal of additional information.

CHAPTER 4

Spotting Early Reversal Signals Using Candle Charts

STEVE NISON

"A prudent man has more than one string to his bow."
—JAPANESE PROVERB

Japanese candle chart analysis, so called because the lines resemble candles, has been refined by generations of use in East Asia. Such charts have been used longer than bar charts and point and figure charts, but were unknown to the Western world until I introduced them in 1990. These charting techniques are now used internationally by traders, investors, and premier financial institutions here and abroad. Most technical analysis Web sites, real-time trading systems, and technical analysis software have candle charts, attesting to their popularity and usefulness.

Some of the reasons for the explosive interest in these heretofore secret techniques include:

● *Candle chart techniques are easy to understand.* Anyone, from the first-time chartist to the seasoned professional can easily harness the power of candle charts. This is because, as will be shown later, the data required to draw the candlestick chart is the same needed to draw the bar chart (the high, low, open, and close).

● *Candle charts provide earlier indications of market turns.* Candle charts can send out reversal signals in a few sessions, rather than the weeks often needed for a bar chart reversal signal. Thus, market turns ascertained with the aid of candle charts will frequently be in advance of traditional indicators. This should help you to enter and exit the market with better timing.

● *Candle charting signals furnish unique market insights.* Candle charts not only show the trend of the move, as does a bar chart, but, unlike bar charts, candle charts also show the force underpinning the move.

● *Candle charting tools enhance Western charting analysis.* As noted above, candle charts use the same data as bar charts—open, high, low, and close. This means that any Western technical tools you now use can also be used on a candle chart. However, candle charts can also give you timing and trading benefits not available with bar charts.

Candle charting strategies are a tool, not a system, and they are best used in conjunction with those Western technical techniques you are most comfortable with.

As the Oriental proverb states, "The journey of a thousand miles begins with the first step." This chapter is a first step, albeit an important one, on the road to candle chart analysis. You will see how the candles can help make your market analysis more efficient, improve entry and exit timing, and open new, effective, and unique avenues of analysis.

Constructing Candle Lines

Figures **4.1** and **4.2** show samples of candle lines. The broad part of the candle line, called the *real body,* is the range between the session's open and close. If the close is higher than that session's open, the real body is empty (see **a** in **Figure 4.1**). A black real body (see **b** in Figure 4.1) occurs when the close is lower than the open.

The thin lines over and under the real bodies are, respectively, the *upper and lower shadows* (see Figure 4.1). The top of the upper shadow is the high of the session; the bottom of the lower shadow is the session's low.

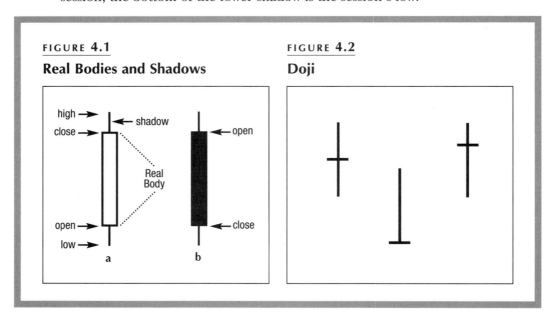

FIGURE 4.1

Real Bodies and Shadows

FIGURE 4.2

Doji

Notice how the candle lines in **Figure 4.2** do not have a real body. Instead they have a horizontal line. These lines that look like crosses are called *doji*. A doji indicates that the open and close are the same (or almost the same). The doji signifies that the market is in balance between the forces of supply and demand. The emergence of a doji in a trending market could be an indication that it is losing its momentum. Doji are discussed in more depth beginning on the next page.

Candle charting techniques can be applied to whatever time frame you now use, from intraday to weekly. Thus, on a 60-minute chart, the real body is the range of the open and close of that 60-minute segment and the top of the upper shadow and the bottom of the lower shadow are the highs and lows of that 60-minute period. Most traders in the West use the candles for daily and intraday analysis.

A critical and powerful advantage of candle charts is that the size and color of the real body can send out volumes of information about whether the bulls or bears are in control of the market. For example:

- A long white real body visually displays that the bulls are in charge.
- A long black real body signifies that the bears are in control.
- A small real body (white or black) indicates a period in which the bulls and bears are in a "tug of war" and warns that the market's trend may be losing momentum. With this in mind, you can use single candle lines to gauge the underlying supply/demand balance of the market.

Using Individual Candle Lines

Figure 4.3 shows that in early to mid-January the bulls were able to maintain this stock near its $117–$118 highs. But a series of candle lines sent out visual clues that the bulls didn't have full control. Specifically, the diminutive size of candle lines at points 1, 2, and 3 reflected hesitation as Procter & Gamble stock approached the upper end of its recent trading zone. These small real bodies showed that either the bulls were retreating or supply was strong enough to absorb the demand. This scenario made the stock vulnerable to a correction.

Figure 4.4 displays how single candle lines helped signal the all-time bottom of IBM stock in 1993. First, one sees the long lower shadow at candle 1 and then a tall white real body at candle 2. This visually showed that demand was entering near $10 a share. At period A, as the market descended, a series of gradually shrinking black real bodies displayed that the selling pressure was evaporating.

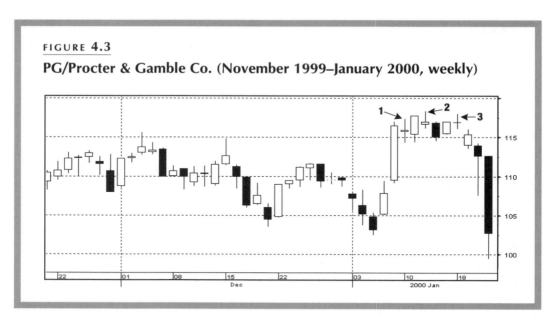

FIGURE **4.3**

PG/Procter & Gamble Co. (November 1999–January 2000, weekly)

The long white candle 3 showed the bulls had regained control of the market. The especially attractive feature about this opportunity was that it posed relatively little price risk. If IBM had closed under the pivotal support area near $10 you would have had to reconsider the bullish outlook. This is a major advantage of charts: there is always a price point at which you would recognize you are wrong in your assessment. Properly used candle charts, and technical analysis in general, can help foster a risk and money management approach to the market.

Doji

The Japanese say that with a doji, especially after a very tall white candle (as in Figure 4.3 at point 1) or in an overbought environment, the market is "tired."

Because doji are so simple to find, some analysts may use the doji as a signal to immediately buy (in an up trend) or sell (during a decline). However, a doji represents a market in a state of transition. The doji changes a bull trend to a more neutral stance. But it does not mean that a rally, for instance, will reverse itself into a decline. During a rally the chances of a doji forecasting a market reversal are increased if:

● The doji confirms other technical clues (e.g., the market is near resistance or support, at a 50 percent retracement level).

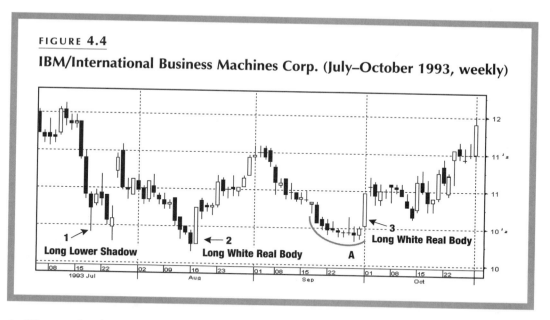

FIGURE 4.4

IBM/International Business Machines Corp. (July–October 1993, weekly)

- The market is overbought or oversold. This is also true for most of the other candle patterns and lines discussed below. Because candle charting tools are mainly reversal indicators, the market must be vulnerable to a correction and investors overextended to increase the chances for a turn, even if it is only temporary.

Figure 4.5 shows that as the Dow Jones Industrial Average ascended from a rally that began in late June 1999 near 10,550, it did so via a series of long white candles. This illustrated that the bulls were in full control. The indication changed entirely with the emergence of a single candle line—the doji at the arrow. Before the doji, the white candles echoed a strong, vibrant market. The doji showed that the rally had now been short-circuited.

Figure 4.5 exemplifies a key asset of candle charts; they send out signals not available with Western technical approaches. For instance, when a bar chart of a session's open and close shows that they are the same, it has no forecasting implications. However, in candle charts, when the open and close are the same it does indicate that the prior trend may be stalling. Specifically, to the Japanese such a session, especially after a sharp advance, indicates that the stock is, as the Japanese say, "separating from its trend."

As previously mentioned, candle charts can be used in any time frame, including small intraday segments. In **Figure 4.6** each of the candle lines repre-

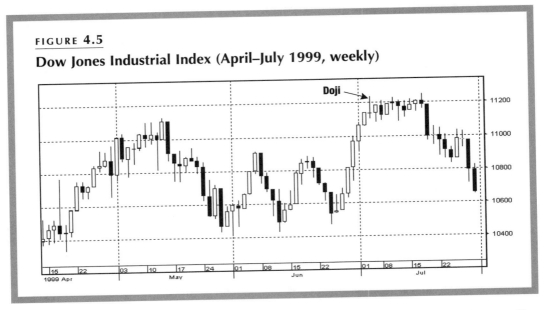

FIGURE 4.5

Dow Jones Industrial Index (April–July 1999, weekly)

sents the open-high-low and close of a five-minute period. Two tall white candles show a forceful rally early on December 30. A warning flag was hoisted via the doji at the arrow. This doji was a valuable warning that as the index got near its recent peak at 3,750 it had met enough supply to checkmate all the demand. In doing so, the index had formed a doji.

This chart highlights another use of a doji. If there is a doji after a long white candle you can use the highest high of the tall white candle or the doji (including their shadows) as signals of resistance. Note how the 3,745 area (the highest high between the doji and the prior long white candle) became resistance, based on a close during the next candle line.

Another example of this technique can be seen on the previous chart, Figure 4.5. Observe how the high of the doji became resistance. This chart shows how resistance can be penetrated intraday, as it was on July 17th. But if the bulls cannot maintain enough force to hold the market above resistance into the close, then the resistance area is still valid. A close over this resistance level would mean a bullish breakout. Just as the market is "tired" with a doji after a tall white candle, so it is said to be "refreshed" with a close over the resistance area.

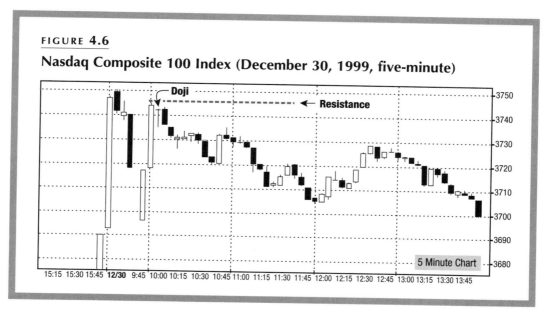

FIGURE 4.6

Nasdaq Composite 100 Index (December 30, 1999, five-minute)

Shadows

Although the real body is an important aspect of the candle line (the Japanese refer to the real body as the "essence of the price movement"), there is also substantial information to be gained from the length and position of the shadows.

For example, candle **a** in **Figure 4.7** is a relatively tall white candle. If this real body did not have any shadows, it would be viewed as a positive indication. But when the complete candle is considered, including the shadows, you get a different sense of the market's strength. Because of the white candle's long upper shadow, the rallying strength has been slightly suppressed. The long upper shadow reflects a session in which the market rallied intraday to the top of the upper shadow, but by session's end the bulls were unable to sustain these highs.

Normally two dual black real bodies would be a negative signal. But the lower shadows in both candles shown at **b** in Figure 4.7 show that the bears did not have enough force to keep the market on its lows into the close. Additionally, for both black candles shown at **b** in Figure 4.7, the lows were the same, which could be another warning against being too bearish in this market.

FIGURE 4.7

Shadows

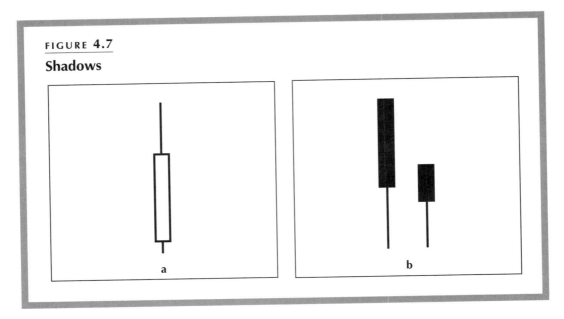

a   b

Hammers and Shooting Stars

Some patterns have so-called one-sided shadows. These are candle lines with very long lower shadows. Examples of these one-sided shadows include *hammers* and *shooting stars*.

The Hammer

If the line in **Figure 4.8** appears during a downtrend, it is a potential bottom reversal signal called a *hammer*, as if the market is trying to hammer out a base. The criteria for the hammer include:

- A small real body (black or white) at the top end of the trading range
- A long lower shadow (at least two to three times the height of the real body)
- Little or no upper shadow
- Appearance during a decline (because it is a bottom reversal signal)

The bullish visual clues are sent by the hammer's shape. Its long lower shadow displays that the market had sold off, but by session's end it had pushed back up to close at or near the highs. It is an indication that the market has rejected lower levels.

Figure 4.9 shows an ideal hammer with its extended lower shadow and close at the day's high and no upper shadow. This hammer's long lower shadow was a positive indication insofar as it markedly showed that demand had overwhelmed supply. However, from a trading perspective the longer the lower shadow the farther you are from buying at the lows. As such, from a risk/reward perspective it may not be appropriate to buy on the hammer's completion (the close of the session). For example, in this hammer, by the time it was completed, Wal-Mart Stores (WMT) closed almost $5 off the lows. This would mean the risk is almost $5 if you bought at this hammer's close. With this in mind, it is usually wise to wait for a correction to within the

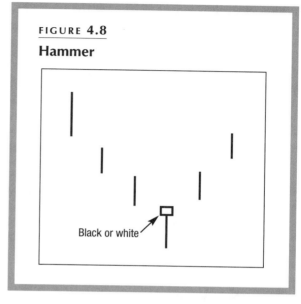

FIGURE **4.8**

Hammer

Black or white

lower shadow (if such a correction occurs) before considering a long position. Doing so decreases the risk of the trade since you are buying near a potential support level. In this chart the stock declined the day after the hammer and suc-

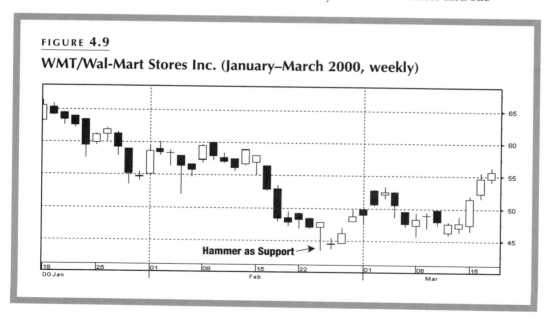

FIGURE **4.9**

WMT/Wal-Mart Stores Inc. (January–March 2000, weekly)

Hammer as Support →

cessfully held support near the hammer's low. That session's small real body was an indication that the bears were losing momentum. A close under the hammer's low would turn the trend back down.

Figure 4.10 shows another value-added aspect of candle charts—what one analyst aptly calls "negative selection"; that is, knowing what *not* to buy or sell. This is important because capital preservation can be just as important as capital accumulation. In this chart, on August 24th a doji following a tall white candle presaged a trend reversal. This decline found a floor with a hammer. This hammer held as support (based on the close) over the next few days. On October 15th a large black candle echoed strong bearish momentum. While this would be a risky time to buy (because of the long black real body), this stock was at the hammer's support. Because of this I would avoid selling this stock in spite of the long black candle, demonstrating negative selection. You can see how well that hammer's support managed to hold as the stock bounced up the session after the long black candle.

The Shooting Star

Figure 4.11 illustrates a candle with an extended upper shadow, little or no bottom shadow, and a small real body (white or black) at the bottom end of the range. This candle line is called a *shooting star* and is potentially bearish if it

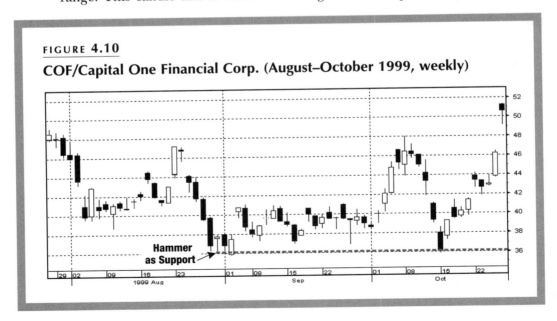

FIGURE 4.10
COF/Capital One Financial Corp. (August–October 1999, weekly)

appears during a price ascent. The shooting star's long upper shadow displays that the bears are aggressive enough to drag prices well off the highs of the session and to close at, or near, the lows.

Because as noted previously, most of the candle charting signals are reversals, they are more effective when a market is overextended. **Figure 4.12** uses the Relative Strength Index (RSI) as the overbought/oversold indicator. When the stock was at an overbought level (circled) a shooting star emerged. The RSI indicator added extra significance to the concurrent individual candle line. This is

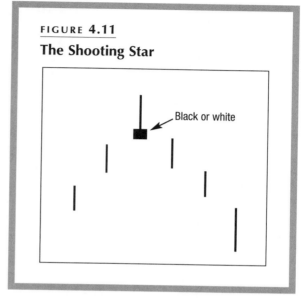

FIGURE 4.11

The Shooting Star

Black or white

another example of how merging candle charting tools with a Western technical tool (such as oscillators) can serve to reinforce the validity of each. Remember—candle charts enhance Western technical tools; they don't replace them.

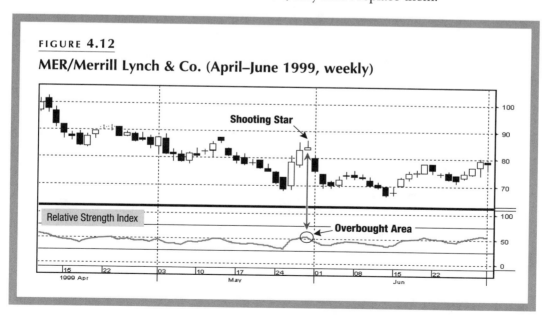

FIGURE 4.12

MER/Merrill Lynch & Co. (April–June 1999, weekly)

Shooting Star

Relative Strength Index

Overbought Area

Engulfing Patterns

An *engulfing pattern* is a two-candle line pattern. A bullish engulfing pattern (see **Figure 4.13**) is formed when, during a downtrend, a white real body wraps around or "engulfs" a black real body. The engulfing pattern illustrates how the candles can help provide greater understanding of the market's behavior. For example, a bullish engulfing pattern reflects how the bulls have wrested control of the market from the bears.

A bearish engulfing pattern (see **Figure 4.14**) is completed when, during a rally, a black real body wraps around a white real body. This pattern shows how a superior force of supply has overwhelmed demand. The Japanese say, for instance, that with a bearish engulfing pattern the "bulls are immobilized."

A trading technique with the engulfing patterns is to use the lowest low of the two sessions that form the bullish engulfing pattern as support. For a bearish engulfing pattern, use the highest high of the two lines as resistance.

For example, **Figure 4.15** shows that Dell Computer Corp. stock completed a bullish engulfing pattern in early August 1999 (interestingly the first part of this pattern was a hammer). The bullish engulfing pattern established a support level near 37½. In mid-October DELL touched this support with a doji. This was a clue that the stock was separating from its trend. More significant was the doji's

FIGURE 4.13
Bullish Engulfing Pattern

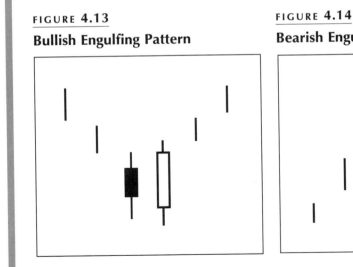

FIGURE 4.14
Bearish Engulfing Pattern

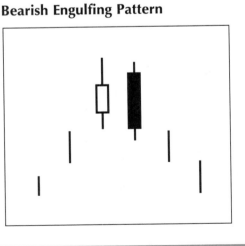

high volume. The heavy volume indicated that there was heavy supply, but the small real body (i.e., the doji) visually proved that all this supply was being absorbed by equally aggressive demand. This was a classic example of "accumulation" (where, supposedly, the smart money is buying from weak hands). This chart shows how powerfully Western technical analysis can reinforce Eastern charting analysis. The high volume (a Western tool) coupled with the doji (a candle signal) confirmed the anticipated support level at the bullish engulfing pattern (a candle pattern).

Figure 4.16 shows a bearish engulfing pattern in mid-July. By the close of the bearish engulfing pattern the Oil Service Index was well off the highs of that session. So it may not have been an attractive time (from a risk/reward perspective) to sell when the bearish engulfing pattern was completed. A more conservative strategy would be waiting for a rebound (which may or not unfold) to use the top of the bearish engulfing pattern as a resistance area. The bearish engulfing pattern held as resistance on the index's next two attempts over 8,200 (on the second attempt the index pushed over resistance intraday, but it did not close over it). A market closing over the bearish engulfing pattern (or under a bullish engulfing pattern) is viewed as a breakout. This brings up an important aspect about candle charting patterns: a recognized candle signal does not necessarily mean that a trade is warranted at that time. You need to assess the risk/reward aspect of the trade.

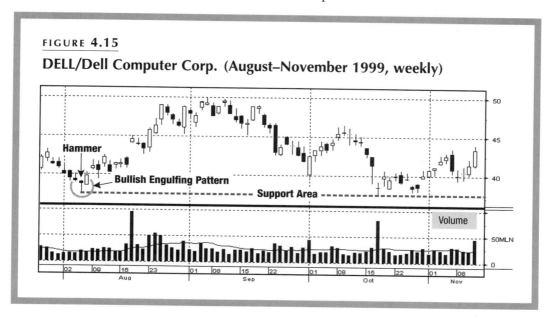

FIGURE 4.15

DELL/Dell Computer Corp. (August–November 1999, weekly)

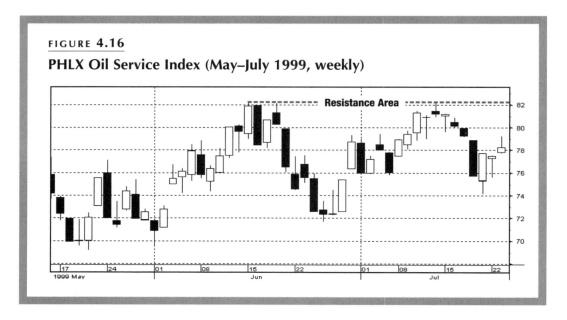

FIGURE **4.16**

PHLX Oil Service Index (May–July 1999, weekly)

Windows

A *window* is the same as a gap in Western technical analysis. A rising window (see **Figure 4.17**) occurs when yesterday's high is lower than today's low. That is, there is a price vacuum between yesterday and today's price action. A falling window (see **Figure 4.18**) means that the low of yesterday's session (the bottom of the lower shadow) is above the top of today's upper shadow (the high of the day). Windows provide a visual clue about the market—they show that the sentiment is one-sided.

A rising window is viewed as a bullish pattern and a falling window a bearish signal. The way to trade with windows is to use them as support (for a rising window) or resistance (for a falling window). There is a saying used in Japan about windows: "The reaction will go until the window." This means that somewhere within a rising window should be support on a correction. With a falling window, there should be resistance on a bounce.

Figure 4.19 shows windows at points 1, 2, and 3. Window 1 is a regular rising window that became support. Note how the low of the window was penetrated, but since the window's low maintained support based on the close, it was considered a successful test of support. Now consider the rising windows at points 2 and 3. These took on extra importance because they were not only rising windows but they were also both gaps (remember that a gap and window

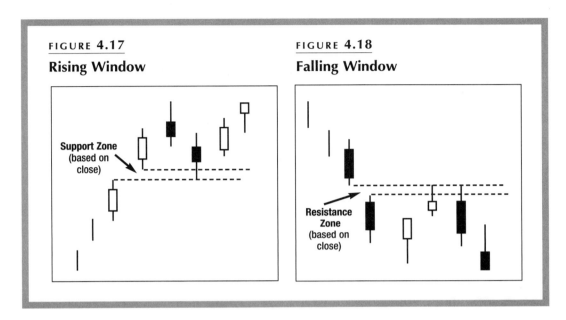

FIGURE 4.17
Rising Window

FIGURE 4.18
Falling Window

mean the same thing) away from a prior resistance area. In Western technical analysis this is known as a breakaway gap (because the market broke away from a resistance level). This is viewed as bullish in classic Western charting tech-

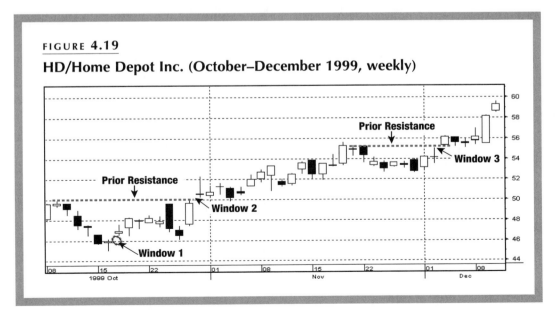

FIGURE 4.19
HD/Home Depot Inc. (October–December 1999, weekly)

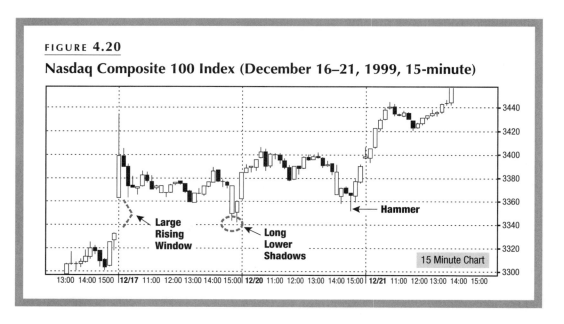

FIGURE **4.20**

Nasdaq Composite 100 Index (December 16–21, 1999, 15-minute)

nique. By adding the insights offered by candles, namely, by incorporating the concept of the rising window as support, windows 2 and 3 (both also breakaway gaps) signal buying opportunities.

Support could fall anywhere within a rising window. A small window provides a tight zone of support (in the case of a rising window) or resistance (with a falling window). A large window presents a challenge insofar as that a whole large window is a potential support or resistance zone. **Figure 4.20**, an intraday chart, shows a sizeable rising window. Its support zone from the top of the window (near 3,360) to the window's bottom (near 3,330) spans 30 points. Support should fall somewhere within this 30-point zone. It could be at the top, bottom, or anywhere within the window. Late in the session of December 17 a series of long lower shadow candles give a tentative clue that support would be 3,340. This support was confirmed the following day by a hammer. Generally the most important support of a rising window is the bottom of that window, but this chart displayed that support was entering before the bottom of the window.

Candles and Risk/Reward Considerations

Nison Research International, Inc. (www.candlecharts.com) uses a unique approach to trading called The Trading Triad®. This approach combines three analytical techniques: candles, Western technicals, and capital preservation. The importance of merging candles with Western technicals has already been discussed. Figure 4.21 highlights the importance of the third leg of The Trading Triad®—capital preservation. Should you buy when you see the bullish engulfing pattern in Figure 4.21?

Before deciding, consider the risk and potential reward of this trade. The risk (i.e., the stop) with a bullish engulfing pattern is the low of the pattern. In this example, the low would be near $24. Where is a potential target? Your answer, of course, depends on your outlook technically and fundamentally. But in this example, one thing stands out: a potential resistance area at the small window just before the bullish engulfing pattern at $25½. So with $25½ as first resistance you can assess the risk/reward of this trade. Specifically, if you buy on the completion of the bullish engulfing pattern (at $25¼) you do so near a resistance area. Therefore, this market would not warrant a long position, even with the bullish engulfing pattern. The moral of this story: before using a candle signal to initiate a trade, always consider the risk/reward aspects of the trade.

Figure 4.22 shows a nicely defined hammer that one would generally view as a potential turning signal. But as the Japanese say, the overall technical picture is more important than an individual candle line or pattern. With this in mind, note what happened on the day of the hammer. A falling window also appeared—and

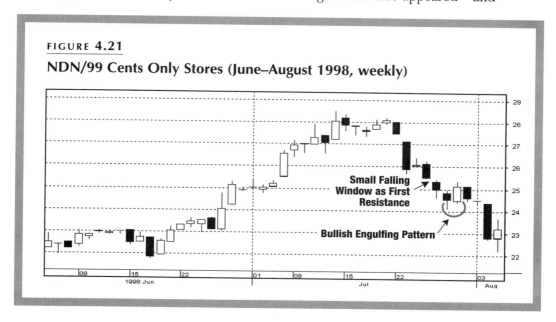

FIGURE **4.21**

NDN/99 Cents Only Stores (June–August 1998, weekly)

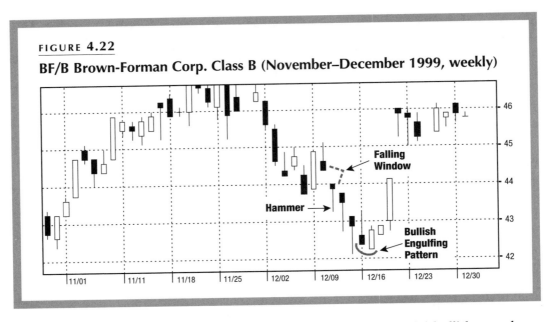

FIGURE **4.22**

BF/B Brown-Forman Corp. Class B (November–December 1999, weekly)

a falling window is a bearish signal. The hammer's potential bullishness, there-fore, would have to be confirmed by a close over that window. After the hammer the market continued its descent (not surprising considering the bearish impli-cations of the window). Can you pick up any clues that the bears were losing momentum as the stock was descending after the hammer? The clues are the long lower shadows on the day of the hammer and the two days after the hammer. Their appearance proved that each of these days the bears could not hold the lows into the close of the session. While these signals are not bullish, they lessen the bearish implications of the lower levels. The reversal signal came with the bullish engulfing pattern in mid-December.

A Japanese proverb states, "His potential is that of the fully drawn bow—his timing the release of the trigger." The timing of the "release of the trigger" depends on many factors beyond those addressed here. For example, there are times when candle signals should be ignored. This is where experience with can-dle charts comes in. Nison Research International analyzes and evaluates candle charting signals with many other considerations, including risk/reward of poten-tial trades, candle patterns in relation to current market conditions, and a mar-ket's action after a trade is initiated. These and other trading aspects allow for the most fully enhanced power of the candles, and such an integrated approach is recommended for their use. May the candles help enlighten your trading.

CHAPTER 5

Reading the Language of the Market with Market Profile

ROBIN MESCH

If you have ever watched an opera in a foreign language without the subtitles, you know you can get a reasonable idea of what is happening from the action and the music. But you would know so much more about the plot and what is going to happen if you had some understanding of what the characters were actually saying. Without the subtitles, you would subjectively impose your biases and experiences on the action. But if you knew the language or were reading the subtitles, you would have direct access to the internal logic of the script, and the degree of subjectivity necessary to understand the meaning would be greatly reduced.

Market Profile tries to provide this internal logic in the context of the market. It is a method of analysis that starts off with the understanding that price alone does not communicate information to the participant, just as words without syntax or context may have no meaning. Volume is an integral part of the direct expression of the market—understand it and you understand the language of the market.

Market Profile was developed by a truly brilliant thinker, Peter Steidlmayer. He found the natural expression of the market (volume) and organized it in a way that is readable (the bell curve), so that objective information generated by the market is accessible to market participants.

Although there is always going to be an art to trading, a reliable trading methodology can minimize the subjective elements and maximize the objective elements. Many market participants do this by considering a number of factors external to the market such as stops, how long it is taking for the trade to move in a certain direction, a schedule that allows trading only during the first two hours the market is open, and so on. These are all external controls to improve trading, and they are mostly geared toward limiting subjectivity. But traders should use information that is internal to arrive at an entry and exit strategy and to discern when a real trading advantage presents itself.

By isolating internal information, technical analysis tries to build a mental framework. To get a feeling for what a mental framework is, consider how the chess masters operate.

If you show a chessboard from any moment in a game to chess masters for one second, they'll be able to reconstruct exactly the position of every piece on the board. However, if you show them a random (nongame) setup of chess pieces on a board for one second, they won't be able to reconstruct it. Why not? Because chess masters understand each piece's position in terms of their mental constructs; a random board doesn't fit any of those constructs, so there is no way for them to structure what they see. Structuring your perception of the market and recognizing the patterns in what is happening are what technical analysis is about. You want to see patterns in the market the way a chess master sees patterns in a chess game.

The most fundamental aspect of structuring the market is in how you represent the data. Just imagine having to trade using only a list of prices like those on a ticker tape instead of using a bar chart. A bar chart, like **Figure 5.1**, facilitates seeing important patterns in the market.

The representation must reveal the patterns that are there. A good exam-

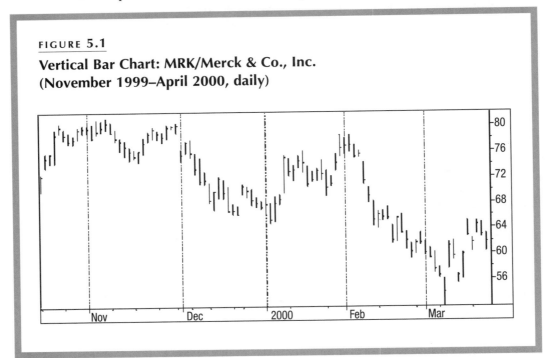

FIGURE 5.1

**Vertical Bar Chart: MRK/Merck & Co., Inc.
(November 1999–April 2000, daily)**

Source: Capital Flow Software

ple of this is numerical representation: Have you ever tried to multiply two Roman numerals?

$$\begin{array}{r} \text{CLVII} \\ \text{x} \quad \text{XVI} \\ \hline \end{array} \qquad \begin{array}{r} 157 \\ \text{x} \quad 16 \\ \hline \end{array}$$

Back in Roman times, multiplication was a highly skilled job. Today a ten-year-old can do it, simply because we have a better way of representing numbers. Roman and Arabic numerals convey the same information, but Arabic numerals are visually easier to manipulate mathematically.

Market Profile uses an alternate representation (as shown in **Figure 5.2**) to provide information on horizontal as well as vertical market movement—and a whole additional set of patterns surfaces.

Organizing and representing the data do not do any good unless some underlying phenomenon exists for us to try to identify. There is in fact an underlying pulse to the market, a fundamental pattern called the cycle of equilibrium and disequilibrium.

FIGURE 5.2

Horizontal and Vertical Chart: ALD/AlliedSignal Inc. (December 1999)

Source: Capital Flow Software

The Cycle of Equilibrium and Disequilibrium

Market Profile measures horizontal versus vertical movement in the market. Let's call that "equilibrium" versus "disequilibrium." This relationship serves as the fundamental organizing principle of the market. A trader's whole style of trading changes based on what part of the equilibrium/disequilibrium cycle the market is in. Market Profile can determine both when the market is going to shift from equilibrium to disequilibrium and how big the move is going to be. But let's first examine some basic Market Profile concepts.

The two basic concepts of Market Profile are:

1. The market is an auction, and will move to bring about a price range in which the buy/sell demand is more or less equal.

2. The market has two phases: horizontal activity and vertical activity. The market moves vertically when buy/sell demand is out of balance, or in disequilibrium, and horizontally when buy and sell demand is in balance, or in equilibrium.

The main purpose of the market is to facilitate order flow. It does so in the form of an auction. That auction is dynamic and constantly fluctuating around efficiency. Simply put, prices rise until they hit a point at which they are too high to attract any more buyers, and then fall until they are too low to attract any more

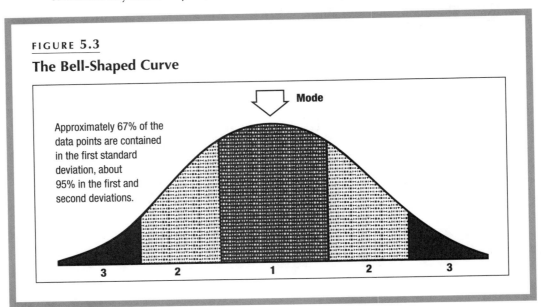

FIGURE 5.3

The Bell-Shaped Curve

Approximately 67% of the data points are contained in the first standard deviation, about 95% in the first and second deviations.

Mode

3   2   1   2   3

sellers. Once a range is established, the market rotates back and forth for a period of time around some widely perceived level of fair value. The market can do only three things: move up, down, or sideways. If it is moving up or down (that is, vertically) it is in a state of disequilibrium. That happens when buy or sell demand is out of balance and either buyers or sellers are in control of the market. When the market moves horizontally, it is in equilibrium, meaning buy and sell demand is in balance. In equilibrium, price is in control of the market, as opposed to buyers or sellers.

A vertical move has a simple structure, but a horizontal move is more complex. To some extent, the behavior of buyers and sellers in an equilibrium market follows some basic statistical principles.

Probably the most basic principle in statistics is the bell-shaped curve, which often appears when you are studying a characteristic that is controlled by certain factors. For instance, if you measured the height of women and put the results in a bar chart, you would get a bell-shaped curve with the peak at the most common height. This peak is called the *mode*. On the bell-shaped curve the middle section labeled 1 in **Figure 5.3**, which contains 67 percent of the data, is called the *first standard deviation*. Sections 1 and 2 combined contain roughly 95 percent of the data. The third standard deviations would be perhaps the woman who is 4 feet 11 inches tall and the woman who is 6 feet 2 inches tall; in terms of the market, it is the price where the instrument spends the least amount of time trading.

In the market the characteristic you are studying is price, and each buy or sell transaction has a price. The market in equilibrium, when charted using Market Profile, tends to form a bell-shaped curve, rotated 90 degrees because of the orientation of the chart.

Let's take a closer look at how to represent the data in Market Profile.

Instead of representing each half-hour segment of a trading day with a bar, in Market Profile each half-hour segment gets its own letter and then is organized in a particular way. Suppose B represents the first half hour. **Figure 5.4** shows a thirty-minute bar chart and how that bar chart would be reorganized into a Market Profile, which is shown on the far right.

Each letter is called a *TPO,* which stands for Time-Price-Opportunity. It means the commodity was offered at that price during that time period. You put a B on the chart at the level of each price that occurs during that first half hour. At the end of the first half hour, you will have a vertical list of Bs covering the range, similar to a half-hour bar.

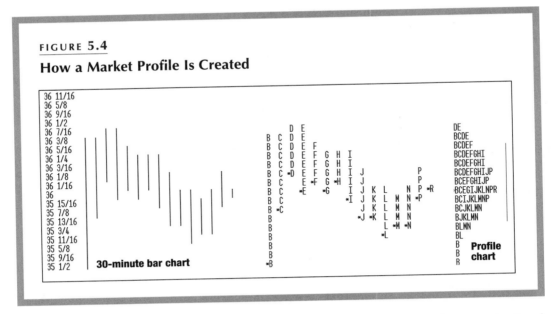

FIGURE 5.4

How a Market Profile Is Created

The second half hour is C period. You put a C in each row where a price level occurs, as far to the left as possible. Places where B and C overlap will now have two letters in their rows. But if C reaches a new high or low it will be placed in the same column as B. Continue with D and the rest of the letters in the same way. You can see that width increases in the rows where the same price occurred in multiple time periods.

A fat profile shows the market has spent a long time at one price. This occurs when the market is in relative equilibrium, since over time there were many opportunities at a given price. A thin profile shows rapid movement to new levels. This occurs when the market is in disequilibrium. The shape of the profile shows the relationship between vertical and horizontal movement and is the key to understanding what the market participants are doing.

Turned on its side, the profile in Figure 5.4 looks roughly like a bell-shape curve, which is typical of a market in balance or in equilibrium. The vertical line on the right in Figure 5.4 shows where the first standard deviation is; this is called the *value area*.

Figure 5.5 shows the 10-year Treasury note profiles for March 2–9, 2000. The profile for day 6 shows a day in equilibrium. The mode is the longest line at 95–150. The bottom of the value area is around 95–125.

Now look at the profile for day 8. Can you identify the mode? It is at 95–205 and 95–190. Can you determine where the value area is? If you take 67 percent of the total TPOs surrounding the mode, you have a value area from 95–240 to 95–165. That is the range in which the bulk of market activity took place. In Figure 5.5 each daily Market Profile forms a variation of the bell curve. Some profiles are almost picture-perfect normal bell curves; others are skewed profiles with the value area at the top of the range or the bottom of the range. You may occasionally come across profiles with very small ranges and large degrees of horizontal activity, and sometimes profiles have extremely large ranges with no horizontal activity whatsoever.

FIGURE 5.5

Daily Market Profile: TYM0/June 2000 10-Year Treasury Futures

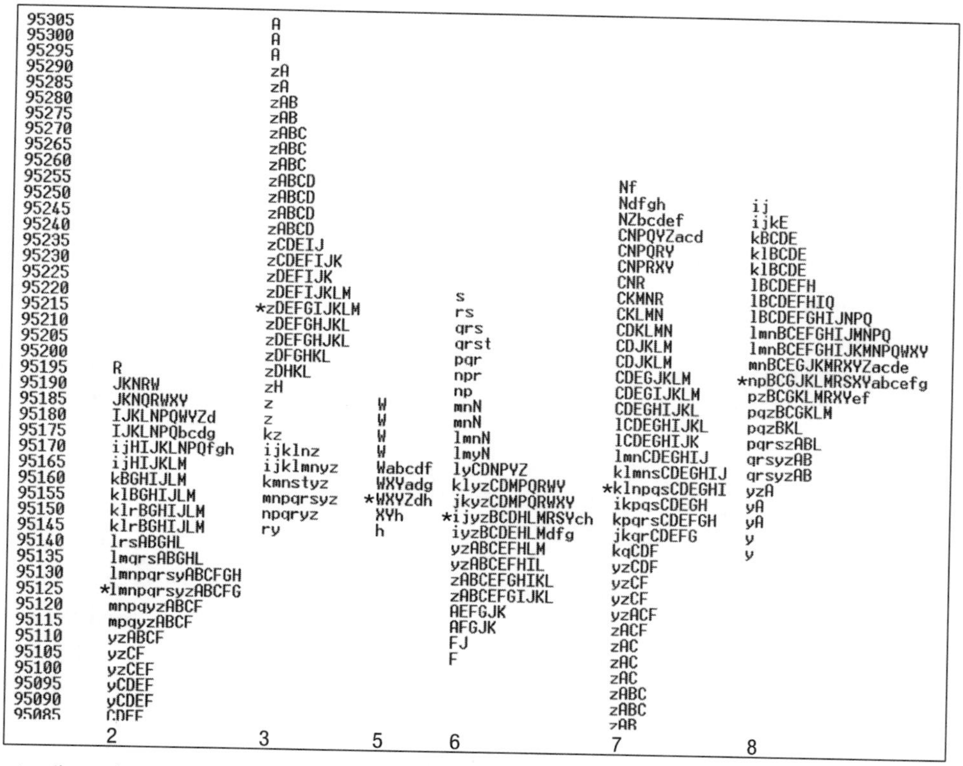

```
95305                    A
95300                    A
95295                    A
95290                    zA
95285                    zA
95280                    zAB
95275                    zAB
95270                    zABC
95265                    zABC
95260                    zABC
95255                    zABCD                        Nf
95250                    zABCD                        Ndfgh            ij
95245                    zABCD                        NZbcdef          ijkE
95240                    zABCD                        CNPQYZacd        kBCDE
95235                    zCDEIJ                        CNPQRY           k1BCDE
95230                    zCDEFIJK                      CNPRXY           k1BCDE
95225                    zDEFIJK                       CNR              1BCDEFH
95220                    zDEFIJKLM                     CKMNR            1BCDEFHIQ
95215                  *zDEFGIJKLM        s            CKLMN            1BCDEFGHIJNPQ
95210                    zDEFGHJKL        rs           CDKLMN           1mnBCEFGHIJMNPQ
95205                    zDEFGHJKL        qrs          CDJKLM           1mnBCEFGHIJKMNPQWXY
95200                    zDFGHKL          qrst         CDJKLM           mnBCEGJKMRXYZacde
95195         R          zDHKL            pqr          CDEGJKLM       *npBCGJKLMRSXYabcefg
95190         JKNRW      zH               npr          CDEGIJKLM        pzBCGKLMRXYef
95185         JKNQRWXY   z                np           CDEGHIJKL        pqzBCGKLM
95180         IJKLNPQWYZd z        W      mnN          1CDEGHIJKL       pqzBKL
95175         IJKLNPQbcdg kz       W      mnN          1CDEGHIJK        pqrszABL
95170         ijHIJKLNPQfgh ijklnz W      1mnN         1mnCDEGHIJ       qrsyzAB
95165         ijHIJKLM   ijklmnyz  Wabcdf 1myN         klmnsCDEGHIJ     qrsyzAB
95160         kBGHIJLM   kmnstyz   WXYadg 1yCDNPVZ   *klnpqsCDEGHI      yzA
95155         k1BGHIJLM  mnpqrsyz *WXYZdh klyzCDMPQRWY jkyzCDMPQRWXY    ikpqsCDEGH       yA
95150         klrBGHIJLM npqryz    XYh    jkyzCDMPQRWXY kpqrsCDEFGH     yA
95145         klrBGHIJLM ry        h    *ijyzBCDHLMRSYch jkqrCDEFG      y
95140         1rsABGHL                    iyzBCDEHLMdfg kqCDF           y
95135         1mqrsABGHL                  yzABCEFHLM    yzCDF
95130         1mnpqrsyABCFGH              yzABCEFHIL    yzCF
95125       *1mnpqrsyzABCFG              zABCEFGHIKL    yzCF
95120         mnpqyzABCF                  zABCEFGIJKL   yzACF
95115         mpqyzABCF                   AEFGJK        yzACF
95110         yzABCF                      AFGJK         zACF
95105         yzCF                        FJ            zAC
95100         yzCEF                       F             zAC
95095         yCDEF                                     zAC
95090         yCDEF                                     zABC
95085         CDEF                                      zAB
                                                        zAB
              2          3        5      6            7                 8
```

* = the mode

Daily Profile Shapes

Using the daily profile shapes to determine the degree of balance and imbalance in the market can be useful and gives you a starting point to understand the shift of control between various market participants. A trading opportunity with the greatest advantage occurs when the shift from balance to imbalance is about to occur. Moreover, if you can identify those trading opportunities and accurately read the potential magnitude of that shift, you can assess the quality of the opportunity and the amount of time you have in the trade.

Balance and imbalance are not absolute; they are relative. As a trader, you are trying to accurately measure their degree of change. If you are working within the one-day time frame, the primary balance of the day is assigned to the first hour's trading range. Using this initial balance range as your reference point, you can measure the degree of change by how this range is disturbed throughout the trading day. In other words, is the first hour's trading range small or large? Is the trading range extended after the first hour, and if so, by how much? Or has the first hour's range stayed roughly intact throughout the day?

This process leads to a classification of the various Market Profile shapes and provides a somewhat mechanical approach to reading the markets. A more natural approach to reading the markets is discussed later. Nonetheless, measuring the degree of change within a day is an excellent starting point to practice reading the shifts between balance and imbalance and identifying the trading opportunities these shifts generate.

Different Market Profile structures represent different opportunities. If there is no net imbalance, the profile structure is classified as either a normal day or a non-trend day.

Normal Days

On so-called *normal* days the balance is established early in the session, and typically there is a wide move in prices during the first hour of trading. This early wide move creates a clearly defined top and bottom to trade against for most of the day. The wider the initial time period move, the more likely it is that you can forecast a normal day's outcome. Typically, the first hour of trading on normal days represents roughly 85 percent of the range for the day and range extension throughout the day is slight or nonexistent. The trading strategy on a normal Market Profile structure is to sell high against the top of the initial balance range and sell low toward the bottom of the range. In **Figure 5.6**, you can see how the extremely wide y and z period on day 5 kept a lid on any further range extension throughout the day. Traders could have sold against the extreme in z period. In fact, the effect of the large initial balance range on day 5 carried over to the following two trading days—on day 7 and 8—as the market on these two days continued to auction within the same trading range as on day 5.

Non-Trend Days

Non-trend days have a fairly small first-hour range in which the initial balance is narrowly, if at all, upset. The bulk of the daily range develops within the first hour's range to create a horizontal and small-range day. Although the actual trading day

---

FIGURE 5.6

Normal Day: USM0/June 2000 30-Year Treasury Futures

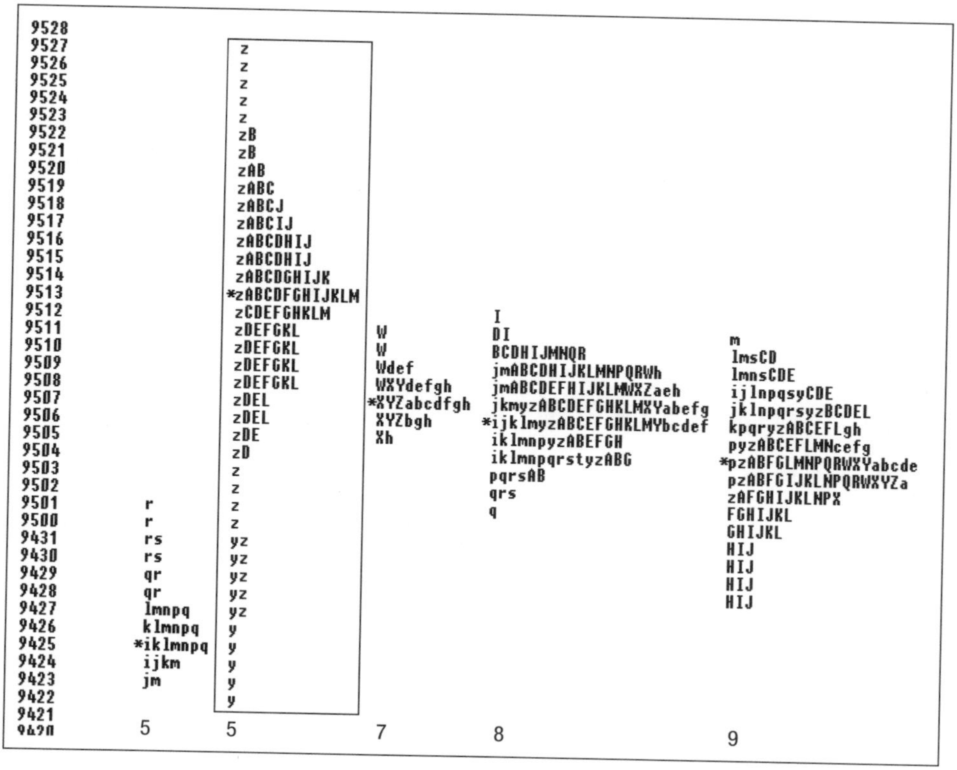

```
9528                      z
9527                      z
9526                      z
9525                      z
9524                      z
9523                      z
9522                      zB
9521                      zB
9520                      zAB
9519                      zABC
9518                      zABCJ
9517                      zABCIJ
9516                      zABCDHIJ
9515                      zABCDHIJ
9514                      zABCDGHIJK
9513                      *zABCDFGHIJKLM
9512                      zCDEFGHKLM
9511                      zDEFGKL               I
9510                      zDEFGKL      W       DI                       m
9509                      zDEFGKL      W       BCDHIJMNQR               lmsCD
9508                      zDEFGKL      Wdef    jmABCDHIJKLMNPQRWh       lmnsCDE
9507                      zDEL         WXYdefgh jmABCDEFHIJKLMWXZaeh    ijlnpqsyCDE
9506                      zDEL        *XYZabcdfgh jkmyzABCDEFGHKLMXYabefg jklnpqrsyzBCDEL
9505                      zDE          XYZbgh  *ijklmyzABCEFGHKLMYbcdef kpqryzABCEFLgh
9504                      zD           Xh      iklmnpyzABEFGH          pyzABCEFLMNcefg
9503                      z                    iklmnpqrstyzABG        *pzABFGLMNPQRWXYabcde
9502                      z                    pqrsAB                  pzABFGIJKLNPQRWXYZa
9501           r          z                    qrs                     zAFGHIJKLNPX
9500           r          z                    q                       FGHIJKL
9431           rs         yz                                           GHIJKL
9430           rs         yz                                           HIJ
9429           qr         yz                                           HIJ
9428           qr         yz                                           HIJ
9427           lmnpq      yz                                           HIJ
9426           klmnpq     y
9425          *iklmnpq    y
9424           ijkm       y
9423           jm         y
9422                      y
9421
9420           5          5            7       8                       9
```

Source: Capital Flow Software

does not offer good intraday trading opportunities, non-trend days are typically good days to enter a position in anticipation of a directional move to come. Directional moves initiated out of non-trend days are typically solid, "go-with" trades. The fact that the market is "stuck" on non-trend days is due to the fact that participants lack information. When they receive that information, they are primed to commit to a directional move. In **Figure 5.7** the tiny y and z range on day 9 carried on through the night trading session and formed a high mode line around 93–18. Note how a strong directional move initiated out of the high volume level.

If the profile structure is imbalanced, the profiles can represent either a normal variation of a normal day or, if the imbalance is at its maximum, a trend day.

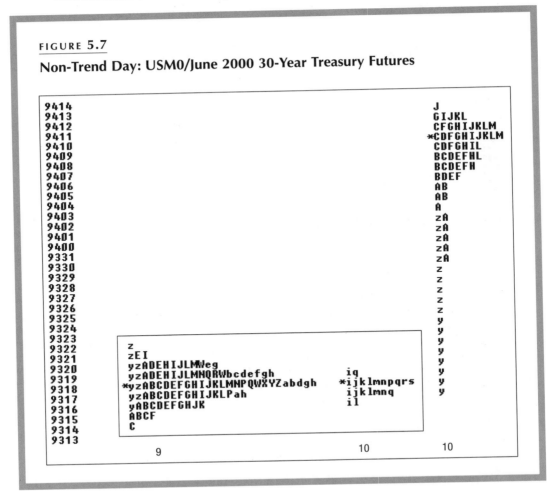

FIGURE 5.7

Non-Trend Day: USM0/June 2000 30-Year Treasury Futures

Trend day opportunities require a completely different approach from one that you would use on a normal day.

Normal Variation of a Normal Day

In normal-variation days the first hour of trading represents about 50 percent of the range, and range extension throughout the day basically doubles the initial balance range. Range extension on this type of day is accomplished in fewer periods and typically occurs earlier than on a trend day. The strategy for trading on a normal-variation day is to watch for the range to double. In **Figure 5.8** the y and z range on day 15 was large, but when B period began to extend this range,

FIGURE 5.8

Normal Variation of a Normal Day: USM0/June 2000 30-Year Treasury Futures

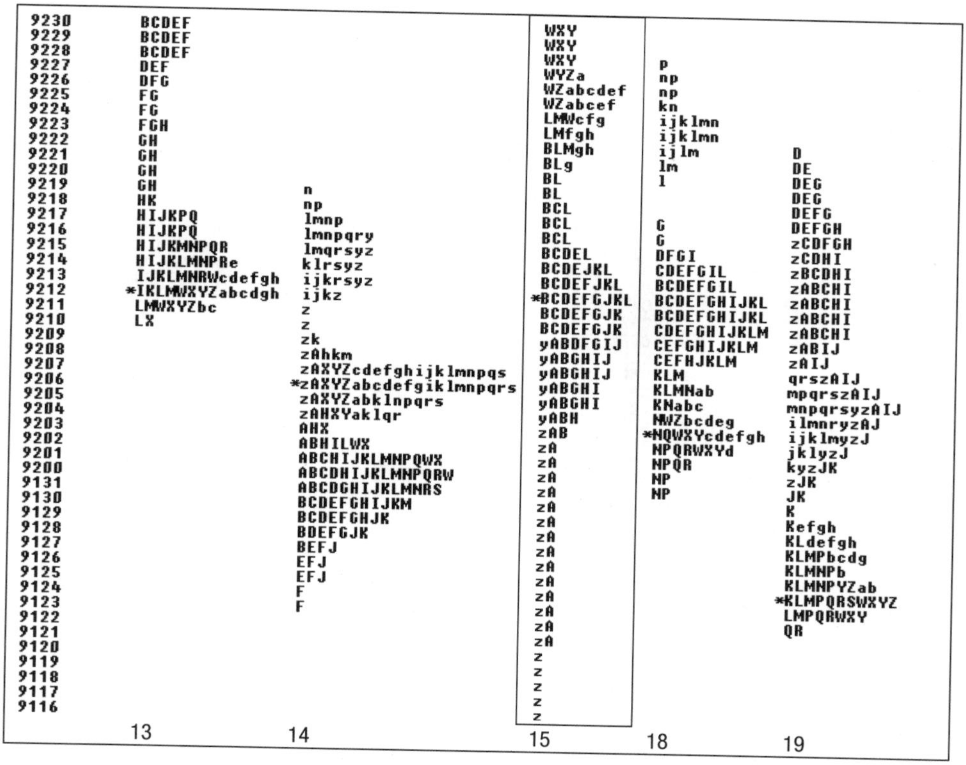

Source: Capital Flow Software

there was a strong possibility that a normal variation day was in the making. Buying pullbacks in G, H, or I period toward the bottom of the developing value area was an appropriate strategy in anticipation of the doubling of the initial balance range, which ultimately occurred during the evening trading.

Trend Days

Trend days are characterized by very little horizontal activity throughout the range (typically no more than four to six TPOs wide), while the vertical range is quite large. Typically on trend days the initial balance range is small and can be easily upset.

FIGURE 5.9

Trend Day: USM0/June 2000 30-Year Treasury Futures

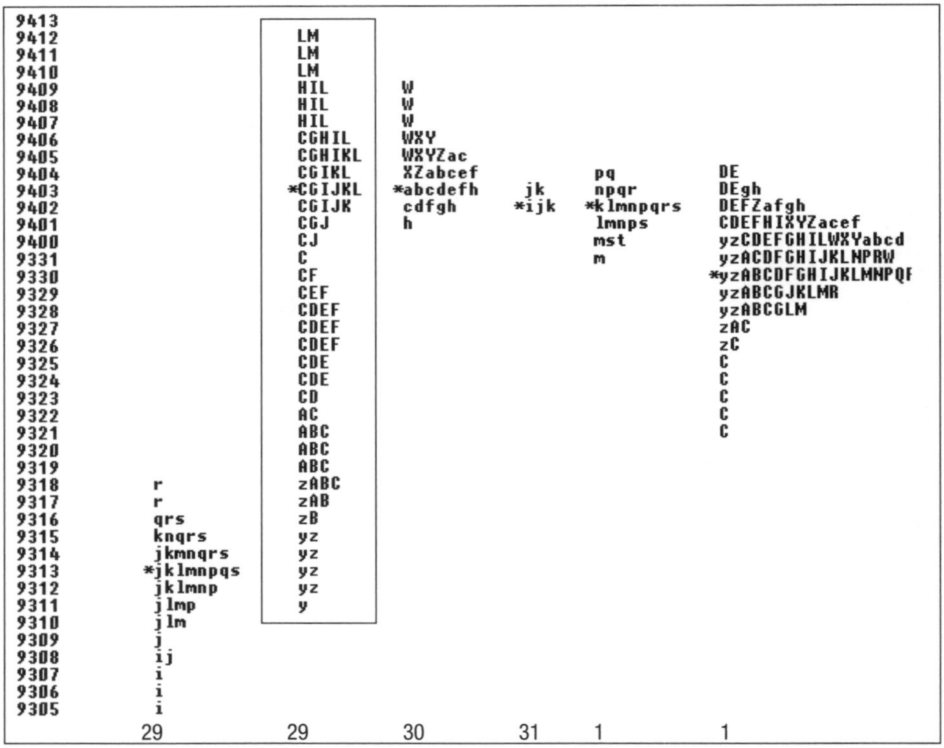

Source: Capital Flow Software

Throughout a trend day market activity continues to move in one direction and ultimately closes toward the extreme of the directional move. Trading strategy on trend days is to buy pullbacks if the direction is up and to sell into rallies if the volatility is down—and never to go against the direction of the day. After a strong trend day, you can expect a normal day or normal-variation day to develop. Failure to show follow-through after a trend day is an alert that the buying or selling has been shut off and a reversal is near.

Day 29 in **Figure 5.9** is a classic trend day in which a small initial balance range was upset early in the day. By C period it was clear that a trend day was in the making, and traders could have bought pullbacks in this market in D and E period in anticipation of range extension throughout the day. One way to monitor the trade is to note sideways activity. When no more than six TPOs occur in one line, which is consistent with a trend day, traders know to stand aside.

This is only a sampling of the day type classifications, and to some degree they enable you to work with the fundamental organizing principle of equilibrium and disequilibrium (or balance and imbalance). Although much market information generated by these daily profiles is useful, classifying them into various types of days is arbitrary. As market hours have expanded and different types of participants have been lured into trading, Market Profile traders continue to see wider ranges and more volatility, and the beginnings and endings of the equilibrium and disequilibrium cycle have expanded beyond the confines of the individual day.

Profiles of Equilibrium and Disequilibrium Cycles

When a fundamental change occurs from balance to imbalance, it is not useful to continue to incorporate the old data into the new—you must start to change your approach to the market, no longer organizing the data according to the day, but rather according to the cycles of equilibrium and disequilibrium.

The market normally moves in a cycle from disequilibrium to equilibrium. After a strong vertical move, the market usually begins to go sideways for a while, in equilibrium, generating up a bell-shaped curve in the Profile. When the bell-shaped curve is complete, the market is ready for another directional move—which is not necessarily accomplished at the end of a trading day. The one-day time frame is an artificial division of market activity because it does not really reflect the natural cycle of market activity. The start of a disequilibrium is a "new beginning": the natural place to start a new profile.

Remember, you are trying to represent the data in the way that makes the patterns clearest. **Figure 5.10** shows profiles that are organized by the day time frame. It contains all the information, but it is difficult to extract all the understanding you need from it.

If you group your data according to periods of equilibrium versus those of disequilibrium, instead of using the daily time frame as the basic organizing principle, you combine a number of days together. The area within Box A is roughly all part of the same cycle of equilibrium. Something new began where Box B begins: a disequilibrium cycle.

Now that you know where the equilibrium and disequilibrium cycles are,

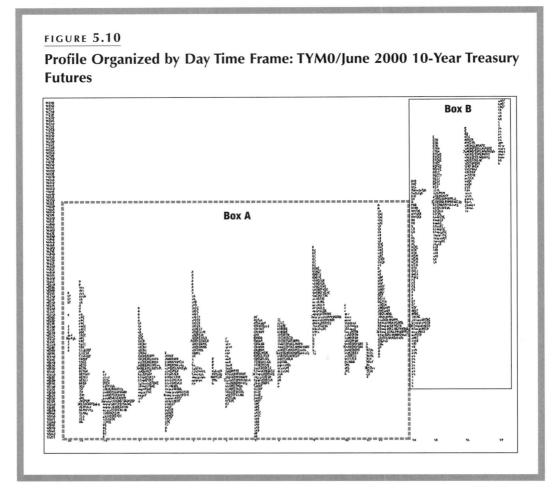

FIGURE **5.10**

Profile Organized by Day Time Frame: TYM0/June 2000 10-Year Treasury Futures

Source: Capital Flow Software

let's see what the profile looks like when it is organized according to the natural cycles of market activity.

Figure 5.11 shows the same profiles organized according to the disequilibrium and equilibrium pattern, and you can see the bell-shaped curve that naturally develops. Within the larger boxed region of Figure 5.10 two distinct bell curves have formed. On days 9 and 14, a cycle of disequilibrium surfaced and initiated a new directional move out of the mode, or high-volume line, a typical pattern for new periods of disequilibrium. As shown in 5.11, the auction from the end of day 23 through day 9 on the following month was part of the development of the initial disequilibrium. By the end of the 23rd, all the profiles collapsed together,

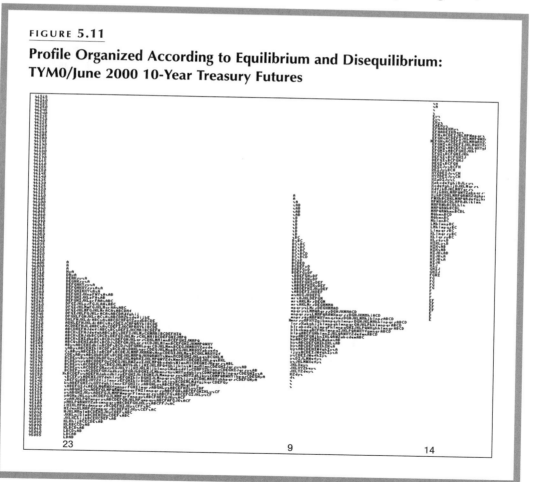

FIGURE **5.11**

Profile Organized According to Equilibrium and Disequilibrium: TYM0/June 2000 10-Year Treasury Futures

Source: Capital Flow Software

FIGURE 5.12

The 4x4: IBM/International Business Machines Corp. (March 2000)

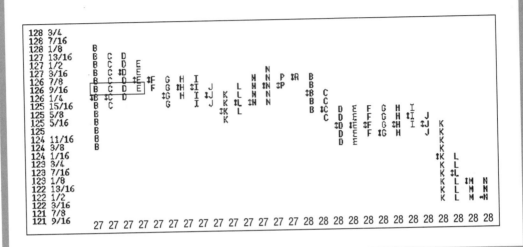

FIGURE 5.13

4x4s on a 30-Minute Bar Chart: SPM0/June 2000 S&P 500 Futures

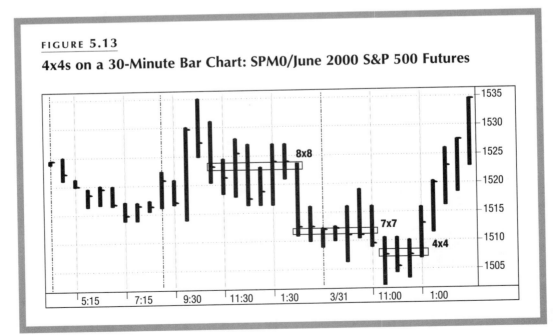

Source: Capital Flow Software

showing that the "cup is full," and the market was ready to spill over into disequilibrium again.

Why is it so important to know how to recognize equilibrium and disequilibrium and to know when one is ready to end and the other is ready to begin? The reason is that you use completely different trading styles and strategies in these two types of markets. It is important to understand the causes of the equilibrium/disequilibrium cycle and how the cycle unfolds. Before looking at the actual anatomy of the cycles from equilibrium to disequilibrium, let's define some terminology.

Non-Price Control and Price Control Phases

Another way of talking about equilibrium and disequilibrium is in terms of price control and non-price control: Non-price control is the phase of market activity when no price is able to limit the extent of the market's vertical movement. In other words, non-price control is disequilibrium. On the other hand, a market that is moving more horizontally than vertically is exhibiting price control. In such a case, there is a price that tends to keep the market in the same area. On a completed bell curve, the control price is another name for the mode. A market that is moving vertically is looking for the price that is going to shut off the buying or selling. When the market finds that price, it becomes price controlled and begins to move horizontally to develop that initial range, and when it is in

FIGURE 5.14

The 4x4 Horizontal Ratio: UTX/United Technologies Corp. (March 1, 2000)

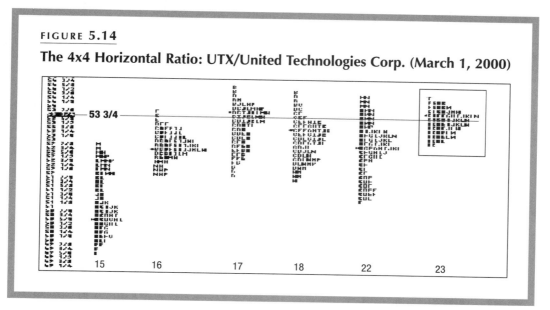

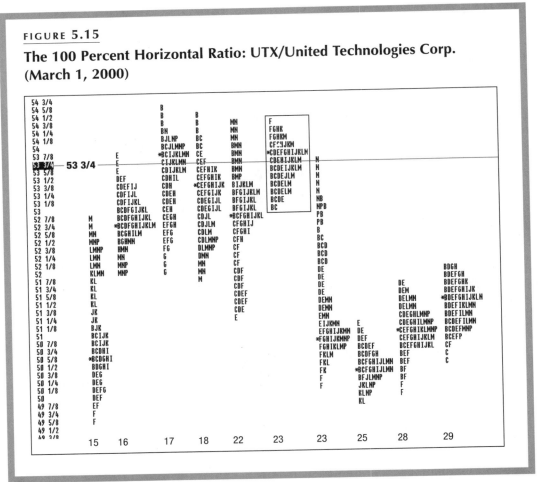

FIGURE 5.15

The 100 Percent Horizontal Ratio: UTX/United Technologies Corp. (March 1, 2000)

the price control phase the market starts to develop the bell-shaped curve.

Let's take a closer look at the price control phase of market activity, starting with the smallest possible time frame.

The 4x4 Formation

In **Figure 5.12** the profile is expanded into single bars (each is equivalent to a thirty-minute bar) to make it easier to see what is going on. On the smallest time frame, the existence of what is called a 4x4 is evidence of price control, or horizontal motion. A 4x4 has a 100 percent ratio of possible width to actual width. A high horizontal ratio (an 8x8 or 10x10) is evidence of extreme price control.

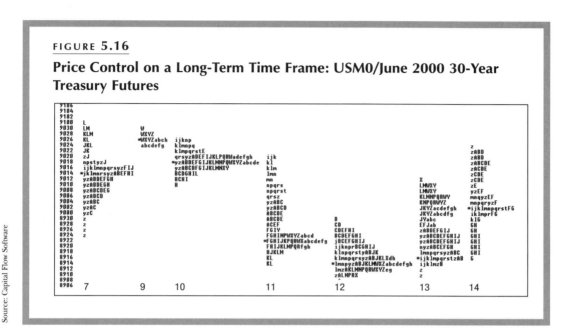

FIGURE 5.16

Price Control on a Long-Term Time Frame: USM0/June 2000 30-Year Treasury Futures

Note that it is easy to pick out a 4x4 on a thirty-minute bar chart: just check whether you can draw a horizontal line that crosses four consecutive bars. **Figure 5.13** marks the areas where there are high horizontal ratios on a thirty-minute Standard and Poor's (S&P) bar chart. You can see that strong directional moves came out of these areas of price control.

Toward the end of the data series in Figure 5.13, the market was in its vertical, non-price–controlled phase, and no 4x4 surfaced. The 4x4 helps you determine when the vertical phase of market activity is nearing completion. The idea of the horizontal ratio can be extended to larger time frames. It is unusual to find a 100 percent horizontal ratio as we analyze an entire day, or several days, but the higher ratios still characterize a price control regime in the market.

In **Figure 5.14**, there are a number of 4x4s. But on the 23rd, the market built a very high horizontal ratio (11x11) which is boxed on the chart. Here the section in the box has eleven letters, C through M, and thus eleven potential slots, all of which are filled: there is a single line that contains all eleven letters. This gives a 11x11 an almost 100 percent horizontal/vertical ratio, which indicates that, on a short-term time frame, the market is in equilibrium, or extreme price control. Because the profile also formed a completed bell-shaped curve, you can expect that the market is ripe for a directional move.

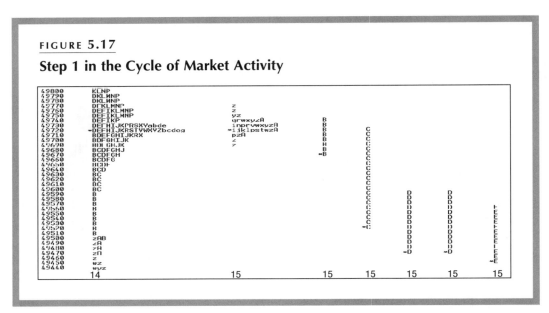

FIGURE 5.17

Step 1 in the Cycle of Market Activity

As **Figure 5.15** shows, one directional move started in N period on the same day directly out of the control price, or mode line, which is the typical pattern. A market establishing extreme price control usually heralds a change in direction or, at minimum, a shift from equilibrium into disequilibrium.

Figures 5.14 and 5.15 demonstrate price control on a very short-term time frame. Let's take a look at what price control looks like on a very long-term picture. In **Figure 5.16**, the period from March 7th through March 14th is all part of the same price-controlled area.

Within a price-controlled period, there are recognizable stages of development, and within that development in turn occur minor cycles of equilibrium and disequilibrium. The underlying structure of the flow from equilibrium to disequilibrium can be broken down into four major steps.

The Four Steps of Market Activity

Each cycle of market activity consists of up to four of the following steps.

Step 1

Step 1, which is always present, is the move toward disequilibrium: the rapid rally that starts off a cycle. Step 1 is the only step of market activity that is non-price

FIGURE 5.18

Step 2 in the Cycle of Market Activity

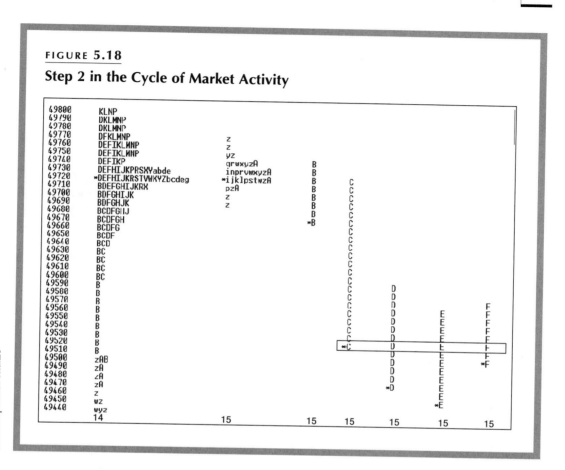

Source: Capital Flow Software

controlled. It represents a market imbalance wherein a large amount of capital has come into or out of the market. Generally, Step 1 of market activity offers the most profitable trading opportunity. In **Figure 5.17**, which shows the S&P futures, you can see the price-controlled region marked by the bell-shaped curve formed by the previous day's trading and augmented by the overnight profile. The Step 1 move came out of the mode in a typical pattern. It gave a strong clue to direction when it broke the ledge of volume on the 15th.

As long as each successive bar is setting a new low, the market is in Step 1. Note the lack of price control during even the shortest time frame in which no 4x4s surfaced.

To review, Step 1:

● Displays strong vertical movement

- Is the only non-price-controlled step
- Offers the most profitable trading opportunity
- Represents a market imbalance: a large shift of capital into or out of the market.

Step 2

Vertical moves, however, cannot go on indefinitely; something has to stop prices, which leads us to Step 2. Step 2 occurs when the vertical move has gone far enough in one direction to shut off the buying or selling—when it reaches a price too high to attract any more buyers or too low to attract any more sellers.

The second step begins with a bar that does not set a new low, in this case the F period bar in **Figure 5.18**. Typically it is marked with a 4x4, the smallest unit

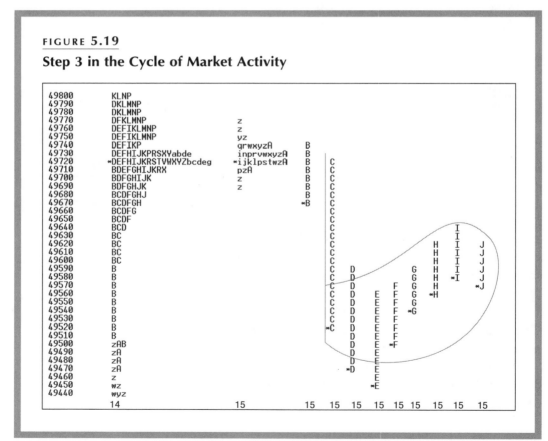

FIGURE 5.19

Step 3 in the Cycle of Market Activity

Source: Capital Flow Software

of price control. In Figure 5.18, you see a 4x4 set up at the bottom of the range. Step 2 is an early warning sign that the market is shifting into development, especially when it includes a 4x4. In other words, Step 2 stops the directional move and begins to build the first standard deviation.

Step 3

Once the vertical move is over, a period of development begins, which is Step 3 of market activity. In Step 3 the market moves horizontally while building the first standard deviation at one end of the initial range of Step I. The bulk of trading will take place near the middle of the range; the extremes will be a price briefly tested but rejected as unfairly high and a price tested and rejected as unfairly low. Little trading will take place at those levels.

In Step 3 depicted in **Figure 5.19**, the market typically does not develop all the way back to the origin of the vertical move. Instead, one end is developed, giving the typical p- or b-shaped profile. Normally this step will continue until it builds up a bell-shaped curve with a distinct mode.

When most of the data is near the top of the range, the shape is called a 3-2-1 up, or p shape, as in **Figure 5.20**. If most of the data is near the bottom, the 3-2-

FIGURE 5.20

The 3-2-1 Up—
The p Profile Shape

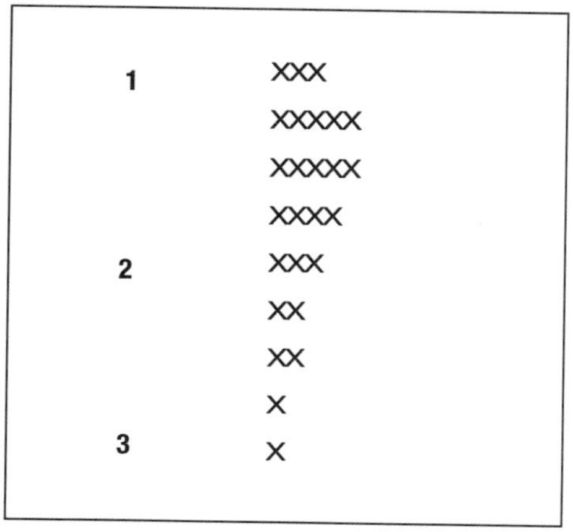

```
1       XXX
        XXXXX
        XXXXX
        XXXX
2       XXX
        XX
        XX
        X
3       X
```

FIGURE 5.21

The 3-2-1 Down—
The b Profile Shape

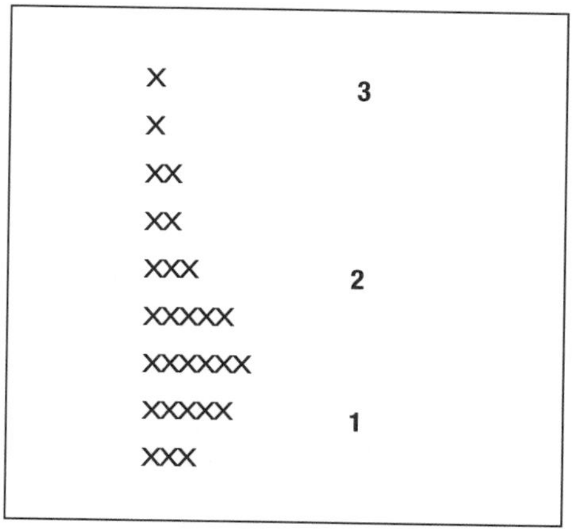

```
        X           3
        X
        XX
        XX
        XXX         2
        XXXXX
        XXXXXX
        XXXXX       1
        XXX
```

FIGURE 5.22

Step 3 of Market Activity: The p and b Shapes

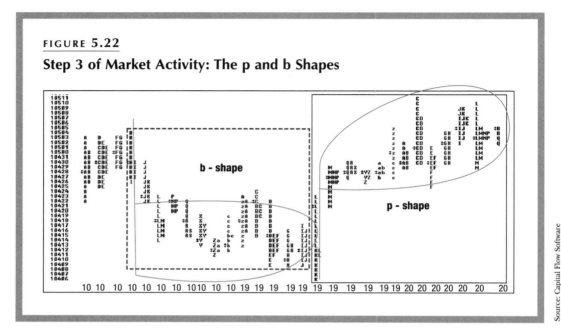

1 down pattern resembles a lowercase b, as in **Figure 5.21**. The numbers refer to the standard deviations: 1 indicates where 67 percent of the data is centering at the mode, 2 is the thinner section containing the second standard deviation, and 3 is the very thin tail.

Can you identify all the Step 3s in **Figure 5.22**? A dotted-line box surrounds a complete b-shaped region, and a solid box surrounds a p-shaped region.

When the two b and p shapes in Figure 5.22 are combined, they form one larger move. Putting the whole together gives a bell-shaped curve, which brings you to the final step of market activity, Step 4.

Step 4

During Step 4 of market activity, the market tries to form a bell-shaped curve over the entire range of Step 1. As this happens, the mode begins to float from one end toward the center of the range.

In Step 4 (see **Figure 5.23**), the market tries to move toward efficiency; the first standard deviation of prices migrates toward the middle of the range that began with Step 1; and the combined profile becomes bell-shaped.

When the data resembles the bell-shaped curve, it arranges itself into a 3-1-3 or D shape (see **Figure 5.24**). The numbers refer to the standard deviations. (Of

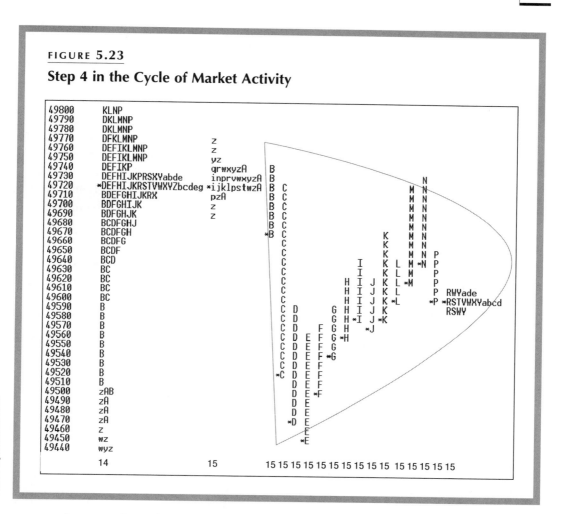

FIGURE 5.23

Step 4 in the Cycle of Market Activity

course, the second standard deviation is also present in the D shape, but it would be too long-winded to say "3-2-1-2-3.")

The Four Steps Complete

Figure 5.25 combines all the bars starting with the b period on March 15 and continuing until the end of overnight trading. With the profile complete, a new move to the upside came out of the mode, giving a new Step 1.

Because you can make the biggest profits during Step 1, you need to be most alert during the late stages of Steps 3 and 4, which will sooner or later lead to a Step 1.

FIGURE 5.24

The 3-1-3: D or Bell Shape

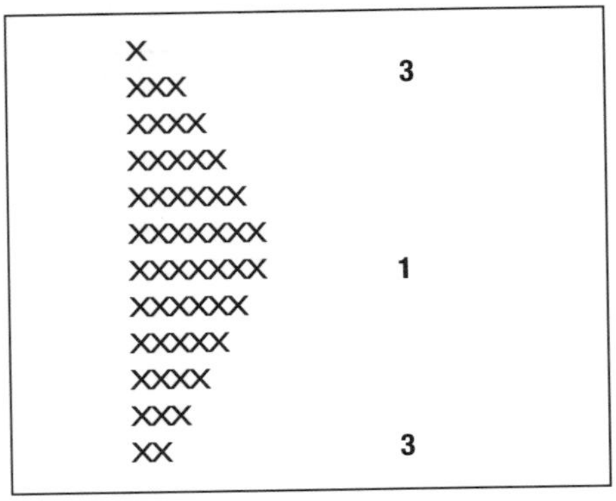

```
X
XXX              3
XXXX
XXXXX
XXXXXX
XXXXXXX
XXXXXXX          1
XXXXXX
XXXXX
XXXX
XXX
XX               3
```

Let's look at this concept in terms of a simple sixty-minute chart. **Figure 5.26** is an hourly bar chart of IBM. Can you visualize the b, p, and D shapes and the various steps of market activity?

In Figure 5.26, all the steps of market activity are present. The four steps begin with Step 1, which starts at A and ends at B, followed by a transition into Steps 2 and 3, which ended at C. At this point you can visualize the entire shape from A to C as a b-shaped pattern in which the lower portion of the range looks like a completed bell-shape curve. Out of the high-volume area at C a new

FIGURE 5.25

The Four Steps Complete

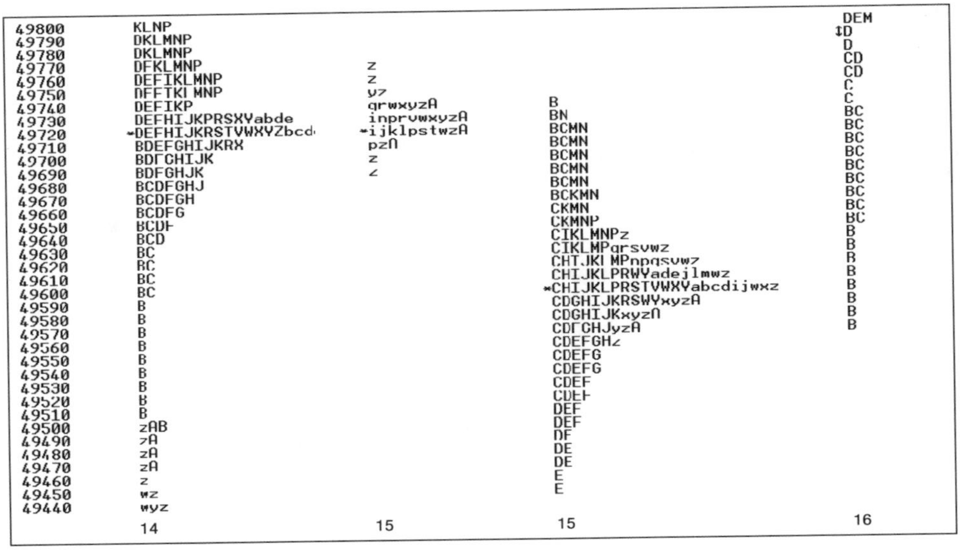

```
49800  KLNP                                                                      DEM
49790  DKLMNP                                                                    1D
49780  DKLMNP                                                                    D
49770  DFKLMNP                z                                                  CD
49760  DEFIKLMNP              z                                                  CD
49750  DEFTKI MNP             yz                                                 C
49740  DEFIKP                 qrwxyzA         B                                  C
49730  DEFHIJKPRSXYabde       inprvwxyzA      BN                                 BC
49720  *DEFHIJKRSTVWXYZbcd    *ijklpstwzA     BCMN                               BC
49710  BDEFGHIJKRX            pzf            BCMN                                 BC
49700  BDrGHIJK               z              BCMN                                 BC
49690  BDFGHJK                ∠              BCMN                                 BC
49680  BCDFGHJ                               BCMN                                 BC
49670  BCDFGH                                BCKMN                                BC
49660  BCDFG                                 CKMN                                 BC
49650  BCDF                                  CKMNPz                               B
49640  BCD                                   CIKLMNPz                             B
49630  BC                                    CIKLMPqrsvwz                         B
49620  RC                                    CHTJKI MPnpqsvwz                     R
49610  BC                                    CHIJKLPRWYadejlmwz                   B
49600  BC                                    *CHIJKLPRSTVWXYabcdijwxz             B
49590  B                                     CDGHIJKRSWYxyzA                      B
49580  B                                     CDGHIJKxyzf                          B
49570  B                                     CDrGHJyzA                            B
49560  B                                     CDEFGHz
49550  B                                     CDEFG
49540  B                                     CDEFG
49530  B                                     CDEF
49520  B                                     CDEr
49510  B                                     DEF
49500  zAB                                   DEF
49490  zA                                    DF
49480  zA                                    DE
49470  zA                                    DE
49460  z                                     E
49450  wz                                    E
49440  wyz
       14                     15             15                                   16
```

Source: Capital Flow Software

FIGURE 5.26

The Four Steps of Market Activity in Sequence: IBM/International Business Machines Corp. (60-minute bar chart)

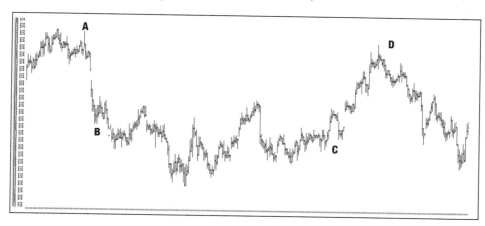

Source: Capital Flow Software

FIGURE 5.27

IBM/International Business Machines Corp. Chart Organized into the Steps of Market Activity

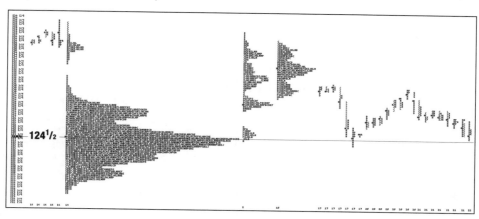

Source: Capital Flow Software

FIGURE 5.28

A Composite Profile: HWP/Hewlett-Packard (June 14–July 21, 1999)

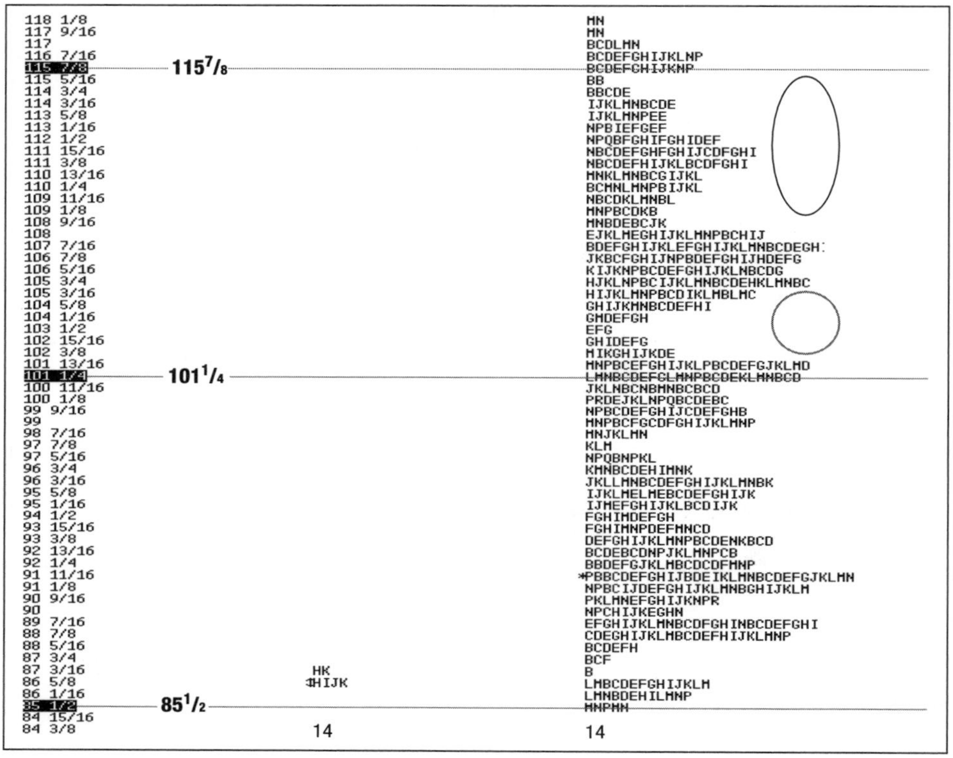

Source: Capital Flow Software

beginning to the upside occurred: a Step 1 to the upside came back to the initiation point of the prior Step 1 decline at A in which the b shape gradually reverted into a D shape, after which the market began to float back to the mode area, a sign of readiness for a new move.

Let's see what the chart of IBM would look like in Market Profile format. We have organized the data of Figure 5.26 into various Profiles: In **Figure 5.27**, points A–C are now combined to form one profile, and you can see the b shape that is in place at the bottom of the Step 1 distribution, as well as a D shape or completed bell curve (b-shapes are completed bell curves, only on a shorter time frame). Once this b shape pattern was complete, a new Step 1 initiated out of the high-volume

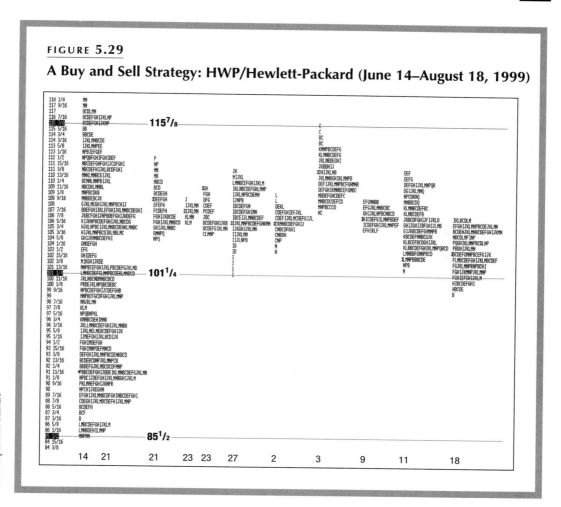

FIGURE 5.29

A Buy and Sell Strategy: HWP/Hewlett-Packard (June 14–August 18, 1999)

Source: Capital Flow Software

area and rallied back to the initiation point of the decline, which began the process of creating a larger-shaped bell curve out of the entire trading range.

Using Market Profile to Create a Buy/Sell Strategy

Now that you have an overview of the complete market cycle, let's look at one last example and apply it to a buy and sell strategy. **Figure 5.28** shows a composite profile of Hewlett-Packard through July 21, 1999. The stock closed toward the top of the value area. Given your understanding of the four steps of market activity, what step is the market in now? What does that imply in terms of a buy and sell strategy, and where do you expect the market to develop next?

You would have to label the entire pattern in Figure 5.28 as a Step 4, which is still underdeveloped. In this profile, you would not expect a directional move to occur until the entire profile reverts into a more fully developed bell curve. But as you can see, much more development is necessary to complete a fully ripe D pattern. Combining the profiles so far shows that the auction in both the upper and lower range is not complete. When trading, it is wise to look for holes in the profile that need to be filled. You have an opportunity to trade the top and bottom of equilibrium until the holes are filled in. The profile needs to develop in the circled areas to form a bell-shaped curve, which is exactly what

FIGURE 5.30

A Completed Bell-Shape Curve: HWP/Hewlett-Packard

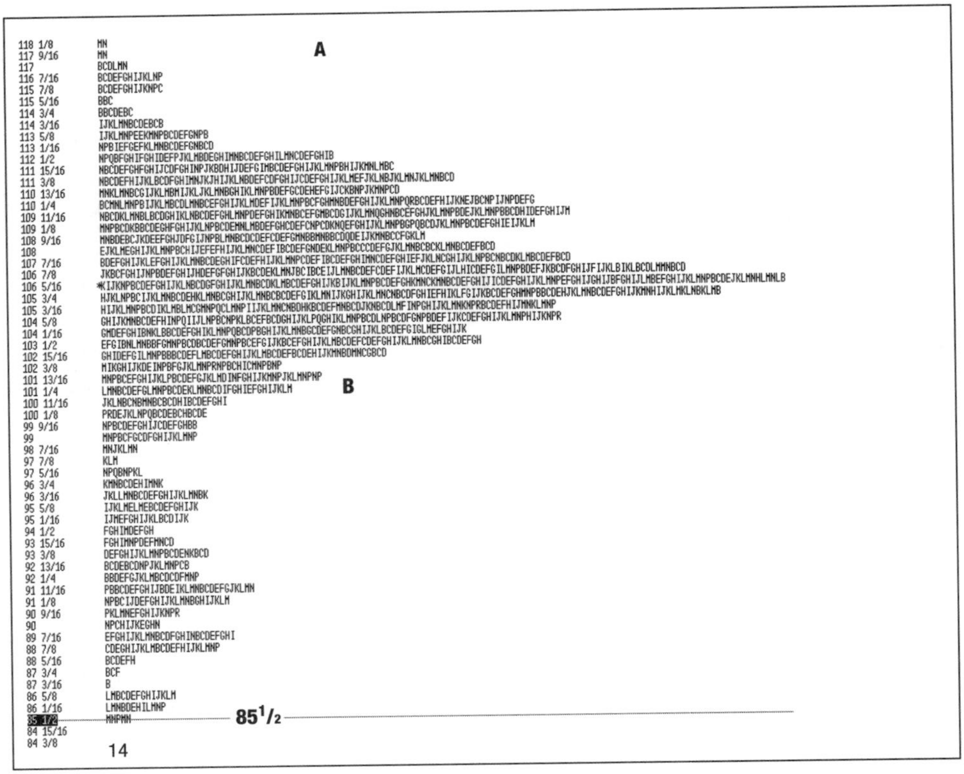

Source: Capital Flow Software

transpired over the next several days. In terms of a buy and sell strategy, you know that markets will typically develop one end of the range into a p or b pattern before developing into a completed bell curve. Because this stock closed toward the upper end of the range, let's assume that the low volume areas in the circled area on Figure 5.28 will be developed first. This means you could buy and sell the top and bottom of the developing value area until a fully developed p shape is in place.

Let's see what happened next. In **Figure 5.29**, the strategy of selling high and buying toward the bottom of the developing value area would have worked quite well for a number of days as the low-volume areas filled in.

FIGURE 5.31

Putting Together the 4 Steps of Market Activity: HWP/Hewlett-Packard

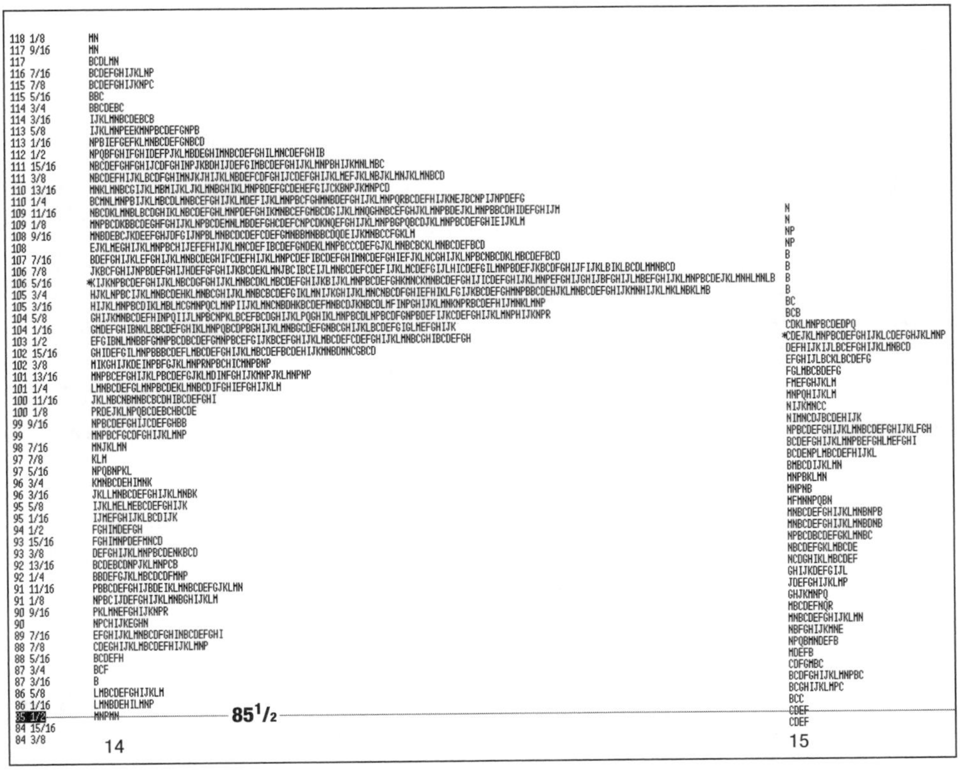

```
118 1/8   MN
117 9/16  MN
117       BCDLMN
116 7/16  BCDEFGHIJKLNP
115 7/8   BCDEFGHIJKNPC
115 5/16  BBC
114 3/4   BBCDEBC
114 3/16  IJKLMNBCDEBCB
113 5/8   IJKLMNPEEKMNPBCDEFGNPB
113 1/16  NPBIEFGEFKLMNBCDEFGNBCD
112 1/2   NPQBFGHIFGHIDEFPJKLMBDEGHIMNBCDEFGHILMNCDEFGHIB
111 15/16 NBCDEFGHFGHIJCDFGHIMPJKBOHIJDEFGIMBCDEFGHIJKLMNPBHIJKMNLMBC
111 3/8   NBCDEFHIJKLBCDFGHIMNJKJHIJKLNBDEFCDFGHIJCDEFGHIJKLMEFJKLNBJKLMNJKLMNBCD
110 13/16 MNKLMNBCCIJKLMBMIJKLJKLMNBGHIKLMNPBDEFGCDEHEFGIJCKBNPJKMNPCD
110 1/4   BCMNLMNPBIJKLMBCDLMNBCEFGHIJKLMDEFIJKLMNPBCFGHMNBDEFGHIJKLMNPQRBCDEFHIJKNEJBCNPIJNPDEFG
109 11/16 NBCDKLMNBLBCDGHIKLNBCDEFGHLMNPDEFGHIKMNBCEFGMBCDGIJKLMNQGHNBCEFGHJKLMNPBDEJKLMNPBBCDHIDEFGHIJM
109 1/8   MNPBCDKBBCDEGHFGHIJKLNPBCDEMNLMBDEFGHCDEFCNPCDKNQEFGHIJKLMNPBGPQBCDJKLMNPBCDEFGHIEIJKLM
108 9/16  MNBDEBCJKDEEFGHUDFGIJNPBLMNBCDCDEFCDEFGMNBBMNBBCDQDEIJKMNBCCFGKLM
108       EJKLMEGHIJKLMNPBCHIJEFEFHIJKLMNCDEFIBCDEFGNDEKLMNPBCCCDEFGJKLMNBCBCKLMNBCDEFBCD
107 7/16  BDEFGHIJKLEFGHIJKLMNBCDEGHIFCDEFHIJKLMNPCDEFIBCDEFGHIMNCDEFGHIEFJKLNCGHIJKLNPBCNBCDKLMBCDEFBCD
106 7/8   JKBCFGHIJNPBDEFGHIJHDEFGFGHIJKBCDEKLMNJBCIBCEIJKLMNBCDEFCDEFIJKLMCDEFGIJLHICDEFGILMNPBDEFJKBCDFGHIJFIJKLBIKLBCDLMNNBCD
106 5/16  *IJKNPBCDEFGHIJKLNBCDGFGHIJKLMNBCDKLMBCDEFGHIJKB IJKLMNBCDKKCMNBCNBCDEFGHKMNCKMNBCDEFGHIJICDEFGHIJKLMNEFGHIJGHIJBFGHIJLMBEFGHIJKLMNPBCDEJKLMNHLMNLB B
105 3/4   HJKLNPBCIJKLMNBCDEHLMNBCDGHIJKLMNBCBCDEFGIKLMNIJKGHIJKLMNCNBCDFGHIEFHIKLFGIJKBCDEFGHMMPBBCDEHJKLMNBCDEFGHIJKMNHIJKLMKLNBKLMB
105 3/16  HIJKLMNPBCDIKLMBLMCGMNPQCLMNPIIJKLMNCNBDHKBCDEFMNBCDJKNBCDLMFINPCGHIJKLMNKNPRBCDEFHIJMMKLMNP
104 5/8   GHIJKMNBCDEFHINPQIIJLNPBCMNPQKLBCEFBCDGHIJKLPQGHIKLMNPBCDLNPBCFGNPBDEFIJKCDEFGHIJKLMNPHIJKNPR
104 1/16  GMDEFGHIBNKLBBCDEFGHIKLNPQBCDPBGHIJKLMNBCDCEFGNBCGHIJKLBCDEFGIGLMEFGHIJK
103 1/2   EFGIBMLMNBBFGMNPBCDBCDEFGMNPBCEFGIJKBCEFGHIJKLMBCDEFGHIJKLMNBCGHIBCDEFGH
102 15/16 GHIDEFGILMNPBBBCDEFLMBCDEFGHIJKLMBCDEFBCDEHIJKMNBOMNCGBCD
102 3/8   MIKGHIJKDEINPBFGJKLMNPNPBCHICMNPBNP
101 13/16 MNPBCEFGHIJKLPBCDEFGJKLMDINFGHIJKMNPJKLMNPNP
101 1/4   LMNBCDEFGLMNPBCDEKLMNBCDIFGHIEFGHIJKLM
100 11/16 JKLNBCNBMNBCBCDHIBCDEFGHI
100 1/8   PRDEJKLNPQBCDEBCHBCDE
99 9/16   NPBCDEFGHIJICDEFGHBB
99        MNPBCFGCDFGHIJKLMNP
98 7/16   MKJKLMN
97 7/8    KLM
97 5/16   NPQBNPKL
96 3/4    KMNBCDEHIMNK
96 3/16   JKLLMNBCDEFGHIJKLMNBK
95 5/8    IJKLMELMEBCDEFGHIJK
95 1/16   IJMEFGHIJKLBCDIJK
94 1/2    FGHIMDEFGH
93 15/16  FGHIMNPDEFMNCD
93 3/8    DEFGHIJKLMNPBCDENKBCD
92 13/16  BCDEBCDNPJKLMNPCB
92 1/4    BBDEFGJKLMBCDCDFMNP
91 11/16  PBBCDEFGHIJBDEIKLMNBCDEFGJKLMN
91 1/8    NPBCIJDEFGHIJKLMNBGHIJKLM
90 9/16   PKLMNEFGHIJKNPB
90        NPCHIJKEGHN
89 7/16   EFGHIJKLMNBCDFGHINBCDEFGHI
88 7/8    CDEGHIJKLMBCDEFHIJKLMNP
88 5/16   BCDEFH
87 3/4    BCF
87 3/16   B
86 5/8    LMBCDEFGHIJKLM
86 1/16   LHNBDEHILMNP
85 1/2    MNPMN                    85 1/2
84 15/16
84 3/8          14                              15
```

Right-hand day column (day 15):
```
N
N
NP
NP
B
B
B
BC
BCB
CDKLMNPBCDEDPQ
*CDEJKLMNPBCDEFGHIJKLCDEFGHJKLMNP
DEFHIJKIJLBCEFGHIJKLMNBCD
EFGHIJLBCKLBCDEFG
FGLMBCBDEFG
FMEFGHJKLM
MNPQHIJKLM
NIJKMNCC
NIMNCDJBCDEHIJK
NPBCDEFGHIJKLMNBCDEFGHIJKLFGH
BCDEFGHIJKLMNPBEFGHLMEFGHI
BCDENPLMBCDEFHIJKL
BMBCDIJKLMN
MNPBKLMN
MNPNB
MFMNNPQBH
MNBCDEFGHIJKLMNBNPB
MNBCDEFGHIJKLMNBDNB
NPBCDBCDEFGKLMNBC
NBCDEFGKLMBCDE
NCDGHIKLNBCDEF
GHIJKDEFGIJL
JDEFGHIJKLMP
GHJKMNPQ
MBCDEFNQR
MNBCDEFGHIJKLMN
NBFGHIJKMNE
NPQBMNDEFB
MDEFB
CDFGMBC
BCDFGHIJKLMNPBC
BCGHIJKLMNPC
BCC
CDEF
CDEF
```

Source: Capital Flow Software

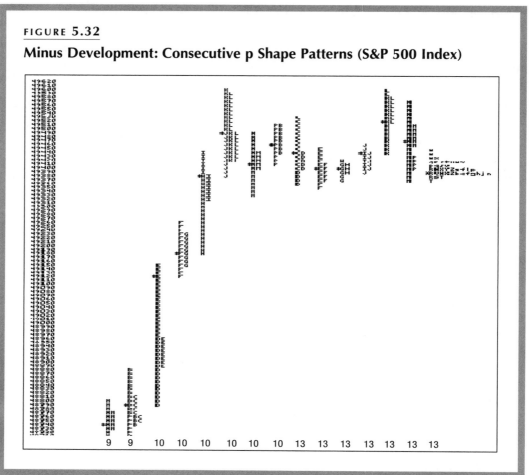

FIGURE **5.32**

Minus Development: Consecutive p Shape Patterns (S&P 500 Index)

When you put all the data together into one composite profile (see **Figure 5.30**), you can clearly see that a completed bell-shape curve has formed at the top of the range. Finally, the cup is full and ready to spill. The market has formed a completed bell-shaped curve and Step 4 is ready to yield to a new Step I. But in which direction?

At this point, with development of the bell curve complete, your strategy must shift away from buying the bottom of value and selling the top. The steps of market activity indicate when to use a congestion-trading strategy versus a trend-following strategy.

Consider the longer-term picture from the beginning of the chart. The mar-

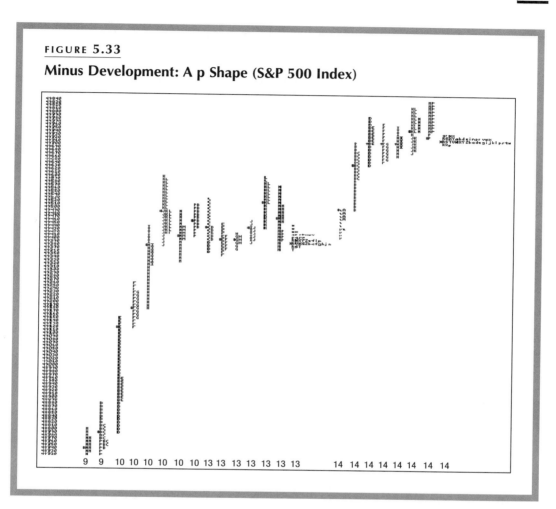

FIGURE 5.33

Minus Development: A p Shape (S&P 500 Index)

ket on the longer-term time frame is in a Step 3 or a p pattern. What, then, can you expect to happen? What type of market activity would indicate that you were right or wrong?

When trading the steps of market activity, you must not lose sight of the larger picture, which will start to influence market direction once the smaller time frames have completed their cycle of market activity. The larger picture is the background or context in which the shorter-term equilibrium is unfolding.

At this point in your trading strategy, Figure 5.30 indicates you should no longer play for range trade, but opt for a Step 1 directional move instead. Typically those moves are initiated from the high-volume area. Important clues in terms of

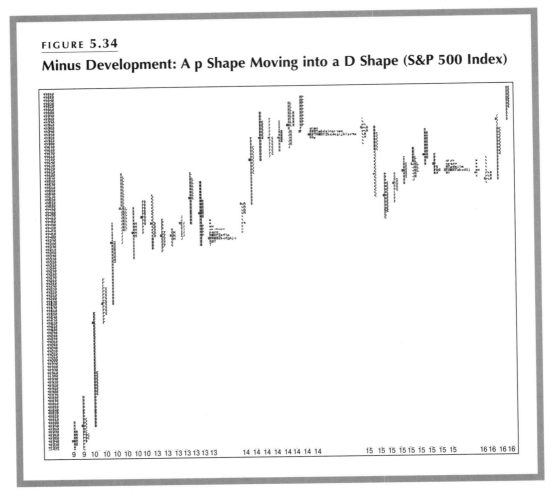

FIGURE 5.34

Minus Development: A p Shape Moving into a D Shape (S&P 500 Index)

the steps of market activity and volume analysis can help you determine a buy and sell strategy and the next directional move of the market. Notice the ledge of volume at A and B in Figure 5.30. This is the top and bottom of value. If the market started to move dynamically over one of those points, it would be fairly safe to assume the next direction. In light of the fact that the bottom portion of this profile is still in need of development and you've identified the entire pattern as an underdeveloped Step 4, a fairly low risk strategy would be to sell the mode line for a move down to the bottom of the developing value area in anticipation of a larger D-shaped bell curve forming. If you are right, the market should not rally higher than the ledge of high volume at the top of the value area at A.

FIGURE **5.35**

Minus Development: A p Shape of Composite Profiles (S&P 500 Index)

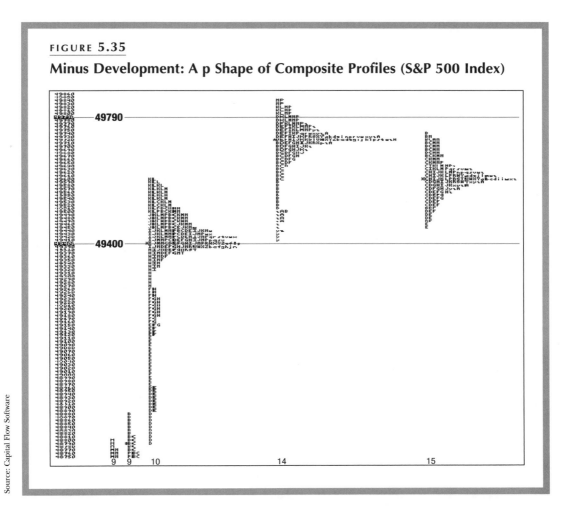

Indeed, as **Figure 5.31** shows, a new directional move came right out of the mode, and the downside target was the bottom of the range.

Minus Development

Unfortunately the market does not always follow the four steps of market activity. Sometimes a market fails to develop into one of the four steps. This deviation from "normal" market behavior is called minus development.

Minus development means that some stages of development have been skipped before the next cycle of disequilibrium starts. It occurs in many different forms and has different implications depending on which step is skipped and

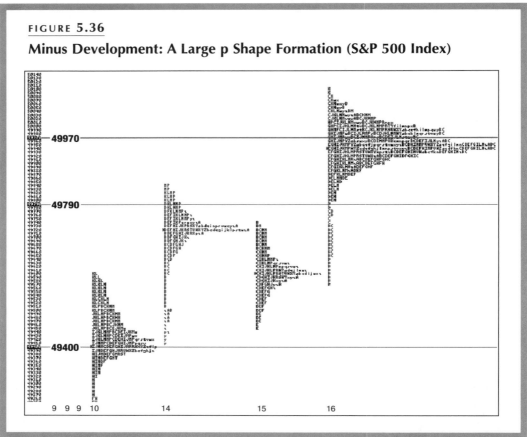

FIGURE 5.36

Minus Development: A Large p Shape Formation (S&P 500 Index)

Source: Capital Flow Software

in what time frame. The most commonly skipped step, however, is Step 4. In such a case, minus development is characterized by consecutive p or b patterns.

What the market does not do is often more important than what it is supposed to do—it means that the opposite is happening. For example, the implication of the p shape (or multiple p shapes) that fails to shift into a D-shape is very bullish (and vice-versa).

Figure 5.32 shows the market in a Step 3 on the big picture but in a completed Step 4 on the short-term picture. Normally, you would expect the market to shift into a Step 4 to incorporate all of the data in the chart into a D-shaped bell curve. If the market breaks below the ledge of high volume (the mode line), in a directional fashion, you would have confidence that the normal steps of market activity were in process. In Figure 5.32 a bell-shaped curve

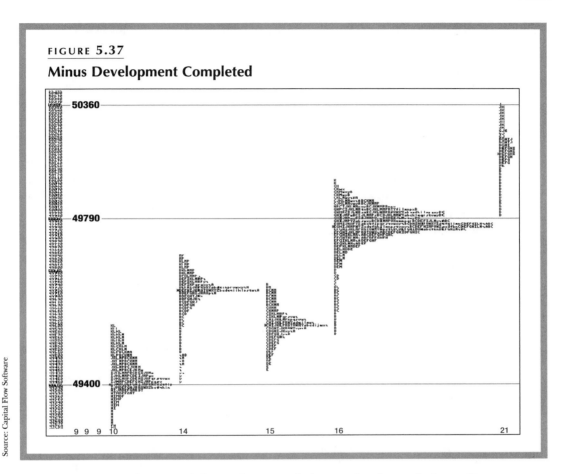

FIGURE **5.37**

Minus Development Completed

Source: Capital Flow Software

has developed at the top of the p shape, and the market is ready for a directional move within the smallest time frame. If the directional move is to the downside, a Step 4 is under way toward the initiation point of the rally; if the next directional move is to the upside, a new Step 1 is likely—and a case of minus development.

The high-volume region is the key—if the market starts to move below it, it will be a signal to sell, while a move above is a signal to buy. In a strongly bullish move, there will be p shape after p-shaped formations as the market rallies, develops, rallies, and develops, with perhaps an occasional small-scale D shape. A series of p shapes is the signature of a strong trend.

In **Figure 5.33**, the market made an initiating move to the upside out of the mode line on day 14. The background of the market shows signs of minus development. There are now two consecutive p patterns where Step 4 would have formed.

The move out of the first p pattern was to the upside, leading to a second p shape that eventually went into a D shape (see **Figure 5.34**). In the context of the first p shape, however, minus development is still the overall situation. If you group all of the data so far into separate profiles, the picture looks like **Figure 5.35**.

If you collapse all of the Profiles in Figure 5.32, they form a completed bell curve at the top of the range. Even though the final stage of development was the D shape, it was against an overall background of minus development in which the D merely represented the completion of a larger p shape. **Figure 5.36** combines the Profiles in Figure 5.35 into a single unit that clearly shows that what has occurred to date has been part of the original Step 1 distribution.

How would you describe the background of the market in Figure 5.36? Will the background influence the foreground? Is this a situation in which the foreground can actually make a dent in the background? As discussed above, the mode line should be a key reference point in determining the next directional move of the market, and indeed it was in this example. A new Step 1 initiated out of the control price to begin the cycle of market activity once again (**Figure 5.37**).

Summary of Principles Underlying Market Profile

Some of the basic principles that underlie Market Profile include the following:
- Volume is the natural expression of the market.
- The market is two-dimensional: vertical and horizontal.
- Market Profile is a relational database that captures the two-dimensional nature of the market and constantly makes a comparison between the vertical and horizontal activity.
- The cyclical flow of the market consists of four steps of market activity.

Learning to use volume is learning to read the language of the market. Relying simply on price to trade is like relying solely on notes to make music. Price continues to be confused with the content it carries, but in reality price is only the messenger, and it is relevant only in the context of the steps of market activity, price control or non-price control, and volume. As traders rely more on the internal dynamics of the market and grasp the meaning of trading volume, they will move closer to an objective means of trading where control is less dependent on personality and more a by-product of properly understanding the language of the market.

CHAPTER 6

Using Oscillators to Predict Trade Opportunities

TOM DeMARK

There are three distinct levels of chart analysis. Very simply, the first and most common involves the quick perusal of a chart and a "gut feeling" interpretation. Whatever may strike the viewer as important at that particular point in time colors the interpretation. There exists no sound, "scientific" basis for the conclusions drawn, which are primarily subjective and rooted in guesswork; terms such as "flags" and "head and shoulders" often are used to describe patterns.

The second level of analysis involves the use of an indicator or a series of indicators whose application is intended to provide a substantive method whereby to analyze the market. Although the indicators' construction may be clear-cut, their implications are still subject to the viewer's interpretation. However, by using indicators, there is greater likelihood that the interpretations will tend to be consistent, uniform, and less subjective than those formulated on the first level through primarily guesswork and intuition.

Finally, the third level of analysis is totally objective and mechanical. The indicators used are included in a defined regimen of interpretation that includes a set of prescribed rules for systematic interpretation and trading execution. The rules are clear and the steps in the analytical process are rigid and straightforward. No gray area or equivocation exists, because the interpretation is defined for the user. In analyzing the market I prefer to operate on level 2, along with using a few level 3-style indicators with which I have considerable experience and confidence.

To be successful as a trader it is critical that one conduct individual research and create and apply one's own disciplined market timing methodology with the objective of ultimately becoming responsible for the considerations that determine one's trading decisions. Relying on a group of indicators but not understanding their construction or proper application will impede a trader from progressing toward this goal. A thorough appreciation of both these indicators' strengths and their weaknesses is needed to apply them effectively. Just as a journeyman carpenter quickly becomes aware of the restrictions and limitations of using various tools, so too the trader must recognize shortcomings of various market timing tools and respect the scope of their intended usage.

Traditional Oscillator Interpretation

Most traders have had at least a casual experience with overbought or oversold oscillators. By and large, their perception is more than likely that oversold zones typically coincide with market lows and overbought zones occur simultaneous with market highs. The approach is simple and crude, as most people associate an oversold reading with low-risk buying and an overbought reading with low-risk selling. This commonly held interpretation is partially correct. The research of Market Studies Inc. indicates that some of the time when a market is either overbought or oversold, the market reverses direction just as most people expect. However, some of the time markets continue their outstanding trend and the expectation of a reversal is totally incorrect.

Importance of Duration Analysis vs. Divergence Analysis
The secret in distinguishing between those two outcomes, that is, when a market will reverse its trend and when it will maintain its current course, resides in the amount of time an oscillator remains in its oversold or overbought state. This important factor is referred to as *duration*. In August 1982, for example, the stock market became quickly overbought for an extended period of time, as the magnitude of the advance off the market low was dynamic and prolonged. Many market pundits were looking for a major correction due to the intensity of the overbought readings, but, as history proved, none occurred, which had to do with the amount of time—as evidenced in consecutive price bars—the market remained overbought. Extensive research has shown that extreme overbought or oversold readings that last for more than six consecutive price bars imply intense buying or selling and forewarn of the likely continuation of the ongoing trend.

Many traditional chartists incorrectly attribute a market's failure to reverse when in either an oversold or overbought state to the fact that no positive "divergence" has occurred between price action and oscillator movement. For example, let's say that an oscillator moves into oversold territory while the underlying security declines in price. Subsequently, the oscillator moves out of oversold territory and into the neutral zone, then declines again into oversold territory—but not quite as deep as the original oversold reading—while the price of the underlying security itself declines deeper than it had the first time the oscillator declined into oversold territory. Traditional chartists would say there was a divergence between the oscillator and the price movement and that the market is positioned to reverse upside.

Because this view is based on the belief that divergences between oscillator and price are always resolved in favor of the oscillator, price should now rally. Conversely, when an oscillator is overbought, returns to neutral, and then returns to a lower overbought level while the underlying security's price records a higher high at the second penetration than the first high, a divergence occurs and price typically declines. This may in fact occur, but rather than being the cause of the market reversal, divergence is merely a symptom of this result; duration is its cause. It is the amount of time in which the oscillator remains in overbought or oversold territory that dictates whether the reversal or the continuation of the trend will occur.

Common Overbought and Oversold Oscillators

The most commonly used overbought/oversold oscillators are the Relative Strength Index (RSI) and Ralph Dystant's Stochastics. The secret to the success of these two oscillators has to do with the fact that they were the only two oscillators in the public domain in the 1970s. At that time, the introduction and the usage of chart books were widespread and many of their publishers included charts with these indicators to fill pages. In addition, the electronic chart services that were introduced in the early 1980s, such as Comtrend, included the same chart displays on their monitors.

No research studies had been conducted to determine whether these particular indicators produced effective results or were better at doing so than others. Reliance on these indicators resulted largely from their wide availability, acceptance, and following among traders. In retrospect, though, no legitimate reason existed for applying such indicators to the interpretation of markets. Nothing special distinguished these indicators beyond whether they were exponentially calculated or whether a particular relationship between the indicator and corresponding closing prices suggested an advance or a decline. To meet the need for validated tools of interpretation, over the past thirty years Market Studies Inc. has researched and developed its own suite of market timing indicators, experimenting with various price relationships and oscillator movements in the process. Initially, TD Range Expansion Index (TD REI) was developed, but many others soon followed.

TD Range Expansion Index™

Many, if not all, oversold/overbought oscillators work well in trading range markets; however, they often become prematurely oversold or overbought in trending markets and consequently prove to be ineffective. An ideal indicator would not record overbought or oversold levels as quickly as conventional indicators do; an ideal analytical method would more easily distinguish between a trading range or a trending market.

One key reason for traders' inability to distinguish between trading range and trending markets has to do with their applying divergence analysis to the relationship between an indicator and an underlying security movement, rather than applying the concept of duration analysis in its place. Part of the problem also has to do with their using certain imprecise indicators whose components are not as sensitive to price activity as other indicators.

To gain the needed precision to reduce the likelihood of an indicator prematurely moving into oversold or overbought zones in a trending market, TD Range Expansion Index (TD REI) requires that certain price bars overlap with price levels of prior price bars, thereby indicating a slowing of a trend. If they do not intersect, the price bar's measure of indicator activity for that particular price period is assigned a zero. This practice in and of itself reduces the risk of moving into oversold or overbought territory too quickly in a trending market.

Furthermore, most, if not all, oscillators in the public domain relate consecutive closing prices to calculate their indices. However, there is nothing especially significant about comparing closing prices. To gain more meaningful price information, why not compare highs and/or lows? Why not alternate the comparisons? TD REI does exactly that and thus achieves sensitivity to extreme price movement while not moving an oscillator prematurely into an oversold or overbought zone. It makes comparisons between successive highs and lows and their counterparts two price bars earlier. TD REI analysis compares every other bar's high and low to remove some of the volatility that arises from unexpected, short-term news developments and events of a fleeting nature, which can cause overly aggressive purchases or sales of large blocks of a security. If one compares the highs and lows with the highs and lows two price bars earlier, this eliminates most spontaneous emotional and short-lived market responses and trading outbursts. These are reactions to news that prove to be inconsequential when observed over more than one price bar.

Construction of TD REI

The TD REI indicator is calculated arithmetically by comparing alternating market highs and lows. At the same time, current price activity is compared with prior price activity to determine if price has intersected or overlapped with prior price movement or is trending away from those price levels. Once the TD REI is plotted with the underlying security price activity occurring at the same time, various techniques can be applied to time both low-risk buy and low-risk sell opportunities in the market.

● **Step 1** compares the high and the low of the current price bar with the high and low two price bars earlier. As mentioned above, this procedure diminishes the impact of one price bar's market spikes or news flares that are accompanied by short-lived buying or selling stampedes. The TD REI comparison gives credence to and acknowledges only those price moves or bursts that appear to be more durable and persist for more than just one price period. Additionally, comparing the two price bars makes an arithmetically calculated oscillator appear more fluid and consistent than would be the case if a one-price-bar comparison were used instead. More definite conclusions can be reached than if one were relying on daily price comparisons alone.

For this first phase, you must subtract the high two price bars ago from the high of the current price bar and subtract the low two price bars ago from the low of the current price bar. These two differences are then added to create a value. This value can be either positive or negative, depending on whether the current high and the current low are above or below the prior high and the prior low, and also on how much above or below the current high and current low the prior two comparable price levels are.

● **Step 2** determines whether or not the calculations performed in Step 1 are to be considered for the purpose of analysis. In other words, if the qualifiers included in this phase are not met, a strong possibility exists that the market is in a trending mode; therefore, a zero value is assigned to the TD REI oscillator total for that particular price bar rather than its calculated value determined in Step 1. Assigning a zero value reduces the likelihood of a market prematurely becoming oversold or overbought and reduces the likelihood that a trader will exit or enter a trade prematurely. This step is critical because it monitors whether current prices overlap or intersect prices during an earlier price period. If they do, the market is in a trading range. When price do not overlap, the market is trending.

The qualifiers require that either (1) the current price bar's price range must overlap with the price activity five or six price bars earlier—in other words, the current price bar's high must be greater than or equal to the low five or six price bars earlier and the current price bar's low must be less than or equal to the high five or six price bars earlier; or (2) the price range two price bars ago must overlap with the close located either seven or eight price bars from the current price bar. In other words, the high of two price bars before the current one must be greater than or equal to the close seven or eight price bars earlier; and the current price bar's low must be less than or equal to the close seven or eight price bars earlier.

● **Step 3** includes either the value calculated in Step 1, because the required price intersection occurred, or the disqualified value of zero, because the required price overlap did not occur. In turn, this value is combined with the price calculations of the prior four price bars' calculations to arrive at the current TD REI five-bar price reading. Note that this five-price-bar reading can include a series of positive, negative, and zero values. By adding the individual values over the five-bar period, the numerator of the TD REI equation is completed. The denominator is the summation of the absolute value of the five consecutive price bars, assuming each price bar has fulfilled the intersection requirement. In other words, the direction of the difference, positive or negative, is ignored and only the distance in positive terms is added to arrive at the denominator value.

The numerator can be positive, negative, or zero, but the denominator cannot be zero unless the highs and the lows over a period of seven consecutive price bars are equal—this includes the five price bars required to calculate TD REI, as well as the two price bars prior to the first price bar. Finally, once the numerator and denominator values are calculated, the positive or negative ratio is multiplied by 100. This percentage is then plotted on a chart; the value fluctuates between -100 and 100.

● **Step 4** establishes the band that defines when the TD REI indicator is either overbought, oversold, or neutral. Generally, -40 and +40 are selected as the oversold or overbought thresholds for a five-price-bar TD REI; any value in between is rated neutral.

● **Step 5** is designed to warn traders when it is likely that time for a trend reversal has expired and that the oscillator's continuation within either overbought or oversold territory means the ongoing market trend will continue. Typically, given the oversold or overbought parameters of -40 and +40, and the construction of a five-price-bar TD REI, the number of consecutive price bars deemed reasonable for a market to remain either oversold or overbought and for the market to respond by reversing trend is six or fewer. The occurrence of more than six consecutive price bars implies that the "duration" limit has been exceeded and the market oscillator has recorded an extreme or an excessive overbought string of consecutive price bars.

To relieve this extreme reading, the oscillator must return to neutral and then attempt to record a "mild" or a "moderate" oversold or overbought reading within six or fewer consecutive price bars. Combined with suggested entry techniques (discussed below), the concept of duration gives a trader a real market timing advantage. As noted previously, duration explains market behavior at prospective turning points or price reversals more fully than divergence analysis, which is merely a manifestation of duration.

An alternative approach is available to the standard treatment of Step 2 when price bars fail to intersect any of a series of prior price bars, thereby suggesting a trending market. The alternative, more conservative, method assigns a value of zero not only to the price bar plot where the intersection of price bars fails to occur, but also an additional zero value to the prior price bar as well, to further ensure that a premature oversold/overbought reading is not recorded.

The standard (as described above) and the alternate option (which includes zero assignment to the prior price bar) are the two selections available in the "type" category of most TD REI variable settings. Market Studies Inc. recommends using the standard method, but some traders may prefer the alternate setting because it reduces the possibility of early oversold or overbought readings even further. Because the trader's goal is to remain in a trade as long as possible, without assuming the risk of missing a reverse indication or an exit, the alternate option is a viable way of safeguarding trades.

Using TD REI

The Dow Jones Industrial Average June 2000 futures contract illustrates a series of potentially short-term profitable trades based on the relative positions of the TD REI indicator and the price activity of the Dow Jones contract (see **Figure 6.1**). The interpretation is straightforward. The approach is trend following, rather than one of price exhaustion, because the low-risk buy entries occur after the closing low is followed immediately in the next price bar by an up close. Moreover, the low-risk sell entries occur after the closing high is succeeded immediately on the next price bar by a down close.

In both instances, the former at a low and the latter at a high, the indicator must be below -40 and above +40 for the two-price-bar period (these thresholds

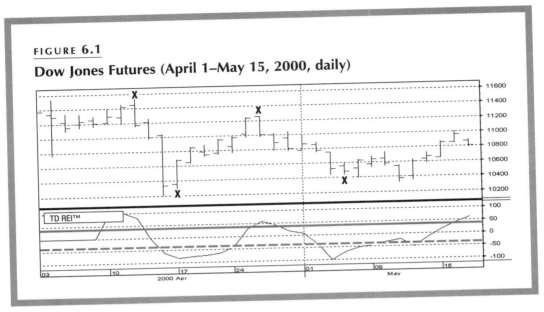

FIGURE 6.1

Dow Jones Futures (April 1–May 15, 2000, daily)

can be reduced slightly to increase trade activity, however). Additionally, at a market bottom, the open on the price bar after an up close at the low should be lower than the up close price bar's high, and ideally the high on that same price bar should be above the prior price bar's high. Similarly, at a market top, the open on the price bar after a down close at the low should be greater than the down close price bar's low, and ideally the low on that same price bar should be below the prior price bar's low.

In Figure 6.1 April 11 and 12 show oscillator values above +40, and the close on April 12 is lower than the close on April 11. The following day's open is above the low of April 12, and the low is below the April 12 low. That is all that is required to produce a low-risk sell indication. The down close day's low must be exceeded downside, since it is not uncommon to record the first two requirements only to record an open above the prior down close day's low but not record a low below it. This last requirement often fails to occur in the case of a low-risk buy indication. In this instance, the open on the price bar subsequent to the up close day's high must be exceeded upside with a higher high.

Figure 6.2 shows the June 2000 10-year Treasury note futures contract. For both February 10 and 11 the oscillator values were below -40. The first day's close was lower than both the prior day's close and the same day's open. February 11's close was greater than that of February 10. The next trading day was February 14,

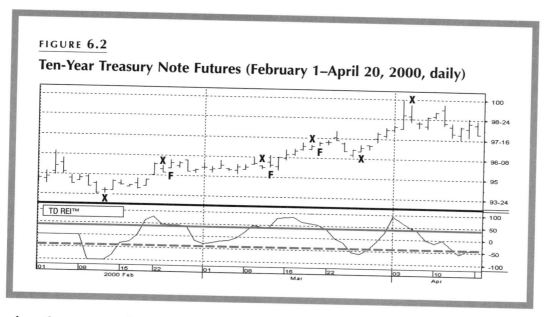

FIGURE 6.2

Ten-Year Treasury Note Futures (February 1–April 20, 2000, daily)

when the open was lower than the prior day's high and the high was above the prior day's high, thereby signaling a low-risk entry. If the open had been above the prior day's high there would have been a risk of a one- to two-day price peak; therefore, a subdued open—one lower than the prior day's high—is a preferable signal, although it is not essential.

From mid-February through the end of March, there were three potential sells, but in each instance, after the two-day setup in which an up close was followed by a down close compared to the prior trading day's close and the opening price level, the following day failed to produce a signal (as marked by an **F**) because the low did not exceed the prior trading day's low. Also, a duration of six appeared during that period, which was the extreme limit for expecting a signal without recycling the oscillator. The first week of April provided a low-risk sell, and this signal did not reverse during the month. One attempt was made on April 13, but the close was up and the prior day's oscillator reading was not below -40.

Figure 6.3 shows that on March 14 and 15 IBM's up close and down close pattern was accompanied by five-day TD REI oscillator readings above +40. However, the next day did not produce a decline below the prior day's low. This was fortuitous because IBM rallied. At its high a sell pattern was finally fulfilled, that is, two days above +40, first an up close and then a down close, followed the next day by an open above the prior day's low, accompanied by a lower low. On

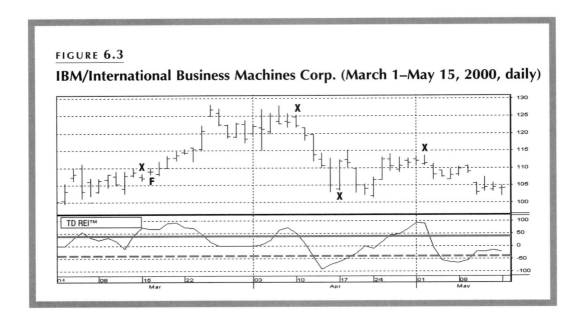

FIGURE 6.3

IBM/International Business Machines Corp. (March 1–May 15, 2000, daily)

April 18 the low-risk buy signal was not perfected because the open that day was above the prior trading day's high, suggesting short covering. These aggressive openings often are accompanied by one- to two-day pullbacks. The same pattern occurred at the sell on May 3, only in reverse, but this trade worked despite the aggressive selling. The duration of greater than six days marked the conclusion of any attempt to identify another low-risk signal.

TD DeMarker I™

TD DeMarker I, another oscillator researched and developed by Market Studies Inc., is intended to be used to identify potential market reversal opportunities based on oversold and overbought oscillator readings. Similar to TD REI, DeMarker I distinguishes between trading range and trending markets and confirms the underlying direction or trend of a market. Whereas most commonly used overbought/oversold indicators are exponentially calculated and focus only on daily price change from closing price to closing price, TD DeMarker I, like TD REI, compares a series of intraday highs and lows and is arithmetically calculated.

The advantage of using arithmetic calculations of intraday price activity instead of exponential calculations of consecutive closing prices is that the indicator will not be influenced permanently by any extraneous, nonmarket-related factors. Such factors may artificially affect the closing price of a market and therefore contaminate the indicator's values until the specific security is either delisted or expired. Some unexpected, nonmarket-related events may force an early market closing, such as a presidential assassination, electrical failure, or bad weather, and therefore may influence values shown by an indicator. Because these indicators are arithmetically calculated, however, such factors are soon eliminated once the period of time for which the indicator was designed has been exceeded. On the other hand, exponentially calculated indicators influence the values forever. Furthermore, because research indicates that there is nothing relevant or more reliable about daily consecutive closing price comparisons, intraday price comparisons of highs and lows have been chosen as reference prices in TD DeMarker I instead of the conventional closing prices used in other oscillators.

In trading range markets, most overbought/oversold oscillators identify market reversal points. However, in a trending market, premature overbought or oversold readings also appear. Most conventional market timers deal with these conditions by applying divergence analysis, or successively comparing lower price movements with concurrent oscillator values at prospective lows, and successively higher price movements with concurrent oscillator values at potential highs. This type of analysis is helpful but misleading; duration is the true signal for the occurrence of market reversal, and when it occurs in a situation of divergence, this is merely coincidental.

Specifically, duration, or the amount of time in which the oscillator remains in overbought or oversold territory, is more important than comparing divergence. For example, the occurrence of a standard period of six or fewer units of time typically differentiates between a mild or modest overbought or oversold period and a period marked by an excessive or extreme reading of more than six consecutive units of time. Excessive consecutive periods of time warrant the oscillator's recycling and recording a neutral value. Then, once the oscillator returns to overbought or oversold territory, the same analysis is applied. In other words, if the oscillator resides in a zone of six or fewer units of time, there is a greater chance that it is coinciding with a price reversal point.

More important, oscillators are intended to identify ideal low-risk buy and low- risk sell opportunity zones. Specifically, low-risk buy opportunities are associated with mildly oversold markets, as well as severely overbought markets that have exceeded the duration limit, or the number of consecutive trading price bars in the overbought zone. Conversely, low-risk sell opportunities are associated with mildly overbought markets, as well as those severely oversold markets that have exceeded the duration limit, or the number of consecutive trading price bars in the oversold zone. Just as the same interpretation is assigned to other TD oscillators, such as TD REI and TD DeMarker II, it is similarly true that the duration, or lapse, of time the TD DeMarker I oscillator remains in the overbought or the oversold zone is critical in distinguishing between a likely pending price reversal or the continuation of a trend.

As with many of the TD oscillators, TD DeMarker I is calculated arithmetically by comparing alternating market highs and lows, as well as determining whether current price activity has intersected or overlapped with prior price movement or is trending away from those prices. Once they are plotted, a series of oscillators can be compared to confirm suspicions regarding low-risk buy or sell market opportunities. Various market timing techniques can be applied and combined to time low-risk market entries, regardless of which indicator or oscillator is used.

Construction of TD DeMarker I

TD DeMarker I compares the current and the previous price bar's highs, as well as the current and previous price bar's lows. If the current price bar's high is greater than the previous price bar's high, the difference is calculated and recorded. However, if the difference is either negative or equal, the price bar is given a value of zero. A similar comparison of highs and calculations is conducted over an additional thirteen consecutive price bars, the respective differences are added, and this value becomes the numerator of the TD DeMarker I equation. The value of the denominator is the numerator plus the sum of the differences between the previous price bar's low and the current price bar's low over thirteen consecutive price bars. If the prior price bar's low is less than or equal to the current price bar's low, a value of zero is assigned to that price bar's value. Next, the value of the numerator is divided by the denominator value and this result, which can fluctuate between 100 and 0, is then plotted on a chart beneath the underlying price bar activity.

Using TD DeMarker I

The TD DeMarker I indicator can be constructed over various time periods. Because TD REI is usually applied to five price bars, it is often preferable to combine it with a variety of longer term indicators. For example, a thirteen-bar period TD DeMarker I indicator serves this purpose well. **Figures 6.4–6.6**

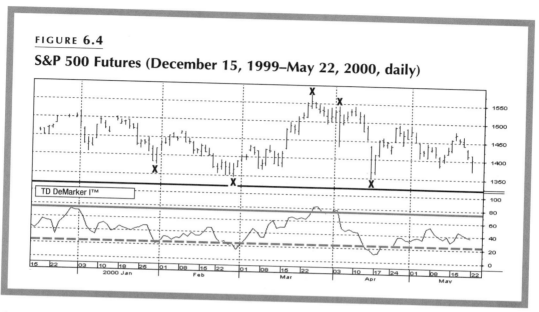

FIGURE **6.4**

S&P 500 Futures (December 15, 1999–May 22, 2000, daily)

demonstrate how this indicator interacts with the underlying price activity of a security to generate low-risk buy and sell signals.

The Standard and Poor's (S&P) June future daily chart (see **Figure 6.4**) identifies instances where the TD DeMarker I oscillator moves below 25 and where it moves above 75. The former represents the oversold zone and the latter the overbought zone. The movement into oversold and overbought territory alone is insufficient to identify low-risk buy and sell opportunities. Rather, the interplay of price movement once the oversold and the overbought levels are exceeded justifies entry and exit. For example, in this case, the thirteen-bar TD DeMarker I moves below the oversold boundary on January 28 and 31, February 24, 25, 28, and 29, and April 12 through 18. To identify the ideal low-risk buy opportunities to enter the market, (1) the underlying close must be lower than the low either one or two price bars earlier, (2) the close must be lower than the prior trading day's close and the current open, and (3) the next period's open must be lower than or equal to one of the prior two closes. Once price trades one tick above that close, the opportunity to buy exists. The ideal low-risk entry buy days are marked on Figure 6.4. On the contrary, from March 24 through March 28 and then from March 30 through April 3, low-risk sell environments exist provided that (1) the underlying close is greater than the high either one or two price bars earlier, (2) the close is greater than the prior trading day's close and

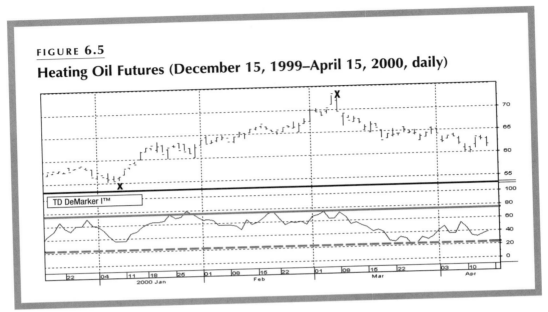

FIGURE 6.5

Heating Oil Futures (December 15, 1999–April 15, 2000, daily)

the current open, and (3) the next period's open is greater than or equal to one of the prior two closes. Once price trades one tick below that close, the opportunity to sell exists. The ideal low-risk entry sell days are marked on Figure 6.4.

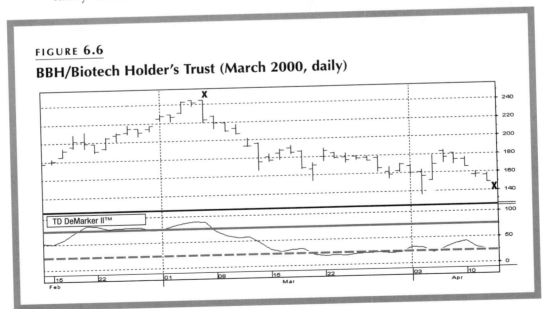

FIGURE 6.6

BBH/Biotech Holder's Trust (March 2000, daily)

After April 18 the sixth day of duration expired along with the identification of a low-risk buy.

Figure 6.5 identifies only two ideal low-risk entry levels—a buy at the low and a sell at the high. As you can see, the large number of days involved in the construction of TD DeMarker I reduces its frequency in entering oversold and overbought territory. When it is within those zones the price activity of heating oil must perfectly indicate the oversold or overbought condition. Consequently, only two opportunities occurred over a three-month trading period. Meanwhile, a discernible trend did exist, and more trading would likely have proven detrimental to one's portfolio.

Figure 6.6 illustrates the low-risk sell and low-risk buy opportunities in the Biotech Holder's Trust (BBH) (which tracks the AMEX Biotechnology Index). Although they are not always the absolute high and low, the indications are nevertheless usually at important trend reversal points. The completion of the duration period marked the last day for identifying a low-risk buy signal.

TD DeMarker II™

Construction of TD DeMarker II

Whereas TD REI and TD DeMarker I measure buying and selling impulses from one price bar to the next, and also to all other price bars, TD DeMarker II is constructed very differently, because it relates price movement from various price levels to determine the levels of supply and demand. The value of the numerator is composed of two measures of buying pressure. The difference between the current price bar's high and the previous price bar's close for a series of price bars is added to the difference between the current price bar's close and the current price bar's low over a similar number of price bars. These two measures relate to the intensity of buying. If the difference between the current price bar's high and the prior price bar's close is negative, a zero is assigned to that portion of the buying pressure component.

The denominator is composed of the calculated numerator value over *x* number of days added to the respective selling pressure values assigned to each price bar. The selling pressure is made up of two measures. The first is calculated by subtracting the difference between the prior price bar's close and the current price bar's low, and if this value is negative, a value of zero is assigned to that portion of the selling component for the price bar. The second calculation is derived

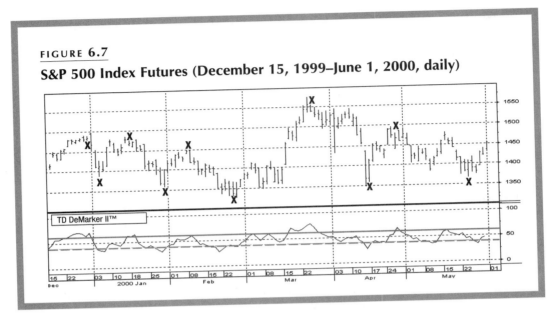

FIGURE 6.7

S&P 500 Index Futures (December 15, 1999–June 1, 2000, daily)

by subtracting the close from the same price bar's high. Then these values are added to the value of the numerator to arrive at the denominator. In other words, TD DeMarker II divides the buying pressure over a period of time by the total pressure, whether it is buying pressure or selling pressure.

TD DeMarker II provides another perspective for evaluating security price movement in terms of overbought and oversold conditions. Applying the criterion of duration allows one to interpret this indicator in light of security price, similar to previously described oscillators. Used in conjunction with the other indicators, TD DeMarker II can simplify a trader's evaluation of low-risk buying and selling opportunities.

Using TD DeMarker II

Most oscillators have more than one time setting that can be selected and applied to the markets. TD DeMarker II is no exception. Using an eight-price bar setting, **Figure 6.7** showing the S&P June 2000 futures illustrates how well this setting conforms to the oversold and overbought levels of 40 and 60, respectively. Reviewing the chart from December 1999 through April 2000 shows how well the movement above and below the overbought and oversold thresholds defined market tops and bottoms. For example, the late December 1999 high was predicted, as were the mid-January high and the March and late April highs. The

FIGURE 6.8

IBM/International Business Machines Corp.
(February 1–May 10, 2000, daily)

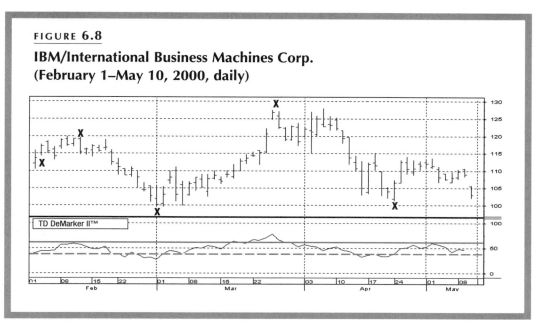

FIGURE 6.9

Eurodollar Futures (January 25–May 15, 2000, daily)

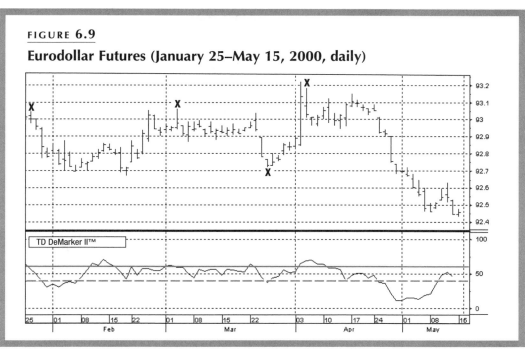

intervening lows in early January and late January, as well as those in February and mid-April, were isolated successfully by following the TD DeMarker II indicator.

Figure 6.8, showing IBM activity, is equally successful in identifying bottoms and tops. The early March low, late March high, and mid-April lows were clearly identified. As with TD REI and TD DeMarker I, dissecting price activity further improves the utility of this gauge. For example, one can improve timing by awaiting a move above the lower threshold after once declining below it and doing the reverse at the high—declining below the upper threshold after first entering this zone. Other techniques (such as those discussed previously) that concentrate on price relationships rather than oscillator movements can be employed as well.

Figure 6.9 again demonstrates the usefulness of this indicator in locating oversold and overbought opportunity zones. The early March and April 2000 Eurodollar highs were identified when the oscillator gave overbought readings. The late March low coincided with an oversold reading. However, in May the amount of time oversold—over six days—suggests extended duration and the likelihood of a move from extreme oversold back to neutral and then another decline into mild oversold before the price bottom is complete.

Key Considerations

Many factors beyond merely using an overbought or oversold oscillator should be addressed before these tools are applied to trading the markets. Not only is the construction of an indicator critical, but also, so are the various interpretations assigned to the indicator as it travels throughout its cycle. For example, the amount of time an oscillator may reside within an oversold or overbought zone is just as significant as the fact that it is overbought or oversold. The concept of duration is therefore very important. If more than one indicator is used, they must be properly synchronized.

The TD REI, TD DeMarker I, and TD DeMarker II are constructed to provide traders with an edge in timing trades. As evident in the chart examples, the oscillators in this chapter can and will work effectively independent of one another. However, combining these oscillators can boost your confidence and greatly simplify the effort involved in the timing and selecting of low-risk buy and sell opportunities.

CHAPTER 7

Using Cycles for Price Projections

PETER ELIADES

The theory of stock market cycles contends that stock prices and stock indices move as a result of a combination of cyclical forces. Fundamental factors also influence stock prices, but their effect is generally smooth and, barring major fundamental developments, unrelated to market timing. The influence of fundamental factors is theoretically sideways or up or down at varying angles of ascent or descent. The cycles fluctuate around the smooth fundamental line and are responsible for a great part of a stock's fluctuations.

Figure 7.1 looks very much like a typical stock chart. Most analysts would consider the movements in the chart to be random, with little if any predictability to the pattern. The fact is that this chart is an exact representation of a combination of four sine waves and a straight line. It is perfectly predictable. For those who are mathematically inclined, it represents the equation: $y = 12 \sin$

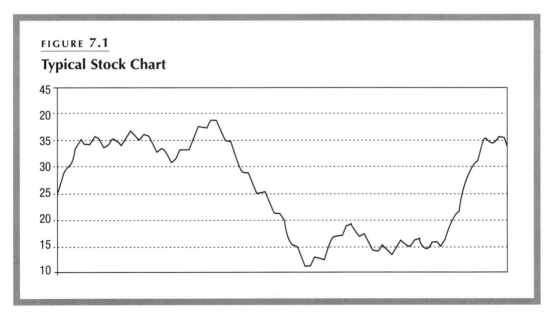

FIGURE 7.1

Typical Stock Chart

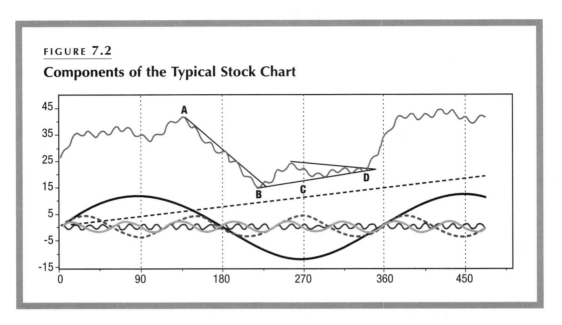

FIGURE 7.2

Components of the Typical Stock Chart

$x + 4 \sin 3x + 2 \sin 6x + \sin 24x + .04x$, where y represents price or the vertical axis and x represents time or the horizontal axis. The concept for the chart is from *The Art of Independent Investing* by Claud Cleeton (New Jersey: Prentice Hall, 1976).

Figure 7.2 is a repeat of Figure 7.1, this time accompanied by the four sine waves and the straight line that determine the exact shape of the chart. The simple combination of four sine waves and a straight line produces some common technical patterns. The decline from point A to point B is delineated by what technicians would call a descending tops line. A move above the line is generally viewed as positive. The price pattern from point B to point D forms a triangle bordered by a rising bottoms line and a declining tops line. Note that when the price breaks out of the triangle formation to the upside, the subsequent move is strongly up, as a technical textbook might suggest. No real-life stock chart is, of course, a strict mathematical formula, but the principles of general predictability apply.

This interpretation of how cycles combine to determine the movement of stocks and stock indices and averages does not imply that only four cycles determine the fluctuations of stocks. There are probably scores of cycles acting simultaneously on the market, making analysis a more difficult procedure than a simple breakdown of mathematical formulas. But the cycle techniques discussed in this chapter require no mathematical skills and can be used to project price objectives for stock indices and, in some cases, individual stocks.

Basic Steps in Generating Price Projections Using Offset Lines

Although analysts have refined the art of cycle projections over the past twenty-five years, it is necessary to acknowledge the foundation built by J. M. Hurst, the man who first kindled the spark of intellectual curiosity within so many analysts with his book entitled *The Profit Magic of Stock Transaction Timing* (New Jersey: Prentice Hall, 1970). Hurst described a technique for deriving price projections in that book, and later improved on that technique to make the analysis more objective.

Figure 7.3 depicts two waves of a theoretical 20-week cycle. In the lower half of the chart, the cycle has been moved forward in time exactly one-half cycle or, in this case, 10 weeks. The dashed line that represents the cycle moved forward intersects the solid, original cycle wave exactly halfway between the bottom and the top of the cycle. Each time the solid line intersects the dashed or offset line, the solid line continues until the advance or decline equals the distance it has already traveled to the point of intersection. In other words, the point of inter-

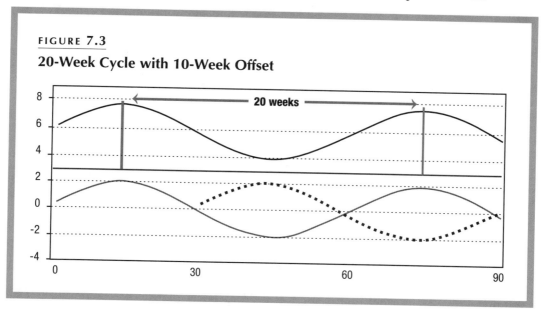

FIGURE 7.3

20-Week Cycle with 10-Week Offset

section marks the halfway point for that particular cycle.

Before the advent of computers sophisticated enough to do the graphics involved, the best way to derive the projections was to use tracing paper. By tracing the chart you wish to analyze, then moving the tracing paper forward in time by varying periods, you can make price projections for the item being analyzed. If we have a bar chart showing the range for the day (or week if it is a weekly chart) marked by the top and bottom of the bar, the most accurate projections are usually derived by preparing the chart as follows. Before tracing the chart, draw a line from the midpoint or median of each bar to the median of the following bar. With a commercially prepared or a computer generated chart, you can substitute the closing price for the median. After drawing a line connecting each bar on the chart, you are ready to do the tracing.

The same concept is presented in **Figure 7.4,** but with a more realistic idealization, using a bar chart. A line is drawn from each day's median or average price to the next day's median or average price. Notice how the average price starts at 10, moves up one point per day for 10 days, then reverses and moves down one point a day for 10 days. The distance from top to top is 20 weeks and the distance from bottom to bottom is 20 weeks—a perfect cycle. If you were doing cycle analysis on this idealized chart, you would place tracing paper over the chart and simply trace a line connecting the midpoints (medians or aver-

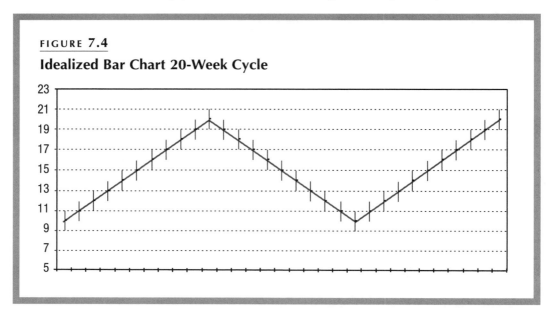

FIGURE 7.4

Idealized Bar Chart 20-Week Cycle

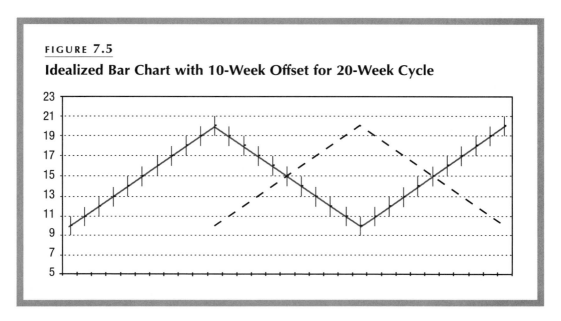

FIGURE 7.5

Idealized Bar Chart with 10-Week Offset for 20-Week Cycle

ages) of each day's high and low. The next step would be to move the tracing paper forward in time the distance equal to one-half the nominal cycle length, in this case 20 weeks, so the offset would be moved forward 10 weeks.

Figure 7.5 shows the principle of all cycle projections made with this technique. After moving the median or average price line forward the equivalent of one-half the distance of the nominal cycle being analyzed, you simply wait for the price in real time to cross above or below this "cycle line" or "offset line." Notice how the price bar line connecting all the medians meets the offset line at a price of 15. To generate a price projection, simply note the price where the price bar line crosses above or below the offset line and that theoretically marks the halfway point of the complete cycle move. In the idealized example the lows of the average or median price are at 10. When they cross above the offset line at 15, the arithmetic is simple. If the move started at 10, and 15 is the theoretical halfway mark, prices would have another 5 points to go before reaching a top. Adding 5 to 15 gives a projection of 20 for the high of the average or median price line.

If you want to generate a projection of price extremes, you would use the highs and lows of the weekly bars, rather than the average. In such an example, prices would bottom at 9, reach a midpoint at 15, and give a projection of 21 (from 9 to 15 is 6 points—15 plus 6 more points equals 21). The opposite is, of

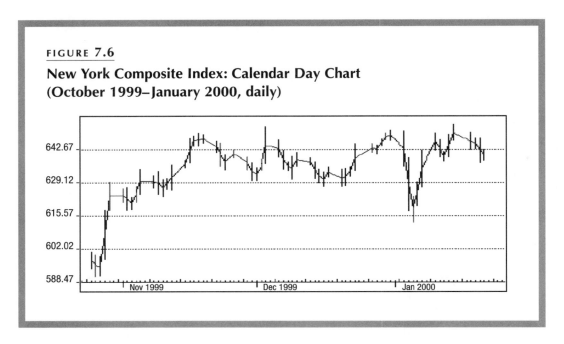

FIGURE 7.6

**New York Composite Index: Calendar Day Chart
(October 1999–January 2000, daily)**

course, true on the way down. Prices start at a high point of 21 on an extreme basis and 20 on an average price basis, move down to a halfway point of 15, and give "downside projections" of 10 on an average or median basis and 9 on an extreme basis.

When Hurst formulated his technique of price projections, the daily charts used were specially constructed charts that left spaces for Saturdays, Sundays, and holidays. **Figure 7.6** is an example of a "calendar day" chart, leaving spaces on the days when the stock market was closed.

Nominal Price Projections and Terminology

Hurst contended that there are so-called nominal cycles in the price fluctuations of the stock market which can be used to give price projections for the various indices and averages. Hurst identified five basic "nominal" cycles that should be analyzed on weekly charts. Those five nominal cycles are:

1) 10 week   3) 40 week   5) 4 year (200–220 weeks)
2) 20 week   4) 78–80 week

The example given previously was of a nominal 20-week cycle and its half-span offset of 10 weeks. When weekly charts are used, there is, of course, no need to draw distinctions between "calendar week" and "market week" charts as is done with the daily charts. In fact, weekly charts are a good place to start learning the technique of calculating price projections. There are also daily cycles shorter than the nominal 10-week cycle. The daily cycles are the nominal 10-day and nominal 20-day cycles, which use 5- and 10-calendar-day offsets to generate projections, and the 35–40 day cycles. Beyond that, the nominal 70–80-day cycle is the same as the nominal 10-week cycle. And the nominal 140–160-day cycle is the same as the nominal 20-week cycle. As you can see, the analysis of daily and weekly cycles overlaps, and it is always interesting to use both daily and weekly analysis for the equivalent time periods (for example, 140–160 days and 20 weeks) to compare the results. They should give similar results.

Key Terms and Concepts

Regarding terminology, a *median* describes the midpoint of a bar when a bar chart is used to represent the price of the item being analyzed. It is simply the average of the high and low points represented by the bar. An *offset* refers to the "shadow line" that is created after the original line connecting the medians is traced and moved forward in time. A good example is the offset line seen in Figure 7.5 that is moved forward, or "offset," 10 weeks as the half-span of the 20-week cycle.

Perhaps the most difficult concept to convey is that of nominal projections. The nominal cycles discussed above are all part of the projection arsenal. The dictionary defines nominal as: "being such in name only; so-called." This is precisely the definition of the term as used in this context. It does not mean that the particular index or particular stock being analyzed necessarily has an actual cycle of that precise length. It is used purely as a reference point. Giving a projection for a nominal 10-day cycle does not imply that the market advance or decline will halt after reaching that initial projection. If or before reached, the nominal 10-day cycle projection could trigger a nominal 20-day cycle projection, which, in turn, could trigger a nominal 5–week cycle projection, and so on. The advance or decline should finally halt when all outstanding projections have been met or, in turn, when an outstanding projection has been invalidated and no further projections have been made in the same direction.

Guidelines for Projecting When Price Extremes Will Occur

When a cycle projection is made, usually it is best not to give a corresponding time target for the projection to be met. Price is a more important indicator than time, except when a consistent time cycle appears to be coinciding with a projected price bottom or top. There are general rules, however, for choosing approximate time periods when projected tops or bottoms should occur. The rules are based on the length of the nominal cycles. For example, a nominal 20-day cycle ideally consists of 10 calendar days up and 10 calendar days down. Theoretically, upside projections are generated at the halfway point, both in time and price, of the advance. Conversely, downside projections are generated at the halfway point of the decline, in terms of both time and price. In the case of the nominal 20-day cycle, any upside projection should be given, in theory, around the fifth day from the bottom of the prior nominal 20-day cycle. Once the projection is given, the implication is that the expected price should be reached in around 5 days.

Another way of arriving at the same general result is to divide the nominal cycle length by four. The result shows the general time period from the date the projection is actually given (by the current price crossing above or below the projection line, or offset line) for the expected projection to occur. Here is an example: assume the market hits a bottom on March 1. Five days later, on March 6, a nominal 20-day cycle projection is given. Because the cycle has already advanced for 5 days, its ideal path would be to advance 5 more days before the nominal 20-day cycle peak is reached, then to decline 10 days to meet the next nominal 20-day cycle bottom. Therefore, the price projection would be met March 11.

An alternate rule can also be used. Let's assume the nominal 20-day cycle projection was generated by price crossing above the offset line on March 3 after a March 1 bottom. Rather than counting the 5 days from the previous bottom, in the alternate case the 5 days would be counted from the actual date the projection was given, or March 3, which leads to an expected projection date of March 8, 3 days earlier than the original calculation. Therefore, the projection would be expected between March 8 and 11. Note, however, that these are general rules and, as noted previously, price is more important than time when predicting cycles.

The converse of the explanation of upward price projections applies to downward price projections. In the case of the initial rule, of course, days would be counted from the prior top, not the bottom, to establish an approximate date for downward projection to be fulfilled. It is also important to reiterate that the fulfillment of short-term price projections is a minimum expectation and does not imply the termination of the advance or decline. We can predict when advance or decline will terminate only after price projections are reached without generating further cycle projections in the same direction.

Applying Market Cycle Projections

With the background in place, let's get to some real-world applications. We will start with a securities index average that most have heard of, but few are acquainted with, the Dow Jones Composite Average. The average is made up of the thirty Dow Industrials, the twenty Dow Transports, and the fifteen Dow Utilities. Analysts seldom work with this chart in real time, but the technique gains an extra aura of respect if it works with a seldom used indicator. Remember that there are five basic nominal cycles to be analyzed for price projections on a weekly chart. Let's start with the nominal 10-week projection chart (5-week offset) then move through the nominal 20-week, 40-week, 78–80-week, and 4-year projection charts.

Dow Jones Composite Average Example

Let's begin at the all-time high of 1,450.10 registered on January 31, 1994. (All of the numbers on the following charts are "actual print" intraday highs and lows as opposed to the "theoretical" highs and lows reported in some newspapers. For example, look at the Dow Jones Composite Average charts in the *Wall Street Journal*. Beneath them a table gives the data for the hour-by-hour averages, and to the far right of the table are listed the highs and lows of the day for each component Dow Jones Industrial Average Stock, followed by the Composite Average. The table distinguishes between "actual print" highs and lows and "theoretical" highs and lows.

Between the second and third week after the 1,450.10 high was reached, the weekly average or "median" price broke below the 5-week offset line, generating a nominal 10-week projection of 1,362.50 ± 8.80 points. **Figure 7.7** should make it clear how the projection was generated. The price at which the line joining the weekly medians crossed below the offset line was 1,406.30. That should mark the halfway point for the nominal 10-week projection. The previous high was 1,450.10, so the distance from the previous high to the halfway mark is 43.8 points. If that is the halfway point, then prices should fall another 43.8 points before reaching the nominal 10-week projection. Projecting another 43.8 points down from the 1,406.30 midpoint gives you the projection of 1,362.50. Note that each time a projection is given, you should allow for a 10 percent margin of

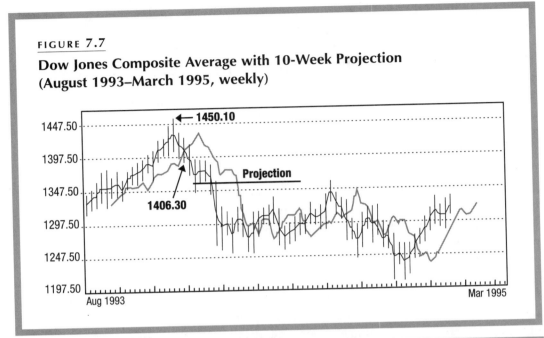

FIGURE 7.7

**Dow Jones Composite Average with 10-Week Projection
(August 1993–March 1995, weekly)**

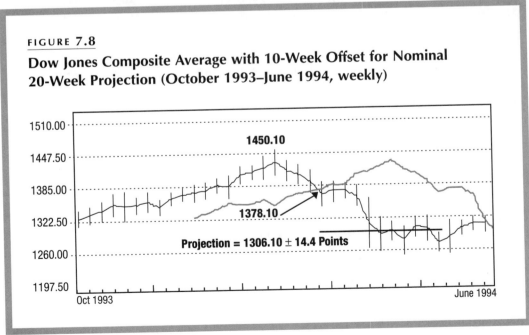

FIGURE 7.8

**Dow Jones Composite Average with 10-Week Offset for Nominal
20-Week Projection (October 1993–June 1994, weekly)**

error. In this case, the complete move from the high at 1,450.10 to the projected low at 1,362.50 would be 87.6 points. Ten percent of that would be 8.76 points. Therefore the final projection would be 1,362.50 ± 8.8 points. Now look at **Figure 7.8**.

One week after the above nominal 10-week projection was given, on its way to the 1,362.50 projection, the weekly median line broke below the 10-week offset, giving a nominal 20-week projection of 1,306.10 ± 14.4 points. All the necessary numbers to calculate the projection are shown in Figure 7.8. Notice that the longer the nominal projection, the more meaningful the projection tends to be. The nominal 10-week projection shown in Figure 7.7 was given in the week ending February 18, 1994 with the Dow Jones Composite Average at a price of 1,398.3. The projection down to 1,362.50 was calling for a decline of an additional 2.6 percent from the closing price on the day the projection was given. The nominal 20-week projection to 1,306.10 was given during the week ending March 4, 1994 with the Dow Jones Composite Average at 1,375.7. This time the projection was calling for an additional decline of 5.1 percent. Now look at **Figure 7.9**.

Four weeks after the nominal 20-week projection was given, as the Dow Jones Composite Average was heading toward its nominal 20-week projection, it broke

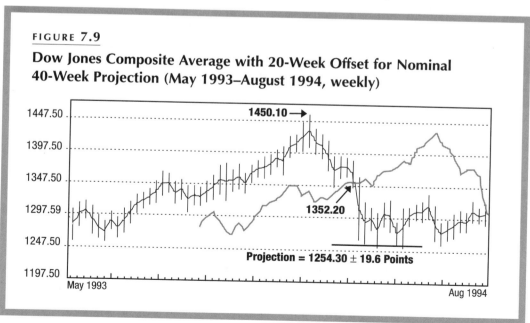

FIGURE 7.9

Dow Jones Composite Average with 20-Week Offset for Nominal 40-Week Projection (May 1993–August 1994, weekly)

below the 20-week offset used to determine the nominal 40-week projection and gave a projection of 1,254.30 ± 19.6 points. That projection was given at the end of the week ending April 1, 1994 with the Dow Jones Composite Average closing at 1,297.8.

This is where the analysis gets more complicated. In the week ending April 22, the Dow Jones Composite Average moved within the "window" of its projection with a low of 1,262.8. Remember, you must allow a 10 percent window for a margin of error with each projection. The nominal 40-week projection given above calling for 1,254.30 ± 19.6 points actually gives a projection within a price window between 1,234.70 and 1,273.9 points. The low of 1,262.80 registered during the week ending April 22, 1994, was located comfortably within the projection window. At the same time, however, it broke below its 39-week offset giving a nominal 78-week projection to 1,134.30 ± 31.6 points, as you can see from **Figure 7.10**.

When New Projections Are Generated

Once an outstanding projection has been met, you should always check to see if any new projections have been given. Note that in the analysis done so far, each time a projection was met, and sometimes even before an existing projection was met (while prices were headed toward the outstanding projection) a new pro-

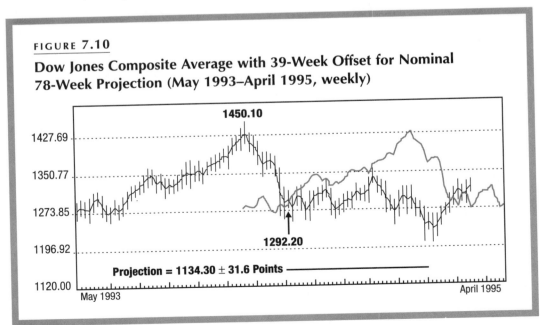

FIGURE 7.10

Dow Jones Composite Average with 39-Week Offset for Nominal 78-Week Projection (May 1993–April 1995, weekly)

jection was generated. There is no way of knowing, even with this projection technique, whether prices will continue down immediately to the latest outstanding projection or attempt to rally first after reaching the level projected by the prior outstanding projection.

In the Dow Jones Composite Average case in Figure 7.9, the decline stopped at the nominal 40-week projection and over the period of the next several months prices attempted to rally. Sometimes, in fact, an interim projection will be given in the opposite direction of the remaining outstanding projection. That is just what happened in this case. Examine Figures 7.10 and 7.11. Figure 7.10 shows a nominal 78-week projection to 1,134.3 ⅞ 31.6 points given in late April 1994. By September 23, prices had moved 22 weeks beyond the time that projection was given without making a significantly lower low. Notice, however, that prices had not crossed back above the offset line on Figure 7.10 despite the rally, and that means the projection down to 1,134.3 ⅞ 31.6 points remained in effect. If the price moved above the offset line, the projections would be "invalidated." That did not happen with the 39-week offset on Figure 7.10.

Now look at an updated nominal 40-week projection chart (see **Figure 7.11**). In the week ending August 26, 1994 the median price line for the week moved *above* the nominal 40-week projection line (20-week offset) at 1,307.89 (the computer is able to determine the exact crossing of the lines to within one-hundredth of a Dow point), giving a projection of 1,352.98 ± 9.1 points. That meant that there were now both upside and downside projections outstanding at the same time.

The general rule is that a projection remains outstanding until it is met or invalidated. As was just noted, the only way to invalidate a projection is for the price to move back above the offset line after a downside projection has been given and before the projection is met, or back below the offset line after an upside projection has been given and before it is met. On August 31, the Dow Jones Composite Average reached a high of 1,352.9, within 0.2 points of an exact projection. If you were doing this projection in real time, it would have been a perfect time to sell or even sell short and take aggressively bearish mutual fund positions. The reasoning behind such a strategy is that all upside projections had been met without generating higher upside projections, while at the same time downside projections remained outstanding.

Let's see how the downside projections were resolved in late 1994. Without taking you through the intermediate steps of showing the 5-week and 10-week offsets associated with generating nominal 10- and 20-week projections, let's look

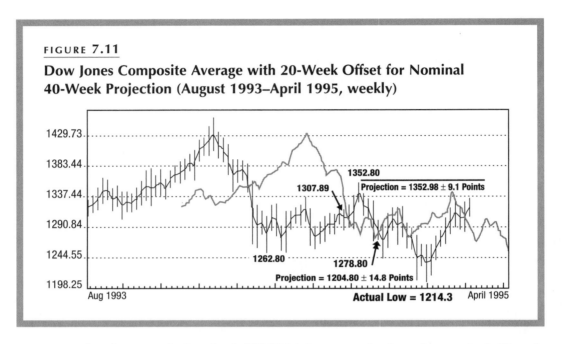

FIGURE 7.11

Dow Jones Composite Average with 20-Week Offset for Nominal 40-Week Projection (August 1993–April 1995, weekly)

at what happened after the 1,352.80 high was reached on the nominal 40-week projection chart (see Figure 7.11).

Notice that, after reaching the interim upside projection almost perfectly, prices started down again, and reaching nominal 10- and 20-week projections (these projections are not shown in Figure 7.11), prices moved below the 20-week offset on Figure 7.11 at a price level of 1,278.8, giving a projection of 1,204.8 ± 14.8 points. Thus the range of the projection was between 1,190 and 1,219.6. In the week ending November 25, 1995, the Dow Jones Composite Average reached a low of 1,219.1, just barely moving into the projection window. Two weeks later, it registered a low of 1,214.3, moving comfortably into the projection window. Remember, however, that there was also a nominal 78-week projection outstanding down to 1,134.30 ± 31.6 points, calling for a move down to at least 1,165.9 points. As it turned out, that projection was never reached, and the low of 1,214.3 turned out to be an important low prior to a very dramatic bull market over the next several years.

Tips on the Success Rate of Projections

A few lessons can be learned about the cycle projection technique as it relates to the failed projection. No scientific study has been done regarding the success rate of projections, but it would be surprising if the success rate were below

65 to 70 percent. Conversely, of course, this means there is a 30 to 35 percent failure rate. Chances are, however, that this represents a far better success rate than other price projection techniques. It is important to remember that the actual final low in the example in Figure 7.11 was given quite closely by the nominal 40-week projection. Any time a longer-term projection (nominal 20-weeks or longer) is met, it is prudent to be continuously on the lookout for signs that the tide could turn, even if there are further projections outstanding. One way to judge whether any further unmet projections have a good chance of being reached is to determine whether all shorter-term projections have been exceeded.

Let's examine an example of that technique. When the nominal 40-week projection window was reached on the Dow Jones Composite Average in the analysis illustrated here, there was still a further downside projection outstanding, the nominal 78-week projection calling for 1,134.3 ± 31.6 points as shown in Figure 7.10. There is a much greater probability that projection would be reached if all shorter downside projections had been exceeded. The nominal 40-week downside projection called for a projection range of 1,190 to 1,219.6 points (see Figure 7.11). If the lowest price in the projection range was exceeded, namely 1,190, the odds of the nominal 78-week projection being reached would have

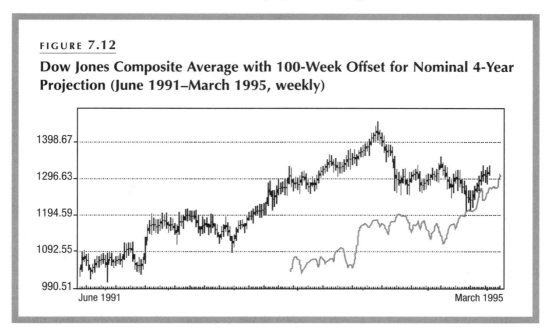

FIGURE 7.12

Dow Jones Composite Average with 100-Week Offset for Nominal 4-Year Projection (June 1991–March 1995, weekly)

increased significantly. That far side of the projection range was not exceeded in this case. Were there any other clues that the nominal 78-week projection would or would not be reached?

Figure 7.12 shows the Dow Jones Composite Average chart and the 2-year (100-week) offset used to generate nominal four-year projections. Notice that when the nominal 40-week projection was being met at the lows on the right side of the chart, prices came down almost exactly to the nominal 4-year offset line. In fact, it would not be an exaggeration to say that the offset line acted as support. This often happens. As one projection is being met, prices will come down to and find support on the offset line of a longer-term projection chart.

Unfortunately, despite the fact that there were some clues that the lower projections for the Dow Jones Composite Average would not be met, a projection remains in effect until it is either met or invalidated. In January 1995, the Dow Jones Composite Average moved above the 39-week offset line (see **Figure 7.13**) to invalidate the nominal 78-week downside projection and simultaneously give a new nominal 78-week upside projection.

Cycle Projections Are Either Met or Invalidated over Time

You have now followed a full sequence of weekly projections from an intermediate high to an intermediate low. Other indices could have been used and far

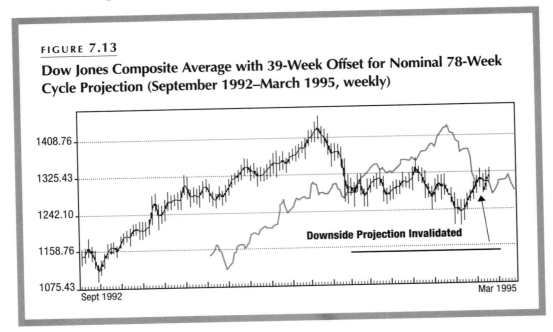

FIGURE **7.13**

Dow Jones Composite Average with 39-Week Offset for Nominal 78-Week Cycle Projection (September 1992–March 1995, weekly)

1408.76

1325.43

1242.10

1158.76

1075.43

Sept 1992

Mar 1995

Downside Projection Invalidated

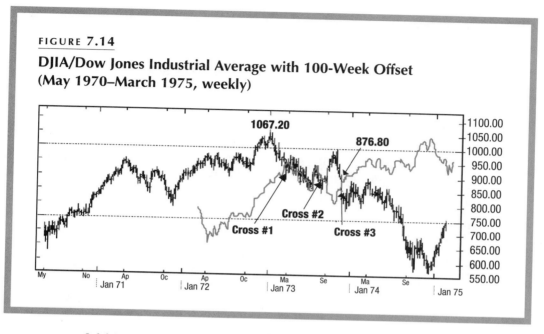

FIGURE 7.14

DJIA/Dow Jones Industrial Average with 100-Week Offset (May 1970–March 1975, weekly)

more successful historical results could have been shown. But using the Dow Jones Composite Average, which is unfamiliar to most people, to show both successful and failed projections is a more realistic way to demonstrate the technique. It is important to note that, at least in theory, cycle projections cannot be wrong for long. A projection will ultimately either be met or invalidated. There are no other options. Once a projection is invalidated, and if there are no other projections outstanding, then there is no further reason to look for prices to move in the direction of the original projection. In fact, the invalidation of a projection causes a new projection to be given in the opposite direction.

Sometimes, however the price will whipsaw above and below the offset line before moving with conviction in one direction or the other. Those situations can try your patience, but ultimately prices will move clearly in one direction or the other. When there are multiple crossings of the offset line, the analysis becomes more complicated. Let's look at a real-world example and consider some of the alternative solutions to the analysis. The worst bear market in the Dow Jones Industrial Average of the past sixty years occurred from January 1973 through December 1974 when the Dow dropped 46.6 percent from theoretical intraday high to theoretical intraday low.

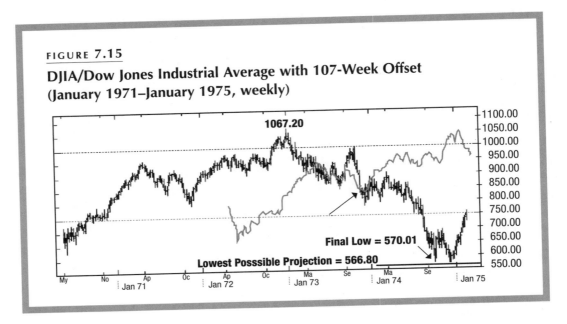

FIGURE 7.15

DJIA/Dow Jones Industrial Average with 107-Week Offset
(January 1971–January 1975, weekly)

Dow Industrials Bear Market Example

Figure 7.14 is a weekly chart of the Dow Jones Industrials including the January 1973 top and the December 1974 bottom. The length of the offset in this chart is 100 weeks. Longer cycles have more variable offsets, and the longest cycle used for price projections, on a practical basis, is the nominal 4-year cycle. Because that cycle has averaged between 200 and 220 weeks in length, the half spans used to generate the projections are 100 to 110 weeks.

Notice that, after the top at 1,067.20 in January 1973, prices moved below the 100-week offset line on three separate occasions. The first crossing (referred to as Cross #1 on the chart) occurred 10 weeks after the top at a price of 944. The next week, prices moved back above the offset line, invalidating any projection given by that first crossing. Four months later, in August 1973, prices again moved below the offset line, this time for only 4 weeks, before crossing back above 5 weeks later. Finally, in November 1973, prices moved below and stayed below the 100-week offset. The cross below the offset occurred at a price of 876.80, giving a projection of 686.40 ± 38.1 points.

In this 100-week offset there were two "whipsaw" crossings below the offset line, then a final decisive move below the line. If you look closely at the third crossing point it is clear that moving the offset to the right further than 100

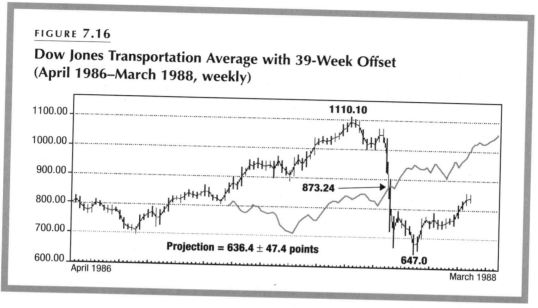

FIGURE 7.16

Dow Jones Transportation Average with 39-Week Offset (April 1986–March 1988, weekly)

weeks would cause prices to cross below the offset line at a lower price, and that would, in turn, generate an even lower projection. Your analysis should try to determine the two extremes where crossings below the offset would occur throughout the complete range of 100- to 110-week offsets.

Figure 7.15 shows the lowest possible crossing that could have occurred using any offset between 100 and 110 weeks. The offset shown is a 107-week offset. Do you see that if the offset were moved further to the right, to 108, 109, or 110 weeks, the crossings below the offset line would have occurred at a higher level?

If only a single crossing occurs above or below the offset line to generate the projection, then the technique described above should be used to finalize the projection. To do this, you would calculate the projection based on the single crossing, then allow for a 10 percent margin of error (not 10 percent of the projected price, but 10 percent of the distance covered from the prior high to the projected low or the prior low to the projected high). In the situation in which there are several crossings above and below the offset line prior to the final penetration, it is usually best to determine what the highest and lowest crossings could have been within the range of the specified offsets, as just shown in Figure 7.15.

It is interesting that the largest bear market reported in the Dow Jones

Industrial Average in the past sixty years was analyzed very capably by the projection technique. The lowest possible projection for the bottom of that bear market was for 566.80. The actual bear market low of the Dow Jones Industrial Average in December 1974 was 570.01, just 3.21 points away from the final theoretical intraday low registered on December 9, 1974.

Let's look at one more compelling example of the prospective accuracy of the cycle projection technique.

Dow Jones Transportation Average Example

Figure 7.16 is the Dow Jones Transportation Average from April 1986 through March 1988. It includes some very dramatic market history—the crash of 1987. Some people would have you believe that there is no possible way to predict where a market that crashes will find a true and important bottom. Frankly, the Dow Industrial Average projection charts were looking for significantly lower lows after the crash of 1987, but people who were doing their cycle projections on the Dow Transportation Average in late 1987 were rewarded with an almost flawless call.

The projection chart in Figure 7.16 is a weekly chart of the Dow Transports accompanied by a 39-week offset to measure the nominal 78-week projection. Prices crossed below the offset line at a price of 873.24. Measuring from the high in August 1987 of 1,110.10, you can see that the Transports declined 236.86 points before crossing the 39-week offset line. The projection thus calls for an equivalent 236.86 points below the crossing point, or 636.38, rounded off to 636.4. As it turned out, after declining over 40 percent from intraday high in August 1987 to intraday low in December 1987, the Dow Transports reached a final low of 647.0 intraday, a mere 1.7 percent away from the exact projected low.

Offsets for Weekly, Daily, and Intraday Cycle Projections

Let's do a final projection exercise by looking at the recent price action of the Dow Industrials going back to 1998. This is also a good time to present a table of the eight principal nominal cycles with the equivalent offsets. Be aware that cycle projection techniques can also be used on intraday charts such as hourly index charts (65 minutes in this case, so there will be exactly six intraday periods each market day or 30-minute charts with exactly 13 periods in each market day). The following table lists the nominal cycles along with the half-span offsets used to generate the cycle projections.

Offsets for Selected Nominal Cycles

NOMINAL CYCLE	WEEKLY	MARKET DAYS	CALENDAR DAYS	CASH CHARTS (30 MINUTE BARS)	FUTURES CHARTS (27 MINUTE BARS)
				2.85-3.25	3.28-3.75
				5.69-6.5	6.56-7.5
				11.38-13	13.13-15
				22.75-26	26.25-30
10 Day		3.5-4.0	5	45.5-52	52.5-60
20 Day		7.0-8.0	10	91-104	105-120
5 Week		12.1-13.8	17.5-20	157.3-179.4	181.5-207
10 Week	5	24.2-27.6	35-40		
20 Week	10	48.4-55.3	70-80		
40 Week	20	96.8-110.6	140-160		
78-80 Week	39-40	189-194	273-280		
4 Year	100-110				

Preliminary versus "Confirmed" Projections

Before reviewing the analysis for the recent Dow Jones Industrial Average charts, let's discuss the concept of how projections are "confirmed." In the table above notice that all of the half-span offsets, except for some of the weekly ones, contain a range of numbers rather than a single number. For example, the "market day" daily offset equivalent to the 10-week offset used to generate nominal 20-week projections shows an offset of 48.4 to 55.3 market days. Suppose you are using the 48.4 offset and prices cross above or below the offset line. That would constitute a "preliminary" projection. Further, let's suppose that prices did not cross the offset line if the offset was moved to the higher end of the offset range, in this case 55.3 days. It is only when the price is above all ranges of the offset line that a projection is considered to be confirmed. Until then, it remains a preliminary projection.

It is common to see a projection met at the same time as a new preliminary projection is given. Those situations are the most challenging for the cycle projection technique. The fact that a projection has been met tells us prices could now turn and head in the opposite direction. On the other hand, because a new "preliminary" projection has been given, it is possible that prices could continue further in the same direction. Only when the projection is "confirmed" does

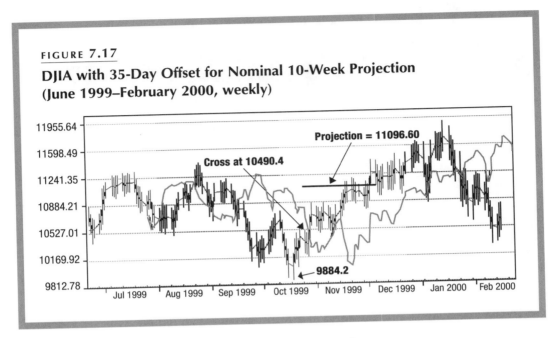

FIGURE 7.17

**DJIA with 35-Day Offset for Nominal 10-Week Projection
(June 1999–February 2000, weekly)**

confidence increase that prices are not yet ready to turn.

Be aware that no aspect of the projection technique can promise results approaching 100 percent accuracy, but as projections are confirmed, the success rate of the projections increases substantially. On the other hand, until a subsequent projection is confirmed, the possibility remains that a turning point is forming based on the fact that the previous projection had been met.

Another way to test the confirmation of a new projection, even before it is technically confirmed (by crossing the half-span offsets for all values of the offset range) is to note whether the extremes of the prior projection have been exceeded. For example, if there is a nominal 10-week downside projection to 10,500 ± 100 points on the Dow Jones Industrial Average, and the Dow moves to 10,500, that projection has been satisfied. Let's say that at the same time the 10,500 projection was being satisfied, a preliminary nominal 20-week projection was given down to 9,800. If the Dow were to move below 10,400, the extreme objective of the nominal 10-week projection, there would be an assumption that the nominal 20-week projection was confirmed at that point, even if prices had not technically confirmed that 9,800 projection by being below all of the possible offsets within the range of the half-span offsets for that nominal 20-week projection. That is because the extreme downside objective of the nominal 10-week projection had

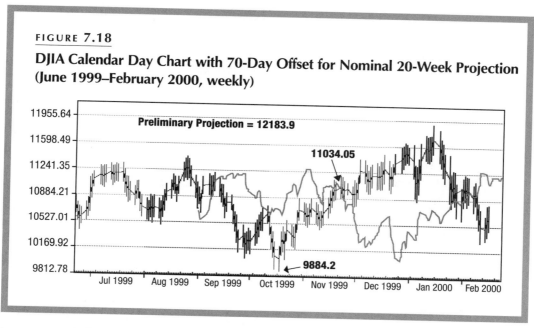

FIGURE 7.18

DJIA Calendar Day Chart with 70-Day Offset for Nominal 20-Week Projection (June 1999–February 2000, weekly)

been exceeded, and, theoretically at least, there had to be another projection allowing prices to go even lower than that extreme objective. For that reason, you could surmise that the nominal 20-week projection was confirmed.

Dow Jones Industrial Average Example

Let's look back at the Dow Jones Industrials from late 1999 to early 2000 to see how the cycle projections would have fared. In the current analysis, let's use daily calendar day charts (calendar day charts leave spaces for Saturdays, Sundays, and holidays) to differentiate this analysis from the earlier analysis of the Dow Jones Composite Average with the weekly price projection charts. The table appearing on page 157 shows that the first five offset groups for the calendar day charts are 5 days, 10 days, 17.5–20 days, 35–40 days, and 70–80 days.

Figure 7.17 starts the analysis with the 35-day offset for projecting the nominal 10-week cycle. A projection to 11,096.60 is given. It is not shown in the figure, but if the far end of the offset were used, namely, a 40-day offset, the projection would have called for a move to 11,543.2. There are two ways to express the projection given by the crossing of prices above the nominal 10-week cycle offset. One way is to use the preliminary projection generated by the 35-day offset and use a plus or minus qualifier based on 10 percent of the total move in points from the prior low at 9,884.20 to the projected top at 11,096.60. Ten percent of that total move (1,212.40 points) would be 121.2 points rounded off to the nearest tenth. The projection could then be stated as 11,096.60 ± 121.2 points.

But there is another more accurate way of stating the projection. Remember, it was just pointed out that the far end of the projection offset, a 40-day offset, would have generated a projection to 11,543.2. Because these represent the two extremes of projections, you can take the average of the two projections, 11,319.9, and add just enough points to the plus or minus qualifier to cover the two extreme projections. In this case the final projection for the nominal 10-week projection would call for 11,319.9 ± 223.3 points.

By the time prices approached the 11,319.9 projection, a higher projection had already been given. **Figure 7.18** shows the nominal 20-week projection chart with a 70-calendar-day offset. Prices broke above the 70-day offset at a price of 11,034.05, giving a preliminary projection up to 12,183.9. Notice, however, in looking at the projection chart with the 70-day offset, that if the offset were moved forward just a few days the projection would actually be lower rather than higher. If you were to experiment with the offsets, it appears that with an offset of 74.5 calendar days, a projection as low as 11,716 would be generated.

The next step is to determine what offset between 70 and 80 calendar days would generate the highest projection and what that projection would be. It turns out that an offset of 71 days would generate a projection of 12,199, which would be the highest or close to the highest projection that could be generated with an offset between 70 and 80 days. There is now enough information to generate a complete nominal 20-week projection. The average of the two extremes, 11,716 and 12,199, is 11,957.5, so the official nominal 20-week projection is 11,957.5 ± 241.5 points. On January 10, 2000 the Dow Jones Industrial Average entered the window of that projection for the first time since the preliminary nominal 20-week projection was initially generated in late November 1999. Four days later, the Dow reached a theoretical intraday high of 11,908.5, completely satisfying the projection and missing an exact hit by fewer than 50 points or 0.4 percent. As of mid-February 2000, the theoretical high of 11,908.5 had been the all-time high on the Dow Jones Industrial Average, and the Dow had fallen 13.5 percent on a theoretical intraday basis to a low of 10,301.12 on February 11, 2000.

Adding Cycle Price Projections to One's Toolbox

There are many subtleties and nuances to the technique of analyzing cycle price projections that have not been discussed in this chapter. But the foundation has been laid for interested technical analysts to pursue their own cycle projections using the techniques shown. The half-span offsets given above have been effective with stock indices and commodities in the past. As a general rule, the more actively traded a particular entity is, the more likely it is to be susceptible to accurate cycle price analysis.

If the offsets do not appear to be working with the instrument you are analyzing, try the procedure in reverse. In other words, look at two obvious consecutive turning points on the price chart of the item being analyzed. What offset would have generated an accurate projection? Do the same reverse analysis on a series of turning points. You should soon arrive at a group of offsets that correspond fairly closely to the ones given in this chapter. It might be worthwhile to try the same analysis on actively traded individual stocks. No matter what instrument you analyze, you should soon be amazed at the prospective accuracy of the price projection technique.

Do not be discouraged, however, to discover that projections are not infallible. Cycles other than the one being investigated can add or subtract from prices at crucial times, leading to an incorrect intersection and an incorrect projection. Prices may cross above and below the projection offset line in a series of whipsaws, confusing the projections (and the one doing the projecting). But working with offset lines is a powerful technique for generating price projections, and it is made the more powerful because so few technicians are doing this analysis. In combination with other techniques you may be fond of, or as a stand-alone tool, the cycle projection technique is one of the most accurate and exciting tools available to a market analyst or technician.

CHAPTER 8

Trading with the Elliott Wave Theory

STEVEN W. POSER

Imagine a technical analysis methodology that can tell you when you are wrong long before your stops are hit. Imagine a technical tool that allows you to make money even when your analysis is wrong. Imagine an analytical framework that permits you to develop a likely road map for prices that you can easily use to support or supplant other technical, or even fundamental, indicators. Imagine that this way of analyzing prices was developed with the basis for technical analysis—crowd psychology—in mind. Imagine a tool so flexible that there is little difference between applying it to five-minute bars and applying it to monthly bars. Imagine a tool that though complex, dovetails perfectly with traditional trendline and pattern analysis as well as the venerable Dow Theory. Imagine that you can use this form of technical analysis on stocks, bonds, currencies, commodities, or virtually any liquid and free market.

This methodology not only exists but has been around for more than seventy years. It is not a black box system. Price is this method's only indicator—not the relative strength index, not a stochastics oscillator. Nobody trades the relative strength index; your trading account is not marked to market based on a stochastics oscillator. Your account is marked based on the difference between the current price of the item you bought or sold and where it stood when the trade was initiated.

This wonderful technical tool is the Elliott Wave Theory, one of the few technical tools that is predictive in nature. The astute trader or investor can employ the principle to accurately forecast market extremes. Most forms of technical analysis, although generally more accurate in terms of price determination than fundamental research, tend to be reactive and lag price action. Moving averages cross price well after the trend has changed. Confirmation of a head and shoulders reversal or triangle breakout occurs long after the most advantageous price levels to enter or exit a trade were achieved. Oscillators are based on smoothed prices and tend to trail price activity. In general, oscillators also work well only during periods of range trading in the markets.

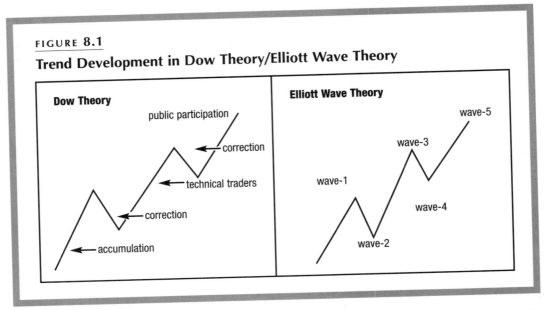

FIGURE 8.1

Trend Development in Dow Theory/Elliott Wave Theory

The wave principle can be used on a stand-alone basis or in conjunction with indicators to help the trader better focus on buying and selling opportunities by identifying likely "energy points" in the market. Elliott Wave Theory's predictive nature means that the trader or investor will be prepared to take action as soon as the market acts according to expectations.

History of Elliott Wave Theory

Ralph Nelson Elliott (1871–1948) developed the Elliott Wave Theory. Elliott was an accountant by trade who spent much of his career working for international railroad companies. He also had an interest in restaurant management and wrote articles and even a book on the subject (*Tea Room and Cafeteria Management*). Elliott fell ill following a stint as Auditor General of the International Railways of Central America in Guatemala. It was during his long convalescence that Elliott began his study of the U.S. stock market.

Elliott had a keen analytical mind. Even in his book on restaurant management, Elliott perceived that markets and the economy moved in cycles, or waves. This perspective led him to the work of Robert Rhea, whose tomes describing Dow Theory are still considered classics. It should come as no surprise that Elliott Wave Theory shares a great deal with its elder cousin, Dow Theory (see also Chapter 1).

It was not just the basic phases of a bull market that Elliott and Dow had in common. Both of these great market analysts detailed the market action based on how investors and traders acted and reacted at each point during a trend's development (see **Figure 8.1**).

The two theories differ in many ways. Dow described bear markets in similar terms to bull markets. A primary bear market had a period of distribution, technical trader entry, and public participation (or in the case of a bear market, more likely, capitulation). Elliott saw bear markets as developing in two broad legs trending lower with a corrective period in between.

The most significant difference between the two theories is that Dow Theory is *reactive*, whereas the Elliott Wave Theory is *proactive*. Dow Theory offers a detailed framework describing how to determine whether or not a trend has *already changed*. To signal the end of a bull trend a lower high and a lower low of some degree is required. Dow Theory offers little guidance with regard to price projections. Dow Theory does offer vague ideas regarding possible retracement targets and equally vacuous ideas regarding how long a primary or secondary trend can be expected to last, but few tools are offered that give the user the ability to pinpoint possible market turning dates, times, and prices.

Elliott approached his analysis from a somewhat different point of view. He fully believed that the markets were deterministic. He argued that, by proper usage of the wave principle, one could accurately forecast market turning points—both in time and price—years in advance. Although no one has achieved that degree of accuracy yet, Elliott Wave Theory does provide an incredibly precise method for finding places of high probability where trend changes may occur. And, to add to its usefulness, its very nature quickly tells the user when the analysis is incorrect.

Description of Elliott Wave Theory

Elliott Wave Theory states that a market moves in two broad phases—a bull market and a bear market. Elliot Wave Theory applies to any freely (not government or monopolistically controlled) traded asset, liability, or commodity. This includes but is not limited to stocks, bonds, oil, gold, or general real estate price levels (but not individual homes or even communities). Elliott proposed that bull markets unfold in five moves or legs. There are three impulsive runs higher that alternate with a pair of nonimpulsive corrective legs. The impulse moves are labeled wave-1, wave-3, and wave-5; the corrective legs are designated as wave-2

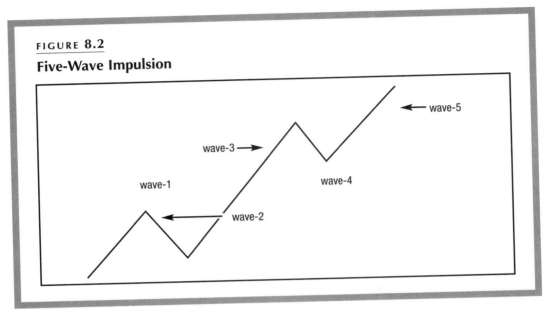

FIGURE 8.2

Five-Wave Impulsion

and wave-4. **Figure 8.2** shows the classic picture of a bull market.

The classic bear market develops in a three-leg pattern. There are two legs with the trend to lower prices. These are called wave-A and wave-C. Wave-B is a corrective affair, as prices rally higher. Wave-B can sometimes exceed the previous wave-5 peak. A stylized bear market move, appended to a five-wave bull market pattern, appears in **Figure 8.3**.

One commonly misunderstood aspect of Elliott Wave Theory is that five-wave and three-wave moves appear throughout all market phases. The preceding descriptions could have equally referred to five-wave patterns to lower prices, and three-wave A-B-C patterns to higher prices. An impulsive move is merely a metaphor for a five-wave price pattern. A three-wave pattern describes a corrective move. There is no reason to attribute a bull market or bear market to five-wave or three-wave structures. This becomes even clearer when you learn that in the most common three-wave correction of an up trend, known as a *zigzag*, wave-A subdivides into a five-wave (impulsive) drop. This fall is part of a correction—a move retracing a larger five-wave pattern (bullish or bearish). It still unfolds in a five-wave pattern. Conversely, wave-B of a bear phase is a three-wave move to higher prices. Wave-B can then subdivide into three smaller waves with the two upward sloping cycles often completed in five-wave runs.

This complexity, and at times, subjectivity, is what often turns people away

FIGURE **8.3**

Three-Wave Decline

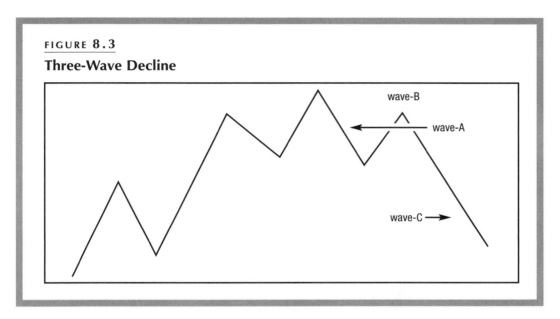

from attempting to apply Elliott Wave Theory to trading and analysis. The fractal nature of Elliott Wave Theory adds a degree of difficulty, but it also adds information that can help the experienced Elliottician (someone who has way too much spare time in which to use the Elliott Wave Theory in trading and/or analysis of market fluctuations).

Here are a general set of rules, concepts, and misconceptions regarding Elliott Wave Theory. The works of market technicians Robert Prechter and A. J. Frost provide a more detailed description of the wave theory:

- Wave-2 can never retrace more than 100 percent of wave-1. This rule has no exceptions.
- Impulse waves are always five-wave affairs. However, when the waves of a terminal triangle subdivide, each wave contains just three legs. A terminal triangle (also known as a diagonal triangle) has the same appearance as a wedge in classical technical analysis. This pattern usually comes at the end of a major market move such as a wave-5 or wave-C.
- Corrective waves either are three waves or develop in a triangle. These triangles are either ascending, descending, or symmetric.
- Wave-4 should not overlap wave-2 unless the whole five-wave cycle is part of a terminal triangle.
- Wave-3 is usually the largest wave. It can never be the shortest wave. During a

with-the-trend move, it is typically at least 1.618 times as large as wave-1. If wave-3 is part of a corrective move (i.e., wave-3 of larger wave-C), it usually is limited to 1.618 times the size of the first wave of wave-C.

- Corrective patterns are often very difficult to count (i.e., identify).
- Irregular corrections are not unusual. They are just as likely to develop as "regular" corrections. An irregular correction occurs when wave-B retraces more than 100 percent of wave-A.
- Using Elliott Wave Theory does not preclude use of classical chart analysis or technical indicators. For example, the classic head and shoulders top is formed via the peaks of wave-3 (left shoulder), wave-5 (head), and wave-B (right shoulder). The neckline is drawn by connecting the nadirs of wave-4 and wave-A.
- Elliott Wave Theory works just as well in markets that have no upward bias (such as the bond market) as in the stock market, which has a long-term upward bias (due to technological change). (In fact, this author developed E-Wave skills by applying the principle to the foreign exchange markets and the bond market.)
- Know your Fibonacci retracements and ratios: 0.236, 0.382, 0.500, 0.618, 0.764, 1.618, 2.618, 4.236. There are others, but these are the most common. Also, know the Fibonacci number series: 1, 1, 2, 3, 5, 8, 13, 21, 34, 55, 89, 144, 233, 377, 610, and so on.

Recognizing Wave Characteristics

Recognizing wave characteristics will help you identify market action. The following descriptions assume the classic bull market and bear market nomenclature for the wave identifiers.

- *Wave-1* occurs when the market psyche is nearly universally bearish. It is the accumulation phase of Dow Theory. The news is still negative. Opinion surveys are still bearish. Market wisdom is to sell rallies. Hints that a bottom might have been achieved (from classical technical analysis) might include: the extreme level of bearishness, momentum divergences at the lows, breaking of down trendlines, and open interest falling during the last part of the previous price drop.
- *Wave-2* occurs when the market sharply retraces its recent hard-fought gains. It is seen as the justification for all the bears' rantings and ravings. It can often retrace nearly 100 percent of wave-1. It can never move below where wave-1 began. Wave-2 shakes out all but the most determined bulls.

- *Wave-3* is what Elliotticians live for (we don't have much of a life). This is the most powerful leg higher. It occurs when price accelerates and volume expands. Open interest should also increase. Wave-3 is typically at least 1.618 times as large as wave-1 and can extend even further than that.
- *Wave-4* is often complex and difficult to identify. It usually retraces no more than 38 percent of wave-3, and its low should not dip beneath the bottom of wave-3's fourth wave. Wave-4's high may exceed the top of wave-3 and is often mistaken for a weak fifth wave. The rule of alternation suggests that wave-2 and wave-4 should "look" different. If one wave is regular, the other should be irregular. Although alternation is called a rule, it is more of a tendency. Do not force a wave-4 identification if alternation is not apparent.
- *Wave-5* is often identified by momentum divergences. It is the period in Dow Theory when the public becomes fully involved and when the smart money might even begin anticipating a market top. In futures markets, open interest might begin falling during wave-5's latter stages.
- *Wave-A* is the distribution phase in Dow Theory. The news is still good, and most traders and investors are still bullish. Wave-A can be either three waves or five waves. Its characteristics are often very similar to wave-1.
- *Wave-B* is often similar to wave-4 and can be very difficult to identify. The top in the stock market in 1929 is often counted as an irregular B-wave. B-waves are often misconceived to be part of the previous bull trend.
- *Wave-C* is the bear market version of wave-3. It is typically highly impulsive (five waves) and often stretches to reach 1.618 times the length of wave-A. Everybody is bearish as this leg completes, resulting in a buying opportunity for the next bull market.

Applying Elliott Wave Theory

Before applying Elliott Wave Theory, the reader should be familiar with the following concepts in addition to Elliott Wave Theory parlance: momentum, relative strength index (RSI), sentiment, trendline, channel, support, resistance, directional index, Bollinger bands, implied volatility, seasonality, and intermarket analysis. The trader can use all of these tools to help solidify the wave counts.

Multiple Time Frame Analysis
Whether you plan on investing in a market for weeks, months, or years, or intend to join the legion of day traders clicking on their mouse buttons to grab

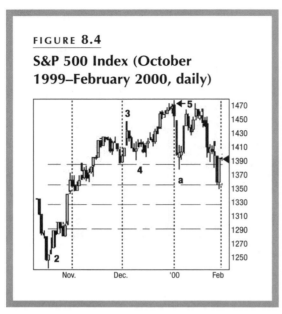

FIGURE 8.4

S&P 500 Index (October 1999–February 2000, daily)

a few points out of a highly volatile stock or futures contract, you must first review several time frames before entering a trade.

A trader who plans to take signals off five-minute bars should be fully aware of what the 15-minute, hourly, and even daily charts look like. Markets have a tendency to find support and resistance at previous highs and lows that may have been reached days, weeks, months, or even years ago. Trendlines drawn on weekly charts and retracements of year-long trends can stop a market cold. These levels will never appear on a five-minute bar chart. The day trader who does not take the time to observe these levels could lose a great deal of money by failing to account for them.

Sometimes the trader needs to look also at closely related markets. For exam-

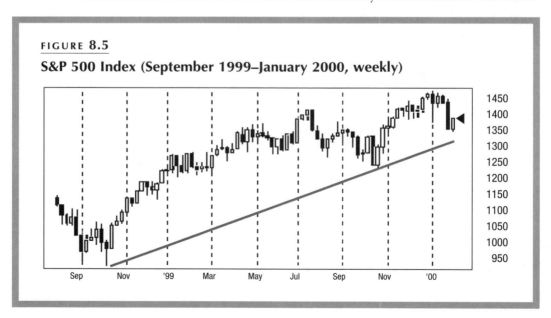

FIGURE 8.5

S&P 500 Index (September 1999–January 2000, weekly)

ple, following the U.S. stock market's sharp drop on January 28, 2000, most commentators were extremely bearish on the equity markets. Most Elliotticians had been looking for an A-B-C correction, but many of the downside targets had already been exceeded. The S&P 500 (cash index), although it had bounced off the 50 percent retracement of the whole rally from October 1999, did not show a clearly completed five-wave pattern lower for wave-C. Some measures pointed to a run into the 1,320 range. This was quite close to the tentative trendline drawn on the weekly chart connecting the lows from October 1998 and October 1999 (see **Figures 8.4** and **8.5**).

This bit of extra work already seemed like a good deal of information that would help the analyst. The trader might have had expectations for only one or two more days of lower prices. By stepping back to a weekly chart, the trader would have confirmed that major support, in the way of a weekly trendline, roughly coincided with an important retracement of the whole rally (62 percent) going back to October 1999. Unfortunately, the coinciding of two levels is no guarantee that prices will actually get there.

When you trade the stock market indices, you must not only be familiar with the index you are trading, but you should also understand how related indices behave. While the Nasdaq and the S&P 500 often diverge, the Nasdaq and the Russell 2000

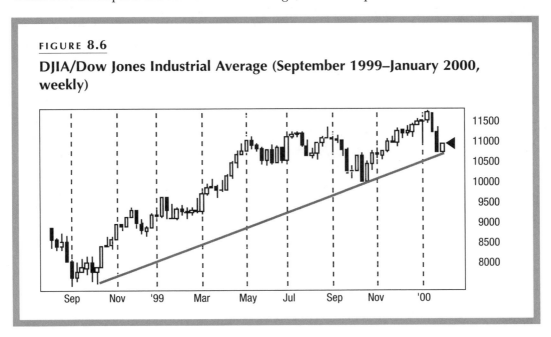

FIGURE **8.6**

DJIA/Dow Jones Industrial Average (September 1999–January 2000, weekly)

might trade in similar patterns. The Dow Jones Industrials typically have a strong correlation with the S&P 500 (see **Figures 8.5** and **8.6**). An extra moment of research over the weekend between January 28, 2000 and January 31, 2000 would have saved day traders a good deal of money. While the weekly trendline for the S&P 500 was nearly 30 points away, the related Dow trendline was much closer and provided support for a major rally higher for the remainder of that day.

This small example highlights the importance of being inclusive in your work. Although you are only marked to market on price, it behooves you to consider multiple factors in your analysis (as long as you do not fall into the "paralysis by analysis" trap). Since all projections pointed to lower prices for January 31, 2000, the day trader should have been trading from the short side. Intermarket work would have warned the trader to be on the lookout for any untoward bullish action. Knowledge of the Dow's weekly trendline would have likely led you to jettison short positions more quickly than would have been possible otherwise.

A consideration of intermarket analysis, then, is an important source of guidance for traders applying Elliott Wave Theory. You should understand as much as you can about markets related to the one you are trading. Whether you use technical analysis as your sole tool for determining entry and exit points, or as an overlay to fundamental research, understanding how markets relate (stocks versus bonds, the dollar versus stocks, commodities and bonds, the Fed and the markets) can only help you in your work. (For a detailed discussion of this topic see Chapter 2.)

From Long-Term Trading to Day Trading: The U.S. Stock Market

In 1999 the U.S. stock market was in the midst of one of the most powerful moves higher in its history. The technology-laden Nasdaq Composite rose more than 85 percent in 1999. The incredible rise in the stock market led most market pundits to compare the nearly meteoric increase to a bubble. Calls for a crash rose in a crescendo to nearly deafening levels. The conservative bears merely suspected that the stock market would tumble about 60 percent, similar to the losses suffered by the Japanese stock market through the 1990s. Even the Chairman of the Federal Reserve Board, Alan Greenspan, opined in a speech he gave on October 14, 1999:

> As I have indicated on previous occasions, history tells us that sharp reversals in confidence occur abruptly, most often with little advance notice. These reversals can be self-reinforcing processes that can compress sizable adjustments into a very short period.

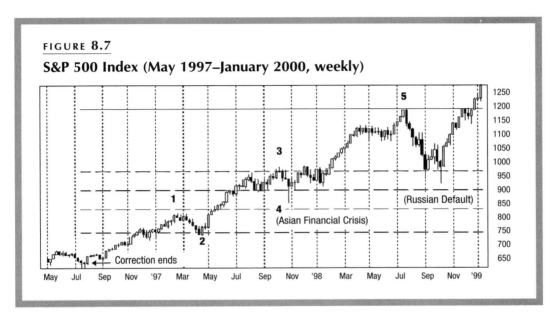

FIGURE 8.7

S&P 500 Index (May 1997–January 2000, weekly)

Panic reactions in the market are characterized by dramatic shifts in behavior that are intended to minimize short-term losses. Claims on far-distant future values are discounted to insignificance. What is so intriguing, as I noted earlier, is that this type of behavior has characterized human interaction with little appreciable change over the generations. *Whether Dutch tulip bulbs or Russian equities, the market price patterns remain much the same.*

We can readily describe this process, but, to date, economists have been unable to *anticipate* sharp reversals in confidence. Collapsing confidence is generally described as a bursting bubble, an event incontrovertibly evident only in retrospect. To anticipate a bubble about to burst requires the forecast of a plunge in the prices of assets previously set by the judgments of millions of investors, many of whom are highly knowledgeable about the prospects for the specific investments that make up our broad price indices of stocks and other assets.

Many followers of Elliott Wave Theory have been attempting to pick a top to this bull market for years. That is one of the dangers of the Elliott Wave Theory—it leads to top and bottom picking. This is great if you get it right, but terrible if your analysis is wrong. That does not mean that you should ignore all the signs of trouble. Often a level that you identify as "the" top proves to be an energy point where the market makes a significant, albeit temporary, trend change. Such possible final tops in price patterns were identified by many Elliotticians in July 1998 and July 1999 (see **Figure 8.7** on which waves 1–5 are marked). Neither of these two points proved to be final tops, but both led to substantial market declines. Overreactions to fundamental events often coincide with already targeted energy points. Wave-4 lower on Figure 8.7 was the culmination of the Asian financial crisis in 1997, and the top of wave-5 in 1998 came in conjunction with the Russian debt default and the subsequent hedge fund debacle involving Long-Term Capital Management.

Elliott Wave Theory can be used to predict the longer term picture for the U.S. stock market and to devise a trading plan for it. Note that there is considerable controversy over long-term wave counts involved. No attempt here is being made to link these counts to a prediction for stock market collapse; such counts are based on assumptions that concatenate very long-term charts of U.S. stocks, U.K. stocks, and even gold prices to attempt to glean a centuries-long perspective on the equity markets. These exercises may be interesting, but they are highly theoretical and of little use in trying to time the stock market from a practical perspective. For the purposes of this chapter, assume that a major five-wave leg higher began in 1982 (labeled wave-I in **Figure 8.8**). (Note that the actual low in the market was in 1975. That might very well have been wave-I. Wave-III then likely began in August 1982.)

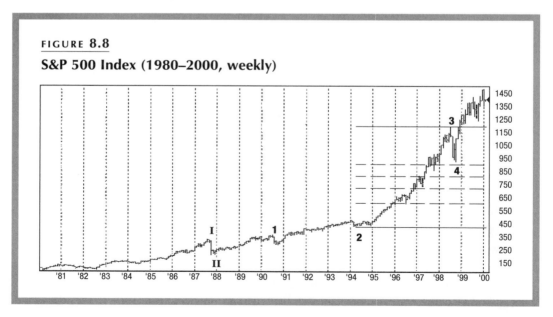

FIGURE 8.8

S&P 500 Index (1980–2000, weekly)

Why should you even attempt to determine the starting point of such a long-term trend? Few people, if any, actually trade off such patterns. Consider long-term investors, such as the baby boom generation, who have their retirement savings locked up in 401(k) plans. If a crash of 90 percent, or even 60 percent, is in the wings, some major asset allocation is needed, and soon. The long-term counts give you a set of assumptions to help you to define the price risks.

The assumed wave count shown in Figure 8.8 is very bullish long-term. Wave-I and wave-II are the longer-term waves; waves 1–4 are part of a five-wave pattern within wave-III. Wave-4 of wave-III ended just above the 38.2 percent Fibonacci retracement of wave-3. (The horizontal lines on Figure 8.8 show possible Fibonacci retracement targets for wave-4.) While the chart shows significant risk for a major *correction* (bear market) ahead after wave-5 completes, the long-term trend is firmly intact. The S&P 500 shows potential to rally toward 3,600 and even could reach 5,000 in the next ten to fifteen years. Note that this agrees with the widely derided books touting "Dow 36,000!"

Such a forecast requires you to understand where it could go wrong and how to recognize when the market deviates from your trading plan. To do this, you must dissect the prior activity and create a road map for going forward.

Creating an Elliott Wave Theory Road Map

When you create an Elliott Wave Theory road map, you need to consider both time and price. Note that wave-1 (of still-active wave-III) took three years to complete. Wave-2 lasted nearly four years, as did wave-3. Wave-4, *which might not be complete*, lasted a matter of months. Assuming wave-4 completed in October 1998, you can project that wave-5 should last approximately as long as wave-1 lasted, or about three years. There is therefore no reason, solely on a timing basis, to believe that the stock market should be due for a serious correction before late 2001.

Before you continue with the immediate-term outlook, you need to complete some further groundwork. First, you should find a reasonable target for where wave-5 of wave-III might complete. The first target can be computed by looking at wave-I, which lasted from the low in 1982 to the high in August 1987. The S&P 500 rose to 337.89 from 102.20 during that time. If you project that wave-III will reach 1.618 times that size, *on a percentage basis,* from the 1987 lows, you get a target near 1,157. The high in 1998 was 1,190. That is fairly close.

Note the labeling for wave-2. Wave-2 actually saw prices rise. This rare occurrence is called a running correction (it is unlikely that many Elliotticians could

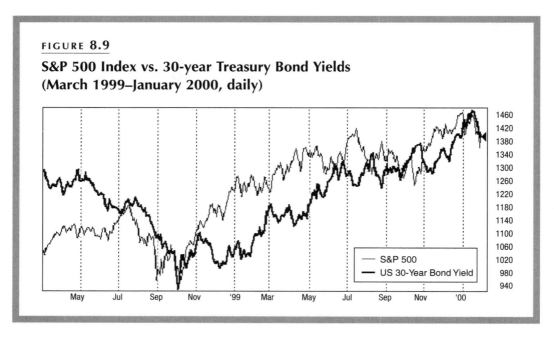

FIGURE **8.9**

**S&P 500 Index vs. 30-year Treasury Bond Yields
(March 1999–January 2000, daily)**

have labeled that correctly as it happened). It implied that the next wave after wave-2 completed would be extremely powerful, which it was. If you measure wave-3 as equal to 1.618 times wave-1, in percentage terms, you get a target at 1,204 on the S&P 500. That is even closer to the 1,190 high that the market achieved. However, a third wave equal to 1.618 times wave-1 after a running second wave is essentially the minimum target for wave-3. The energy point, as bracketed by the twin projections based on wave-I and wave-1 of wave-III, were sufficient to cause a large market correction, but it was not likely the end of wave-III.

Since this pair produced a good projection once, it is worth seeing if any further projections bring you added information. The next target for wave-III based on the wave-I high and the wave-II low is 1,873 (2.618 times wave-I). If wave-3 proves to reach 2.618 times wave-1, you get a target at 1,949. That is very close to 1,873 (unless you shorted 100 S&P 500 futures at 1,873). This also means that wave-3 is probably not yet complete.

Where does that leave the stock market? Shrill calls for a market top can be heard across the land. That has left the contrarians bullish. They say that the stock market can climb a wall of worry. Unfortunately, if prices are rising within a third wave, the climb ought not look like a wall of worry. Remember, impulsive price gains should be relatively easy to count.

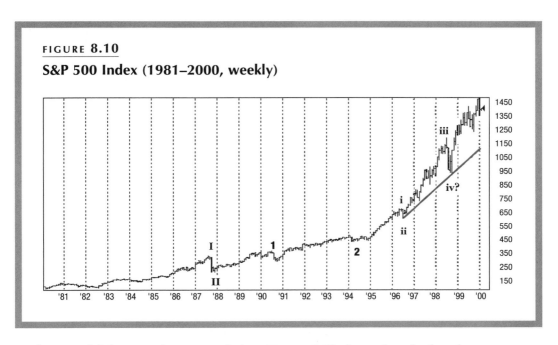

FIGURE 8.10

S&P 500 Index (1981–2000, weekly)

Some quick intermarket research (see **Figure 8.9**) shows that the bond market has been attempting to bottom, even as economists have called for ever larger Federal Reserve Board rate hikes. The correlation between stocks and bonds
for the past few years has varied mostly between none and negative. Bond prices
have not been able to rally significantly any time the stock market has been in
high gear. Bonds have shown a tendency to show strong gains, however, as the
stock market has run through its many brief, but at times deep and volatile, corrective bouts. If bonds are due to rally, then you should expect that stocks might
be setting up for a fall. The correlation is not perfect, but it should make you
stand up and notice. Figure 8.9 shows bond yields versus stock prices. (Bond
yields move in the opposite direction of bond prices.) Note that during the stock
market's range trading between May and October 1999, stock and bond prices
showed a positive correlation. The negative correlation reasserted itself as equities began their sharp ascent in October 1999.

You have now determined that:

● The labeling initially presented showing stocks currently in a fifth wave of
larger wave-III is highly suspect.

● The bond market looks due to rally higher and bonds and stocks have tended to move in opposite directions for the past two to three years.

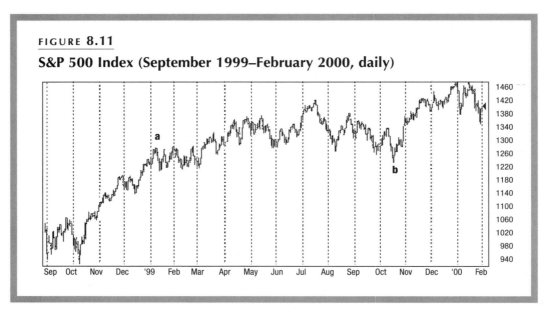

FIGURE 8.11

S&P 500 Index (September 1999–February 2000, daily)

- Despite the huge gains since October 1998, clear five-wave advances are not yet evident.

You can then revise the wave counts to show a new possibility (see **Figure 8.10**). This count removes the difficulty of ending a major third wave at levels too low. Wave-iii is still short, but it is no longer part of a move off a running second wave correction. The question mark next to wave-iv indicates the amount of time spent in that leg seems too short. Furthermore, as noted previously, the wave counts since that low of October 1998, despite some of the most impulsive rallies higher in history, do not afford easy five-wave counts. This implies that although the moves were impressive, they might be part of a larger consolidation. Note also that the downward movement portion of wave-ii was very short and regular. It would not be at all surprising for wave-iv to be long and complex (and irregular).

So far, Elliott Wave Theory has suggested that a 401(k) investor should be sitting tight in the stock market. The waves have also implied that a decent correction may be due soon. Very long-term players holding retirement accounts might not want to take action, as target levels from 1,873 to 1,949 are called for (and as suggested, may be somewhat higher than that over the next ten to fifteen years). Those who have purchased stocks though in the past two to three years might need to seriously consider the upcoming analysis in their investment decisions for the next six to twelve months.

As previously noted, an impulsive rally, especially one that is supposed to be part of a larger third wave, should be relatively easy to identify. The wave count since October 1998 is anything but clear. The huge consolidation during mid-1999 is virtually uncountable. One rule of thumb is that if you cannot count it, it is corrective (i.e., nonimpulsive—remember that, correction has nothing to do with price direction). This argues for relabeling the drop in 1998 as wave-a of wave-iv and not wave-iv as shown in Figure 8.10.

In **Figure 8.11**, wave patterns a, b, and c (with a revised wave-iv on Figure 8.10) do not jump out at you and scream buy or sell. However, if wave-c equaled 62 percent of wave-a (in points, not in percentage terms) you get a target of 1,474. That minor energy point helps explain the January drop. However, targets based on price extensions are not as reliable as percentage moves. Percentage-based computations tend to be more accurate. If wave-c equals 62 percent of wave-a on a percentage basis, the price target is 1,554. Yet, another computation points to 1,573. This pair of price targets in such close proximity poses the significant risk of that area developing into an energy point strong enough to lead to a moderate trend reversal.

With the above analysis in hand, you can devise a robust trading strategy. In early 2000 the market was nervous and climbing a wall of worry. Elliott Wave Theory analysis suggests that it was too early for a major reversal. Further research

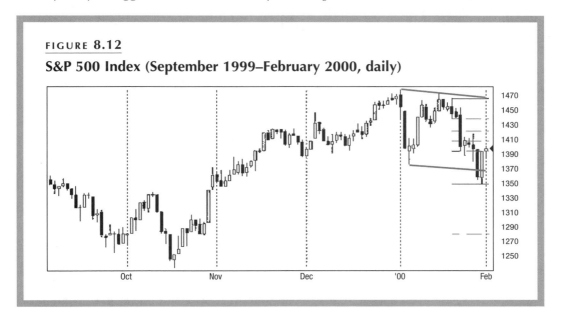

FIGURE 8.12

S&P 500 Index (September 1999–February 2000, daily)

reveals a strong seasonal tendency for U.S. equities to rise through the first quarter on the back of tax advantaged account purchases. Also, based on the past forty-plus years of trading, most of the market's gains occur in the November through April time frame. Put all of these factors together, and the idea of higher prices in general going forward makes sense, with preferred targets near 1,554.

Stops and the Elliott Wave Theory

No strategy is complete without a stop level. Your first attempt at a stop points to the 62 percent retracement of the rally since October 1999, which comes in around 1,327. You could also place it below the weekly trendline from the October 1998 lows at 1,337, but the retracement makes better sense in terms of Elliott Wave Theory.

Now, we can scroll forward and consider whether purchases made sense following the rally on January 31, 2000. In other words, was the low set that morning (see **Figure 8.12**) the end of the drop? Although you have already seen how the trendline on the Dow halted the losses, is the pattern actually complete from the 1,478 high on January 3?

The first quick look would suggest that prices did complete a full a-b-c wave pattern off the highs. Unfortunately, there are several points of concern regarding this analysis:

● The drop exceeded c equals a.
● The fall also moved below the channel line.
● The losses sank well beneath the 50 percent retracement of the rally from October 1999.
● It felt like the bulls were let loose at Pamplona after one day's recovery.

The above conditions were not enough to override the bullish tendencies evident in the powerful rally on January 31, 2000. At the same time, the price surge did little to negate an outside reversal lower on the weekly chart from the prior week. A look at the hourly chart for the month (**Figure 8.13**) revealed the following preferred wave count since the S&P 500 failed to generate a new high on January 14, 2000.

This analysis means that on the next minor move higher, short-term traders should consider establishing new shorts. Stops need to be placed either just above the 38 percent retracement of labeled wave-iii at 1,408, or above the top of the fourth of wave-iii at 1,419. A close watch is needed on this trade. At the moment when the chart was created, the pattern developing off the lows appeared to be a five-wave rally. That is not possible in wave-iv. If prices are rising sharply higher as

FIGURE 8.13

S&P 500 Index (January 2000, hourly)

a target of 1,408 or 1,419 is approached, the recommendation would be to stand aside and look for places to enter long trades.

Assume for the moment that a short trade was entered at 1,406 and that you left latitude for stops at 1,419. As previously mentioned, you can make money trading with Elliott Wave Theory even when you are wrong. You should expect the market to fall fairly sharply from near 1,408. If prices slip, but only grudgingly, quickly tighten stops to below where the initial short trade was made and reverse to long. If prices approach 1,406 with a head of steam, do not even attempt making short trades.

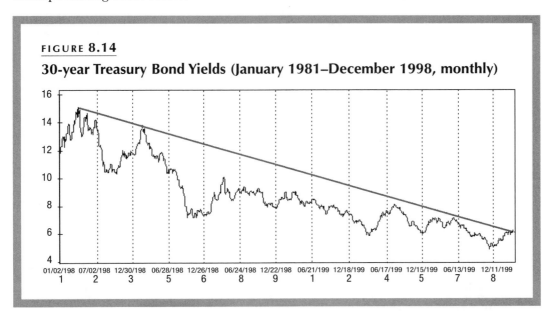

FIGURE 8.14

30-year Treasury Bond Yields (January 1981–December 1998, monthly)

Making Money When Your Analysis Is Wrong

In addition to the preceding theoretical example of how you can be wrong and still make money using the Elliott Wave Theory, here is a detailed example of an incorrect call that still led to very substantial gains.

U.S. Bond Market Example

The benchmark for the U.S. bond market is the 30-year Treasury bond (see **Figure 8.14**). After the Russian debt crisis and the collapse of the large U.S.-based hedge fund Long-Term Capital Management, yields on U.S. bonds fell precipitously. In response to the near-collapse of the global financial system and complete seizing of the non-government-grade debt market, U.S. 30-year Treasury bond yields tumbled from 5.78 percent at the end of July 1998 to as low as 4.69 percent as the stock market bottomed on October 8, 1998. The futures market (U.S. Treasury bond futures are traded on the Chicago Board of Trade) reached past 135. This level was the focus of many long-term Elliott Wave Theory projections.

The speed with which the bond market reversed at that time was absolutely astounding. When the Federal Reserve Board surprised the markets with an intermeeting cut on October 15, 1998, yields never fell even below their lows from the previous day's trading. The bond market had clearly topped. The only question was how high would bond yields rally?

Turn the page forward to the autumn of 1999. Bond yields had been generally rising for a year. The yield on a 30-year Treasury bond reached as high as 6.40 percent, 171 basis points above the October 8, 1998 nadir. Short-term wave projections pointed to a yield peak in the 6.40–6.45 percent range. Market pundits had become increasingly bearish. Suddenly, prognosticators had forgotten about possible psychological yield resistance at 6.50 percent and began projecting that the long bond was due to reach 6.75 percent and even 7.00 percent in short order.

Not only had yields reached a key target area, but also several cycles observed over the years projected that bonds had spent enough time falling in price (rising in yield). With the trendline back to 1981 under attack, this was the perfect spot for a trend change. When yields briefly touched above that eighteen-plus year-old trendline and failed to follow through higher, the alarm (for aggressive traders) sounded to start buying bonds. (One strategy aggressive traders use is to trade the other way when a market fails to produce the "expected" behavior. The break of an eighteen-year-old trendline should have brought in major selling.

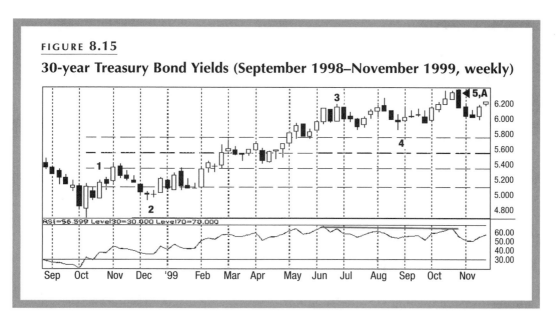

FIGURE **8.15**

30-year Treasury Bond Yields (September 1998–November 1999, weekly)

When it did not, purchases were made.)

The wave counts from the yield lows were not abundantly clear. Momentum divergences, even on the weekly chart, when combined with the trendline and yield targets, were strong hints that a substantial bond market rally was due. Also, seasonal patterns pointed to November and especially December as being two good months for the bond market. Adding it all together resulted in a wave count suggesting that wave-A of a large A-B-C corrective bear run completed at 6.40 percent.

If wave-A had taken yields from 4.69 to 6.40 percent, a substantial bond market rally was due. The five-wave pattern higher in yields shown in **Figure 8.15** portends another major leg higher in yields. First, bonds needed to correct those yield gains. Fibonacci retracement targets are shown as horizontal lines on the chart. The minimum expected rally was 38 percent of the whole rate rise. That targeted 5.85 percent. The probability was for a 50 to 62 percent retracement, which projected yields down to 5.55 percent or lower. Given the continued risks of Fed rate hikes, the 50 percent retracement at 5.55 percent would seem the most likely target.

There was only one reason to have any concern regarding the call for lower yields—the stock market. Bonds had not been able to mount a substantial rally for over two years in the face of a strong stock market. The November to December period was typically very bullish for equities. Furthermore, the stock

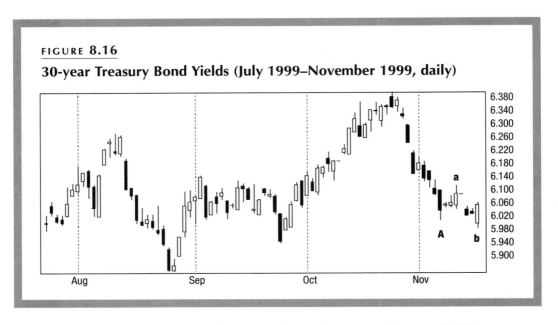

FIGURE 8.16

30-year Treasury Bond Yields (July 1999–November 1999, daily)

market was not seen entering a significant downward phase until 2000, very possibly not before late first quarter or early second quarter of 2000. However, that relatively minor intermarket queasiness was not enough to turn a much stronger technical bullish argument bearish.

Flexibility Is Key

Trading with Elliott Wave Theory permits you to trade aggressively. Once the market shows even the slightest sign of favoring your analysis, upon reaching a turn target, it becomes very easy to enter a trade. When bond yields fell more than 5 basis points intraday, after reaching 6.40 percent, it was easy to enter long. Since safe trading is always recommended, I placed stops above 6.50 percent, a level that seemed unlikely would ever be reached.

Within days of putting the trade on, bond yields tumbled. Just four days later, with two price gaps in hand, yields were down to 6.15 percent. It was time to engage in heavy back patting. Rates did tick higher the next session, touching 6.20 percent, and traded an inside day. An inside day, using Japanese candlestick analysis (see Chapter 4), is a sign that the trend is running out of steam. From that perspective, it was reasonable to expect a corrective increase in yields. Even that moderately negative activity failed to push rates higher. The next session, yields tumbled to a new short-term low. Nine days after rates peaked at 6.40 percent, they

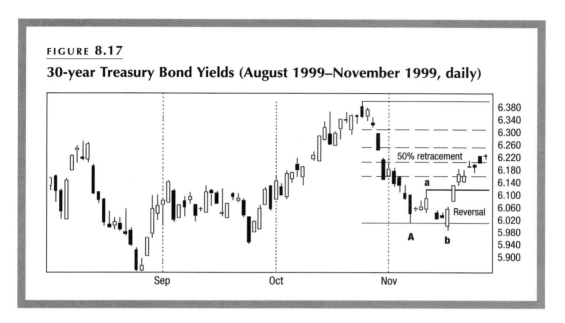

FIGURE **8.17**

30-year Treasury Bond Yields (August 1999–November 1999, daily)

stood at 6.01 percent, completing wave-A lower in yields (see **Figure 8.16**).

So far, so good. The tenth day after rates peaked saw an inside session again, which was followed by a break above the last bullish session's yield high. This probably signaled that wave-A of an expected A-B-C corrective zigzag was now complete (see Figure 8.16). The bond market had already rallied 39 basis points. A typical 50 percent retracement back toward 6.40 percent, and then further rally with wave-C 1.618 times as large as wave-A, would have taken yields to 5.56 percent, or almost exactly the projected 5.55 percent retracement target.

The next few sessions caused a bit of confusion as yields again fell (after first rising to 6.12 percent, well short of the retracement target at 6.20 to 6.21 percent). Rates slipped as low as 5.98 percent before again turning higher (see **b** marked on the above charts). At this point, that had to be considered rather bullish. With a new yield low, an irregular B-wave made the most sense.

Normally, a trader could permit even a 62 percent retracement of the whole rally (meaning yields would have needed to rise past 6.25 percent before covering shorts). But with the new yield low, once yields pushed substantially above the interim high at 6.12 percent (see **a** marked on the above charts), I needed to be on notice, especially since rates reversed with an outside reversal/bullish engulfing pattern. Certainly, a run above the 50 percent retracement level at 6.21 percent should not have been possible under the expectation of a move to 5.55 percent.

Investors who felt the reversal day was significant might have exited there, and others should have considered dropping the long trades above the previous yield rally peak at 6.12 percent. Whether you closed your longs at the close on the reversal day at 6.06 percent, on the break above 6.12 percent, or on reaching above the 50 percent retracement 6.21 percent, using Elliott Wave Theory, you had an extremely incorrect forecast (5.55 percent), and still managed to grab between 50 percent and 80 percent of the whole rally (see **Figure 8.17**).

Fine-Tuning Your Elliott Wave Theory-Based Trading

Applying the Elliott Wave Theory to trading can be extremely challenging. Its apparent subjectivity and multiple scenarios can appear daunting to the novice. Proper understanding of risks and rewards can empower the trader to overcome these disadvantages and actually turn them into tools that lead to profitable trading decisions.

Recall that Elliott Wave Theory counts assume a certain road map. Each wave has a set of characteristics. These characteristics are based on a market mindset. If the market does not develop in the manner forecast, then the wave count is probably wrong. Trading Psychology 101 states that you must always be proactive and flexible. You cannot attach your ego to a trade. You must constantly read the information coming from the market. If the market tells you that your analysis was incorrect, you must take action to ensure that your position profits from the corrected analysis.

Elliott Wave Theory–based trading makes this kind of action easy. As soon as the market fails to develop in a manner that should be expected based on your wave counts, you should quickly adjust your position. This might mean taking profits early, because your expected third wave, for example, is merely wave-B of wave-2. It might mean taking a loss because you put on an aggressive position and the market took out a key retracement that does not fit your wave analysis.

One of the weaknesses of Elliott Wave Theory is that stop placement is by necessity usually in spots where you will have a great deal of company. That means there is significant risk of getting caught in a waterfall of stops, leading to large slippage. Constant monitoring of how the market is trading should help prevent you from ever being forced to take a stop. You should be in a position, by watching how the market trades compared to the proper wave characteristics, to elect to revise your position well before your stops are actually hit. There may be times when you cannot avoid stops, such as when you hold a position over a major data release, leaving the market speeding along too quickly to permit timely trades.

You can also move stops to levels a bit away from places where your wave counts are proven wrong, so that they will be out of harm's way during any stop-running episode. You can place stops beyond the levels where the wave count is wrong, if a reasonable projection would suggest a retracement in your favor before that level is attained. This is not the preferred strategy, however. It can lead to "hoping" for a correction to make you "whole" again, rather than taking action to get the correct trade. You can also tighten stops so that they are in front of the make or break level, if the market has moved against your position sufficiently to make your forecast appear incorrect. The best strategy in such a case is to close the position, rather than waiting for the stop to be hit.

By learning to be inclusive and flexible in your trading, Elliott Wave Theory, when used in conjunction with classical chart analysis, intermarket research, market sentiment studies, and other forms of technical analysis, should take the trader to ever more profitable trading plateaus.

CHAPTER 9

Trading Volatility in the Options Market

LAWRENCE McMILLAN

The game of stock market predicting holds appeal for many traders because those who can do it seem powerful and intelligent. Every trader has favorite indicators, analysis techniques, or "black box" trading systems. Even if you were to prove that the market can't be predicted, most traders would refuse to believe you and would cite new technologies, or combinations of techniques, to keep the debate alive.

Can You Predict the Market?

The astute option trader knows that market prediction falls into two categories:
1. The prediction of the short-term movement of prices
2. The prediction of volatility of the underlying instrument.

Nearly every trader uses something to aid in determining what to buy and when to buy it. Many of these techniques, especially if they are refined to a trading system, seem worthwhile. In that sense, it appears that the market can be predicted. However, this type of predicting usually involves a lot of work, including not only the initial selection of the position, but money management in determining position size, risk management in placing and watching (trailing) stops, and so on. It is not easy.

To make matters even worse, most mathematical studies have shown that the market can't really be predicted. They tend to imply that anyone who is outperforming an index fund is merely "hot"—has hit a stream of winners. Can this possibly be true? Consider this example. Have you ever gone to Las Vegas and had a winning day? How about a weekend? What about a week? You might be able to answer yes to all of those questions, even though you know for a certainty that the casino odds are mathematically stacked against you. What if the question were extended to your lifetime—are you ahead of the casinos for your entire life? This answer is most certainly no if you have played for any reasonably long period of time.

Mathematicians have tended to believe that outperforming the broad stock market is just about the same as beating the casinos in Las Vegas—possible in the short term, but virtually impossible in the long term. Thus, when mathematicians say that the stock market can't be predicted, they are talking about consistently beating the index—say, the S&P 500—over a long period of time.

Those with an opposing viewpoint, however, say that the market *can* be beat, that the game is more like poker—in which a good player can be a consistent winner through money management techniques—than like casino gambling, where the odds are fixed. It would be impossible to get everyone to agree on who is right. There is some credibility in both viewpoints, but just as it is very hard to be a good poker player, so it is difficult to beat the market consistently with directional strategies. Moreover, even the best directional traders know that large swings or drawdowns occur in their net worth during the year. Thus, the consistency of returns is generally erratic for the directional trader.

This inconsistency of returns, the amount of work required, and the need to have sufficient capital and to manage it well are all factors that can lead to the demise of a directional trader. As such, short-term directional trading probably is not a comfortable trading strategy for most traders—and if you are trading a strategy that you are not comfortable with, you are eventually going to lose money doing it.

Is there a better alternative? Or should you just pack it in, buy some index funds, and forget it? As an option strategist, you should most certainly feel that there is something better than buying the index fund. The alternative of volatility trading offers significant advantages in those areas that make directional trading difficult. So if you find that you are able to handle the rigors of directional trading, then stick with that approach. You might want to add some volatility trading to your arsenal, though, just to be safe. However, if you find that directional trading is just too time-consuming, or have trouble utilizing stops properly, or are constantly getting whipsawed, then it is time to concentrate more heavily on volatility trading, preferably in the form of straddle buying.

Volatility Trading Overview

Volatility trading first attracted mathematically oriented traders who noticed that the options market's prediction of forthcoming volatility in the underlying instrument—that is, implied volatility—was substantially out of line with what one might reasonably expect should happen. Moreover, many of these traders

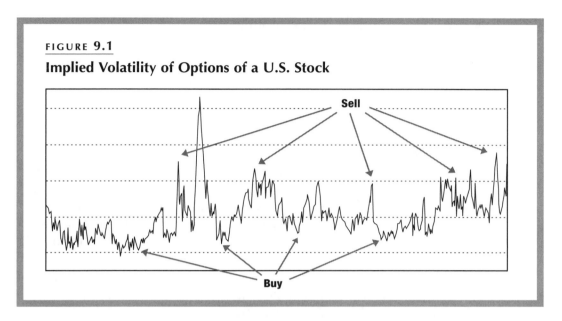

FIGURE **9.1**

Implied Volatility of Options of a U.S. Stock

(market makers, arbitrageurs, and others) had found great difficulties with keeping a "delta neutral" (i.e., fully hedged) position neutral. Seeking a better way to trade without having a market opinion on the underlying security, they turned to volatility trading. They did not expect volatility trading to eliminate all market risk, by turning it all into volatility risk, for example. These traders merely felt that they could handle the risk of volatility with more deference and aplomb than they could handle price risk.

Simply stated, it seems to be a much easier task to predict volatility than to predict prices. That is said, notwithstanding the great bull market of the 1990s, in which all investors who strongly participated certainly feel that they understand how to predict prices. (Remember not to confuse brains with a bull market.) Consider the chart in **Figure 9.1**.

This seems as though it might be a good stock to trade: buy it near the lows and sell it near the highs, perhaps even selling it short near the highs and covering when it later declines. It appears to have been in a trading range for a long time, so that after each purchase or sale, it returns at least to the midpoint of its trading range and sometimes even continues on to the other side of the range. Even though there is no scale on the chart, it appears to be a tradeable entity. In fact, this is a chart of implied volatility of the options of a major U.S. corporation. It really doesn't matter which one (it is CSCO), for the implied volatility chart of nearly every stock, index, or futures contract has a similar pattern—a trading range. Implied volatility will totally break out of its normal range only when something material happens to change the fundamentals of the way the stock moves—a takeover bid, for example, or perhaps a major acquisition or other dilution of the stock.

Many traders who have observed this pattern have become adherents of trying to predict volatility. Notice that if you are able to isolate volatility, you don't care where the stock price goes; you are just concerned with buying volatility near the bottom of the range and selling it when it gets back to the middle or high of the range, or vice versa. In real life, it is nearly impossible for public customers to be able to isolate volatility so specifically. They must pay some attention to the stock price, while establishing positions in which the direction of the stock price is irrelevant to the outcome of the position. This quality of volatility trading is appealing to many investors who have repeatedly found it difficult to predict stock prices. Moreover, this approach should work in both bull and bear markets. Thus, volatility trading appeals to a great number of individuals. Just remember that, for you personally to operate a strategy properly, you must find that it appeals to your personal philosophy of trading. To try to use a strategy that you find uncomfortable will only lead to losses and frustration. So, if this somewhat neutral approach to option trading sounds interesting to you, then read on.

Historical Volatility

Volatility is merely the term that is used to describe how fast a stock, future, or index changes in price. In connection with options, two types of volatility are important. The first is *historical volatility*, which is a measure of how fast the underlying instrument has been changing in price. The other is *implied volatility* —which is the option market's prediction of the volatility of the underlying instrument over the life of the option. The computation and comparison of these two measures can aid immensely in predicting the forthcoming volatility of the underlying instrument—a crucial matter in determining today's option prices.

Historical volatility can be measured with a specific formula. It is merely the formula for standard deviation as contained in most elementary books on statistics. The important point to understand is that it is an exact calculation, and there is little debate over how to compute historical volatility. It is not important to know what the actual measurement means. That is, if you say that a certain stock has a historical volatility of 20 percent, that by itself is a relatively mean-ingless number to anyone but an ardent statistician. However, it can be used for comparative purposes.

The standard deviation is expressed as a percent. For example, the historical volatility of the broad stock market has usually been in the range of 15 to 20 per-cent. A very volatile stock might have an historical volatility in excess of 100 per-cent. You can compare these numbers to each other to determine that, for exam-ple, a stock with the latter historical volatility is five times more volatile than the stock market. So, the historical volatility of one instrument can be compared with that of another instrument to determine which one is more volatile. That in itself is a useful function of historical volatility, but its uses go much farther than that.

Historical volatility can be measured over different time periods to give you a sense of how volatile the underlying stock has been over varying lengths of time. For example, it is common to compute a 10-day historical volatility, as well as a 20-, 50-, and even 100-day. In each case, the results are annualized so that you can compare the figures directly.

Consider **Figure 9.2**. It shows a stock (although it could be a futures contract or an index) that was meandering in a rather tight range for quite some time. At the point marked A on the chart, it was probably at its least volatile. At that time,

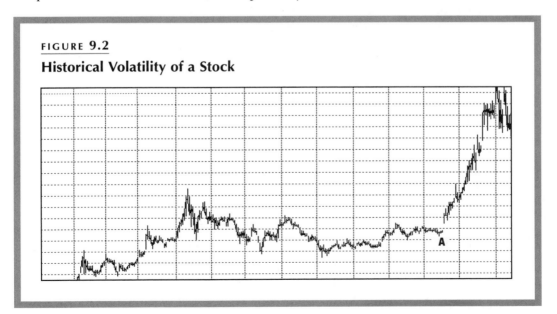

FIGURE 9.2

Historical Volatility of a Stock

the 10-day volatility might have been something quite low—say 20 percent. The price movements directly preceding point A had been very small. However, prior to that time the stock had been more volatile, so longer-term measures of the historical volatility would have shown higher numbers. As seen in Figure 9.2, the possible measures of historical volatility, then, at point A, might have been something like:

10-day historical volatility: 20 percent
20-day historical volatility: 23 percent
50-day historical volatility: 35 percent
100-day historical volatility: 45 percent

A pattern of historical volatilities of this sort describes a stock that has been slowing down lately. Its price movements have been less extreme in the near term.

Again referring to Figure 9.2, note that shortly after point A, the stock jumped much higher over a short period of time. Price action like this increases the implied volatility dramatically. And, at the far right edge of the chart, the stock had stopped rising but was swinging back and forth in far more rapid fashion than it had been at most other points on the chart. Violent action in a back and forth manner can often produce a higher historical volatility reading than straight-line movement can—it is just the way the numbers work out. So, by the far right edge of the chart, the 10-day historical volatility would have increased rather dramatically, while the longer-term measures would not be so high, because they would still contain the price action that occurred prior to Point A. At the far right edge of Figure 9.2, the following figures might apply:

10-day historical volatility: 80 percent
20-day historical volatility: 75 percent
50-day historical volatility: 60 percent
100-day historical volatility: 55 percent

With this alignment of historical volatilities, you can see that the stock has been more volatile recently than in the more distant past. Determining which of these historical volatilities to use as "the" historical volatility input into option and probability models is discussed later. You need to be able to make volatility estimates in order to determine whether or not a strategy might be successful and to determine whether the current option price is a relatively cheap one or a relatively expensive one. For example, you can't just say, "I think XYZ is going to rise at least 18 points by February expiration." You need to have some basis in fact for such a statement and, since you lack inside information about what the company might announce between now and February, that basis should be statistics in the form of volatility projections.

Historical volatility is, of course, useful as an input to the Black–Scholes (or other) option model. In fact, the volatility input to any model is crucial because the volatility component is such a major factor in determining the price of an option. Furthermore, historical volatility is useful for more than just estimating option prices. It is necessary for making stock price projections and calculating distributions, too, as will be shown when those topics are discussed later. Any time you ask the question, "What is the probability of the stock moving from here to there, or of exceeding a particular target price," the answer is heavily dependent on the volatility of the underlying stock (or index or futures).

It is obvious from the previous example that historical volatility can change dramatically for any particular instrument. Even if you were to stick with just one measure of historical volatility (the 20-day historical is commonly the most popular measure), it changes with great frequency. Thus, you can never be certain that basing option price predictions or stock price distributions on the current historical volatility will yield the correct results. Statistical volatility may change as time goes forward, in which case your projections would be incorrect. It is therefore important to make projections on the conservative side.

Implied Volatility

Implied volatility pertains only to options, although you can aggregate the implied volatilities of the various options trading on a particular underlying instrument to produce a single number that is often referred to as the implied volatility of the underlying.

At any point in time, a trader knows for certain the following items that affect an option's price: stock price, strike price, time to expiration, interest rate, and dividends. The only remaining factor is volatility—in fact, implied volatility. It is the big fudge factor in option trading. If implied volatility is too high, options will be overpriced. That is, they will be relatively expensive. On the other hand, if implied volatility is too low, options will be cheap, or underpriced. The terms *overpriced* and *underpriced* are not really used by theoretical option traders much anymore, because their usage implies that you know what the option should be worth. In the modern vernacular, you would say that the options are trading with a high implied volatility or a low implied volatility, meaning that you have some sense of where implied volatility has been in the past, and the current measure is thus high or low in comparison.

Essentially, implied volatility is the option market's guess at the forthcoming statistical volatility of the underlying over the life of the option in question. If traders feel that the underlying will be volatile over the life of the option, they will bid up the option, making it more highly priced. Conversely, if traders envision a nonvolatile period for the stock, they will not pay up for the option, preferring to bid lower—hence the option will be relatively low-priced. The important thing to note is that traders normally do not know the future. They have no way of knowing, for sure, how volatile the underlying is going to be during the life of the option.

That said, it would be unrealistic to assume that inside information does not leak into the marketplace. That is, if certain people possess nonpublic knowledge about a company's earnings, new product announcement, takeover bid, and the like, they will aggressively buy or bid for the options and that will increase implied volatility. So, in certain cases, implied volatility shooting up quickly may be a signal that some traders do indeed know the future—at least with respect to a specific corporate announcement that is about to be made.

However, most of the time there is not anyone trading with inside information. Yet, every option trader—market maker and public alike—is forced to make a guess about volatility when buying or selling an option. That is true because the price traders pay is heavily influenced by the volatility estimate (whether or not traders realize that they are, in fact, making such volatility estimates). As you might imagine, most traders have no idea what volatility is going to be during the life of the option. They just pay prices that seem to make sense, perhaps based on historical volatility. Consequently, today's implied volatility may bear no resemblance to the actual statistical volatility that later unfolds during the life of the option.

For those who desire a more mathematical definition of implied volatility, consider this. An option's price is a function of the following:

Option price = f(stock price, strike price, time, risk-free rate, volatility, dividends)

Suppose that you know the following information:

Current option price: 6

XYZ price: 93

July 90 call price: 9

Time remaining to July expiration: 56 days

Dividends: $0.00

Risk-free interest rate: 6 percent

This information, which is available for every option at any time simply from an option quote, gives you everything except the implied volatility. So what volatility would you have to plug in the Black–Scholes model (or whatever model you are using), to make the model give the answer 6 (the current price of the option)? That is, what volatility is necessary to solve the equation?:

6 = f(93, 90, 56 days, 6 percent, x, $0.00)

Whatever volatility is necessary to make the model yield the market price (6) as its value, is the implied volatility for the XYZ July 90 call. In this case, if you are interested, the implied volatility is 48.8 percent.

Implied Volatility as a Predictor of Actual Volatility

Just because you can calculate implied volatility does not mean that the calculation is a good estimate of forthcoming volatility. As stated above, the options market does not really know how volatile an instrument is going to be, any more than it knows the forthcoming price of the stock. There are clues, of course, and some general ways of estimating forthcoming volatility, but the fact remains that sometimes options trade with an implied volatility that is quite a bit out of line with past levels and therefore may be considered to be an inaccurate estimate of what is really going to happen to the stock during the life of the option. Just remember that implied volatility is a forward-looking estimate, and because it is based on a trader's suppositions, it can be wrong, just as any estimate of future events can be in error.

This question posed above is one that should probably be asked more often than it is: Is implied volatility a good predictor of actual volatility? Somehow, it seems logical to assume that implied and historical (actual) volatility will converge. That is not really true—at least not in the short term. Moreover, even if they do converge, which one was right to begin with—implied or historical? That is, did implied volatility move to get more in line with actual movements of the underlying stock, or did the stock's movement speed up or slow down to get in line with implied volatility?

To illustrate this concept, the following figures show the comparison between implied and historical volatility. **Figure 9.3** shows information for the $OEX Index. In general, $OEX options are overpriced. That is, implied volatility of $OEX options is almost always higher than what actual volatility turns out to be.

There are three lines on this chart: (1) implied volatility, (2) actual volatility, and (3) the difference of the two. There is an important distinction here, though, as to what comprises these curves.

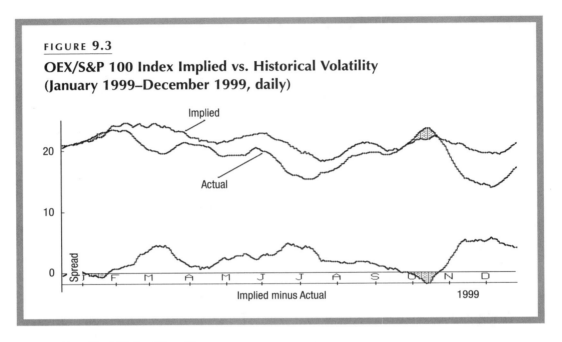

FIGURE 9.3

OEX/S&P 100 Index Implied vs. Historical Volatility (January 1999–December 1999, daily)

Implied Volatility Curve

The implied volatility curve depicts the 20-day moving average of daily composite implied volatility readings for $OEX. That is, each day-one number is computed as a composite implied volatility for $OEX for that day. To smooth out those daily readings, a 20-day simple moving average is used. This daily implied volatility of $OEX options encompasses all the $OEX options, so it is different from the Volatility Index ($VIX), which uses only the options closest to the money. By using all of the options, a slightly different volatility figure from $VIX is arrived at, but a chart of the two should show similar patterns. That is, peaks in implied volatility computed using all of the $OEX options occur at the same points in time as peaks in $VIX. These implied volatility figures are computed using an "averaging" formula whereby each option's implied volatility is weighted by trading volume and by distance in- or out-of-the-money, to arrive at a single composite implied volatility reading for the trading day.

Actual Volatility Curve

The *actual* volatility on the graph is a little different from what one normally thinks of as historical volatility. It is the 20-day historical volatility, computed 20 days later than the date of the implied volatility calculation. Hence, points on the implied volatility curve are matched with a 20-day historical volatility calculation that was made 20 days later. Thus, the two curves more or less show the prediction of volatility and what actually happened over the 20-day period. These actual volatility readings are smoothed as well, with a 20-day moving average.

Difference Curve

The difference of the two is quite simple, and it is shown as the bottom curve on the graph. A "zero" line is drawn through the difference. When this "difference curve" passes through the zero line, the projection of volatility and what actually occurred 20 days later were equal. If the difference curve is above the zero line, then implied volatility was too high; the options were overpriced. Conversely, if the "difference line" is below the zero line, then actual volatility turned out to be greater than implied volatility had anticipated. The options were underpriced in that case. Those latter areas are shaded in Figure 9.3. Simplistically, you would want to own options during the shaded periods on the chart and would want to be a seller of options during the nonshaded areas.

Note that Figure 9.3 indeed confirms the fact once again that $OEX options are consistently overpriced. Very few charts are as one-dimensional as the $OEX chart, on which the options are so consistently overpriced. Most stocks find the difference curve oscillating above and below the zero line.

The important thing to note is that implied volatility is really not a very good predictor of the actual volatility that is to follow. If it were, the difference curve would hover near zero most of the time. Instead, it swings up and down, with implied volatility over- or underestimating actual volatility by wide levels.

This means that using the difference between implied volatility and current historical volatility as a criterion for deciding whether to buy volatility or to sell it is incorrect, and possibly dangerous to your wealth. That is, if you happen to notice that XYZ's options have an implied volatility of 30 percent and XYZ is currently trading with a 20-day historical volatility of 20 percent, you cannot draw much of a conclusion about whether to buy or sell volatility from this information. It is irrelevant.

One is far better served by comparing apples to apples as it were. In other words, compare implied volatility to past levels of implied volatility. This concept is described in more detail later in this chapter.

One thing that does stand out on these charts is that implied volatility seems to fluctuate less than actual volatility. That seems to be a natural function of the volatility predictive process. For example, when the market collapses, implied volatilities of options rise only modestly. This can be observed in case by again referring to Figure 9.3, the $OEX option example. The only shaded area on the

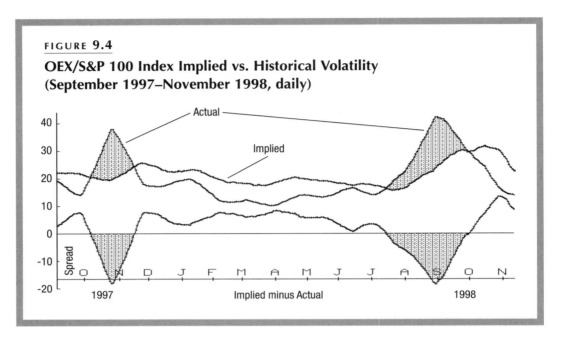

FIGURE **9.4**

**OEX/S&P 100 Index Implied vs. Historical Volatility
(September 1997–November 1998, daily)**

graph occurred when the market had a rather sharp sell-off during October 1999. In previous years, when there had been even more severe market declines (October 1997, or August–October 1998) $OEX actual volatility had briefly moved above implied volatility (see **Figure 9.4**). In other words, option traders and market makers are predicting volatility when they price options, and one tends to make a prediction that is somewhat middle of the road, for an extreme prediction is more likely to be wrong. Of course, it turns out to be wrong anyway, since actual volatility jumps around rapidly.

Spotting Implied Volatility That Is Overvalued or Undervalued
It is the volatility trader's objective to spot situations where implied volatility is possibly or probably erroneous and to take a position that would profit when the error is brought to light. Thus, the volatility trader's main objective is to spot situations in which implied volatility is overvalued or undervalued, regardless of the outlook for the underlying stock itself. In some ways, this is not so different from the fundamental stock analyst who is attempting to spot overvalued or undervalued stocks, based on earnings and other fundamentals.

From another viewpoint, volatility trading is also a contrarian theory of investing. That is, when everyone else thinks the underlying is going to be stable, the volatility trader buys volatility. That is, when everyone else is selling options and option buyers are hard to find, the volatility trader steps up to buy options. Of course, some rigorous analysis must be done before the volatility trader can establish positions, but when those situations come to light, it is most likely that the trader is taking positions opposite to what the masses are doing. The volatility trader buys volatility when the majority is selling it (or at least, when the majority is refusing to buy it), and the trader sells volatility when everyone else is panicking to buy options, making them extremely expensive.

Volatility Extremes

You cannot just buy every option that you consider cheap. You must give some consideration to what the probabilities of stock movement are. Even more important, you cannot just sell every option considered expensive. There may be valid reasons why options become expensive, not the least of which is that someone may have inside information about some forthcoming corporate news (a takeover or an earnings surprise, for example).

In fact, there are analysts and traders who look for large increases in trading volume as a clue to which stocks might be ready to make a big move. Invariably, an increase in the trading volume along with an increase in implied volatility is a good warning sign that someone with inside information is buying the options. In such a case, it might *not* be a good idea to sell volatility, even though the options are mathematically expensive.

The seller of volatility can watch for two things as warning signs that perhaps the options are predicting a corporate event (and hence should be avoided as a "volatility sale"). Those two things are a dramatic increase in option volume and/or a sudden jump in implied volatility of the options. One or both can be caused by traders with inside information trying to obtain a leveraged instrument in advance of the actual corporate news item being made public.

A Sudden Increase in Option Volume or Implied Volatility

The symptoms of inside trading, as evidenced by a large increase in option trading activity, can be recognized. Typically, the majority of the increased volume occurs in the near-term option series, particularly the at-the-money strike and perhaps the next strike out-of-the-money. The activity does not cease there, however. It propagates out to other option series as market makers—who by the nature of their job function are short the near-term options that those with insider knowledge are buying—snap up everything on the book that they can find. In addition, the market makers may try to entice others, perhaps institutions, to sell some expensive calls against a portion of their institutional stock holdings. Activity of this sort should be a warning sign to the volatility seller to stand aside in this situation.

Of course, on any given day there are many stocks whose options are extraordinarily active, but the increase in activity does not have anything to do with insider trading. This might include a large covered call write or maybe a large put purchase established by an institution as a hedge against an existing stock position, or a relatively large conversion or reversal arbitrage established by an arbitrageur, or even a large spread transaction initiated by a hedge fund. In any of these cases, option volume would jump dramatically, but it would not mean that anyone had inside knowledge about a forthcoming corporate event. Rather, the increases in option trading volume as described here are merely functions of the normal workings of the marketplace.

What distinguishes these arbitrage and hedging activities from the machinations of insider trading? First, there is little spreading of option volume into other series in the benign case, and second, the stock price itself may languish. However, when true inside activity is present, the market makers react to the aggressive nature of the call buying. These market makers know they need to hedge themselves, for they do not want to be short naked call options in case a takeover bid or some other news spurs the stock dramatically higher. As mentioned earlier, they try to buy up any other options offered in the book, but there may not be many of those. So, as a last result, the way that they reduce their risk (their "negative position delta," discussed below) is to buy stock. Thus, if the options are active and expensive, and if the stock is rising, too, you have a reasonably good indication that someone knows something. However, if the options are expensive but none of the other factors are present, especially if the stock is declining in price, then you might feel more comfortable with a strategy of selling volatility.

However, there is a case in which options might be the object of pursuit by someone with insider knowledge, yet not be accompanied by heavy trading volume. This situation could occur with illiquid options. In this case, a floor broker holding the order of those with insider information might come into the pit to buy options, but the market makers may not sell them many, preferring to raise their offering price rather than sell a large quantity. If this happens a few times in a row, the options will become very expensive as the floor broker raises the bid price repeatedly, but only buys a few contracts each time. Meanwhile, the market maker keeps raising the offering price. Eventually, the floor broker concludes that the options are too expensive to bother with and walks away. Perhaps the client then buys stock. In any case, the options have become very expensive, as the bids and offers were repeatedly raised, but not much option volume was actually traded because of the illiquidity of the contracts. Hence the normal warning light associated with a sudden increase in option volume would not be present. In this case, though, a volatility seller should still be careful. You do not want to step in to sell calls right before some major corporate news item is released. The clue here is that implied volatility can explode in a short period of time (within one day) and that alone should be enough warning.

The point that should be taken here is that when options suddenly become very expensive, especially if accompanied by strong stock price movement and strong stock volume, there may be a good reason why that is happening. That reason will probably become public knowledge shortly in the form of a news event. Hence a volatility trader should avoid selling in situations such as these. Any sudden increase in implied volatility should probably be viewed as a potential news story in the making. These situations are not what a neutral volatility seller wants to get into.

On the other hand, if options have become expensive as a result of corporate news, then the volatility seller can feel more comfortable making a trade. Perhaps the company has announced poor earnings and the stock has taken a beating while implied volatility rose. In this situation, you can assess the information and analyze it clearly, because you are not dealing with some hidden facts known to only a few insider traders. With clear analysis, you might be able to develop a volatility selling strategy that is prudent and potentially profitable.

Another situation in which options become expensive in the wake of market action is during a bear market in the underlying stock. This can be true for indices, stocks, and futures contracts. The crash of 1987 is an extreme example, but implied volatility shot through the roof during the crash. Other similar sharp market collapses, such as October 1989, October 1997, and August–September 1998, caused implied volatility to jump dramatically. In such situations, the volatility seller knows why implied volatility is high. With that knowledge, you can then construct positions around a neutral strategy or around your view of the future. You must be careful, however, when the options are expensive and no one seems to know why. That is when insider trading may be present, and that's when the volatility seller should defer from selling options.

Cheap Options

When options are cheap, the reasons may be far less discernible. An obvious one may be that the corporate structure of the company has changed—perhaps it is being taken over, or perhaps the company has acquired another company nearly its size. In either case, it is possible that the stock of the combined entity will be less volatile than the original company's stock was. As the takeover is in the process of being consummated, the implied volatility of the company's options will drop, giving the false impression that they are cheap.

In a similar vein, a company may mature, perhaps issuing more shares of stock, or perhaps building such a good earnings stream that the stock is considered less volatile than it formerly was. Some Internet companies are classic cases: in the beginning they are high-flying stocks with plenty of price movement, so the options trade with a relatively high degree of implied volatility. However, as these companies mature, they buy other Internet companies and then perhaps even merge with large, established companies (America Online and Time-Warner Communications, for example). In such cases, actual (statistical) volatility diminishes as the company matures, and implied volatility does the same. On the surface, buyers of volatility may see the reduced volatility as an attractive buying situation, but upon further inspection they may find that it is justified. If the decrease in implied volatility seems justified, a buyer of volatility should ignore the stock and look for other opportunities.

When to Be Cautious

All volatility traders should be suspicious when volatility seems to be extreme—either too expensive or too cheap. Buyers of volatility really have little to fear if they miscalculate and thus buy an option that appears inexpensive but turns out not to be. Volatility buyers might lose money when they do this, and constantly overpaying for options will lead to ruin, but an occasional mistake will probably not be fatal.

Sellers of volatility, however, have to be a lot more careful. One mistake could be the last one. Selling naked calls that seem terrifically expensive by historical standards could be ruinous if a takeover bid subsequently emerges at a large premium to the stock's current price. Even put sellers must be careful, although a lot of traders feel that selling naked puts is safe because it is the same as buying stock. But who ever said that buying stock wasn't risky? If the stock literally collapses—falling from 80, say, to 15 or 20, as Oxford Health did, or from 30 to 2 as Sunrise Technology did—then a put seller will be buried. Since the risk of loss from naked option selling is large, you could be wiped out by a huge gap opening. That is why it is imperative to study why the options are expensive before you sell them. If it is known, for example, that a small biotech company is awaiting

Food and Drug Administration (FDA) trial results in two weeks, and all the options suddenly become expensive, the volatility seller should not be a hero. It is obvious that at least some traders feel that there is a chance for the stock to change in price dramatically. It would be better to find some other situation in which to sell options.

The seller of futures options or index options should be cautious, too, although there cannot be takeovers in those markets, nor can there be a huge earnings surprise or other corporate event that causes a big gap. The futures markets, though, do respond to crop reports and government economic data, which can create volatile situations, too. The bottom line is that volatility selling—even hedged volatility selling—can be taxing and aggravating if you have sold volatility in front of what turns out to be a news item that justifies the expensive volatility.

Vega

An option strategist should have some idea of the general changes that a position will undergo if implied volatility changes. It is important to understand some of the basics of the effect of volatility on an option's price. Technically speaking, the term *vega* is used to quantify the impact of volatility changes on the price of an option. Simply stated, vega is the amount by which an option's price changes when volatility changes by 1 percentage point.

Example: XYZ is selling at 50, and the July 50 call is trading at $7\frac{1}{4}$. Assume that there is no dividend, that short-term interest rates are 5 percent, and that July expiration is exactly three months away. With this information, you can determine that the implied volatility of the July 50 call is 70.0 percent. That is a fairly high number, so you can surmise that XYZ is a volatile stock. What would the option price be if implied volatility were to rise to 71.0 percent? Using a model, you can determine that the July 50 call would theoretically be worth 7.35 if that happened. Hence, the vega of this option is 0.10 (to two decimal places). That is, the option price increased by 10 cents, from 7.25 to 7.35 when volatility rose by 1 percentage point. (Note that *percentage point* here means a full point increase in volatility, from 70 percent to 71 percent.)

What if implied volatility had decreased instead? Once again, you can use the model to determine the change in the option price. In this case, using an implied volatility of 69 percent and keeping everything else the same, the option would then theoretically be worth 7.15, again, a 0.10 change in price (this time, a decrease in price).

This example points out an interesting and important aspect of how volatility affects a call option: if implied volatility increases, the price of the option will increase, and if implied volatility decreases, the price of the option will decrease. Thus, there is a direct relationship between an option's price and its implied volatility.

Mathematically speaking, vega is the partial derivative of the Black–Scholes model (or whatever model you are using to price options) with respect to volatility. In the above example, the vega of the July 50 call, with XYZ at 50, can be computed to be 0.098, very near the value of 0.10 that you arrived at by inspection.

Vega also has a direct relationship to the price of a put. That is, as implied volatility rises, the price of a put will rise as well.

Example: Using the same criteria as in the previous example, suppose that XYZ is trading at 50, that July is three months away, that short-term interest rates are 5 percent, and that there is no dividend. In that case, the following theoretical put and call prices would apply at the stated implied volatilities:

STOCK PRICE	JULY 50 CALL	JULY 50 PUT	IMPLIED VOLATILITY	PUT'S VEGA
50	7.15	6.54	69%	0.10
	7.25	6.64	70%	0.10
	7.35	6.74	71%	0.10

Thus, the put's vega is 0.10, too—the same as the call's vega was.

In fact, it can be stated that a call and a put with the same terms have the same vega. To prove this, you need only to refer to the arbitrage equation for a conversion. If the call increases in price and everything else remains equal—interest rates, stock price, and striking price—then the put price must increase by the same amount. A change in implied volatility will cause such a change in the call price, and a similar change in the put price. Hence the vega of the put and the call must be the same.

As can be done with delta, or any other of the partial derivatives of the model, you can compute a position vega—the vega of an entire position. The position vega is determined by multiplying the individual option vegas by the quantity of options bought or sold. The *position vega* is merely the quantity of options held times the vega times the shares per options (which is normally 100).

Example: Using a simple call spread as an example, assume the following prices exist:

SECURITY	POSITION	VEGA	POSITION VEGA
XYZ Stock	No position		
XYZ July 50 call	Long 3 calls	0.098	+0.294
XYZ July 70 call	Short 5 calls	0.076	−0.380

NET POSITION VEGA: -0.086

This concept is very important, because it tells you if you have constructed a position that is going to behave in the manner you expect. For example, suppose that you identify expensive options, and you figure that implied volatility will decrease and eventually become more in line with its historical norms. Then you would want to construct a position with a *negative position vega*. A negative position vega indicates that the position will profit if implied volatility decreases. Conversely, if you are a buyer of volatility—one who identifies some underpriced situation—you would want to construct a position with a *positive position vega,* for such a position will profit if implied volatility rises. In either case, other factors such as delta, time to expiration, and so forth will have an effect on the position's actual dollar profit, but the concept of position vega is still important to a volatility trader. It does no good to identify cheap options, for example, and then establish some strange spread with a negative position vega. Such a construct would be at odds with your intended purpose—in this case, buying cheap options.

Trading Volatility

Establishing a Delta Neutral Position

Typically, when you trade volatility, you initially establish a position that is neutral. That is, the position does not have a bullish or bearish bias with respect to the movement of the underlying instrument. The reason that this is done is so that the position relies more on volatility as the vehicle determining profits or losses than on the forthcoming movements of the underlying. In reality, though, public customers cannot isolate volatility and completely remove price or time as elements in their profitability. Even if it could be done (and market makers have a difficult time themselves constructing a position that completely isolates volatility), it would cost a great deal in commissions, slippage, and bid-asked spread differential. So, for the public customers to make money trading volatility, they must often make some decisions about the price direction of the underlying instrument. However, by initially establishing a neutral position, the trader can delay those decisions about price for as long as possible. Remember that one of the tenets behind volatility trading is that it is easier to predict volatility than it is to predict the forthcoming price of the underlying. Thus, if that more difficult decision can be deferred, then by all means do so.

When the term *neutral* is used, it is generally meant that the position is *delta neutral*. That is, there are at least two components to the position (perhaps a long put and a long call) that tend to offset each other for short-term movements by the underlying instrument.

Example: Suppose that XYZ is trading at 60, and that you are considering the purchase of volatility, namely by buying a July 60 straddle (the simultaneous purchase of both the July 60 call and the July 60 put). The deltas of the put and the call can be used to construct a completely neutral position. Suppose that the following information is known:

XYZ STOCK	OPTION	OPTION PRICE	DELTA
60	July 60 call	5.50	0.60
60	July 60 put	3.63	−0.40

A delta neutral position would be constructed by buying two of these calls and three of these puts. That is, two of the long calls would have a net position delta of +1.20 (two times 0.60), whereas the three long puts would have a net position delta of −1.20 (3 × −0.40). Whenever only two options are involved in a position, the delta neutral ratio can be computed by dividing the deltas of the two options involved.

Neutral Ratio = (delta of call) / (delta of put) = 0.60/−0.40 = −1.50

Ignoring the minus sign, this ratio is 1.50, so any ratio involving the purchase of 1.5 times as many puts as calls would be delta neutral. It could be three puts and two calls, as above, or it could be 75 puts and 50 calls—any quantity in the three-to-two ratio would be acceptable and would be delta neutral.

As a practical matter, when quantities traded are small, or the delta neutral ratio is only slightly larger than one-to-one, you might simply buy an equal number of puts and calls when establishing a long straddle, for example. The profit graphs in **Figure 9.5** compare the profitability, at expiration, of owning the neutral straddle (three puts and two calls) versus that of a normal straddle (two puts and two calls).

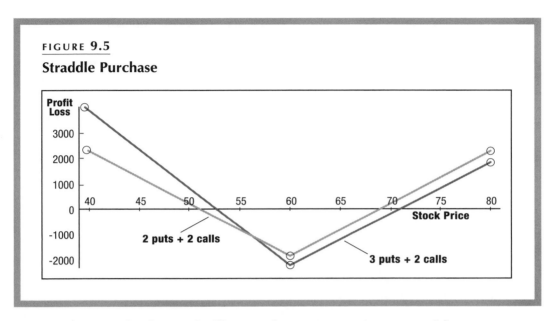

FIGURE 9.5

Straddle Purchase

Determining Whether Volatility Is Cheap, Expensive, or Neither

The first step in trading volatility is to determine situations in which volatility is out of line, that is, when it is either too cheap or too expensive. One way to do this would be to look at a lot of charts such as Figure 9.1. However, that would require a lot of tedious work, and it still does not give a firm definition as to what is cheap or expensive. Another, more rigorous, way is to look at the current level of volatility with respect to where volatility has traded in the past.

Identifying the Current Percentile Ranking

For the moment, let's put aside the question of just which volatility measure to use, in order to define the concept of percentiles. Most people are familiar with percentiles—they are used to tell us where an individual item falls within a broad array of similar items. For example, if a high school senior scored 1300 on the SAT test, he might fall into the 85th percentile—indicating that his score is higher than 85 percent of all of the other people who have taken the test. (For the record, this author has no idea where the 85th percentile really is for the SAT test. This is just a general example.) In a similar manner, if you have a long history of volatility measurements for a particular stock as well as the measurement of today's volatility, then it is a simple matter to determine the percentile that today's volatility falls within.

Example: XYZ options are currently trading with an implied volatility of 54 percent. It is fairly typical to weight the implied volatilities of individual XYZ options to arrive at a composite volatility, such as this one: 54 percent. On the surface, you have no idea whether 54 percent represents an expensive or cheap level of implied volatility. But suppose that you also have saved the daily composite implied volatility reading of XYZ, using closing prices, in a database. Now, you might look at this composite figure for all of the past 600 trading days and then determine into which percentile the current 54 percent reading falls. This would be a typical way of determining the current percentile of implied volatility.

You might also compute the current percentile of historical volatility in the same manner. In any case, if the current reading falls into the 10th percentile or lower, the volatility can be considered to be cheap; if it is in the 90th percentile or higher, the volatility can be considered to be expensive.

Using the Two Volatility Measures

There are only two types of volatility: historical (also called actual or, sometimes, statistical) and implied. Historical volatility tells you how fast the underlying security *has been* changing in price. Implied volatility is the option market's guess as to how fast the underlying *will be* changing in price during the life of the option. It is easy to see that these might rightfully be completely different numbers. For example, take the case of a stock that is awaiting approval from the FDA for a new drug application. Often, such a stock will trade in a narrow range, so historical (actual) volatility is low, but the options will be quite inflated, indicating high implied volatility that reflects the expectation of a gap in the stock price when the FDA ruling is made.

Thus, you are faced with the decision of whether to use historical or implied volatility in your analysis of a prospective position. But, to make things even more difficult, you might need to consider both of these volatilities in more detail. For example, when considering historic volatility traders usually look at the 10-day, 20-day, 50-day, and perhaps even 100-day or 1-year historical volatility. These, too, can be extremely different numbers. Assume, for example, that the following statistical volatilities exist:

XYZ Historical Volatility

10-day: 8 percent
20-day: 13 percent
50-day: 15 percent
100-day: 19 percent

The fact that these numbers are so disparate reflects what has happened to

XYZ prices in the past 100 days. Apparently, 100 days ago prices were quite volatile and were bouncing around a lot. However, the current market action has been very uniform, which indicates a lessened actual volatility. Thus, the numbers get smaller and smaller as the look-back period is shortened.

Furthermore, assume that implied volatility is currently about 20 percent for these XYZ options.

So what are you to do when trying to analyze a volatility trade position? Which volatility out of this myriad of numbers should you use? Obviously, there is no way to say for sure. If there were, then all volatility traders would be millionaires. But some reasonable approaches can be taken.

First, do not assume that implied and historical volatility will be equal. That is, the fact that XYZ implieds are 20 percent and the near-term statistical volatilities are much lower does not indicate that this is a good volatility selling candidate. In fact, in certain markets, implied volatility and historical volatility can remain at disparate levels for long periods of time, perhaps aligning only when the underlying makes a violent move of some sort.

When discussing historical versus implied volatility, it is useful to know that a study recently pointed out that, assuming that historical and implied volatility are the same now and are going to be the same in the future, straddle buying should produce a profit more than 80 percent of the time. Experienced volatility traders can tell you that 80 percent is too high of a general probability estimate for straddle buys. Obviously, individual cases can have probabilities like that, but not all. In other words, the fact that implied and historical volatility happen to be equal to each other does not mean that a good straddle buy is at hand. By inference, it also does not mean that they will be equal in the future.

With respect to implied volatility, you should have some idea of whether the current reading is high or low. If it is low, then option buying strategies should be considered, for if implied volatility were to return to the middle of its range, then positions that contain long options would benefit. If implied volatility is high, then, after ascertaining that no fundamental reason exists why it should be high (takeover rumor, for example), option selling strategies can be considered. That's why percentiles are suggested.

You can determine a good volatility trading situation by initially looking at the percentile of current implied volatility, leaving historical or statistical volatility as a measure to be used in the analysis of any desired trading position to be established. However, for the sole purpose of determining whether options are cheap or expensive, you should use only implied volatility.

Buying Volatility

Having determined that a volatility position is going to be neutral to begin with and that it is going to use the current level of implied volatility to determine where cheap or expensive options exist, you can now lay out the specifics of a volatility buying or selling strategy.

Volatility buying is one of the most attractive options trading strategies that exists. It has limited risk, has the potential for large profits, and is not a high-maintenance strategy, so it can be used by the public customer nearly as effectively as it can by the professional trader.

In particular, *volatility buying* refers to buying straddles when implied volatility is low, and when certain other statistical criteria are satisfied. The straddle should meet four specific criteria before you buy it:

- Implied volatility must be very low.
- A probability calculator of some sort must indicate that the stock has an 80 percent chance of reaching the straddle's break-even points.
- A review of past movements of the underlying must indicate that it has frequently been able to make moves of the required size in the required amount of time.
- A review of the fundamentals must indicate that there is no fundamental reason why volatility is low (a cash tender offer has been received, for example).

This approach is really a concession that market prediction—predicting the magnitude of stock prices—cannot be done. That is, when you buy these straddles, you do not know whether the stock is going up or down (and do not care). In addition, the strategy is easier to manage on a day-to-day basis than is directional trading.

Note that this form of straddle buying is completely volatility related—it is distinctly different from what I consider to be an erroneous notion that you often read in option-related literature: that you should select the straddle based on what you expect the stock can do. If you knew how far the stock was going to move, that is, you were able to predict its volatility, you probably wouldn't need any straddle analysis at all.

The one thing that makes sense about straddle buying is that the large unknowns in the stock market—gap moves related to either a complete new piece of corporate fundamental information or a general market change (read *crash*)—are beneficial to straddle owners. The straddle buyer loves times when the stock moves by a huge amount. Huge moves are seen every day in stocks, usually related to some surprising news event. Moves of that size are so far outside the standard of normal volatility and price movement that they could never be predicted, but at least a straddle owner can benefit from it. Only chaos theory, which states that a small change in a seemingly irrelevant place can have great effects (perhaps even chaotic ones) later, seems to allow for the sorts of moves that are commonplace in stock trading. It applies to many areas of nature, and some people have tried to apply it to the stock market as well, especially after the crash of 1987, which did not seem predictable by any standard branch of mathematics, but did seem possible under chaos theory. If chaos theory says that you cannot predict the stock market, and many say that it does, then perhaps you should stop trying to do so and instead concentrate on building quality strategies. Such a strategy would certainly be straddle buying when implied volatility is low.

A fairly detailed example should help clarify the four steps to buying a straddle. These same concepts can be applied to other volatility buying strategies, such as the purchase of a *strangle* (simultaneously buying both an out-of-the-money call and an out-of-the-money put) or the purchase of a *backspread* (typically constructed by simultaneously selling, say, one in-the-money call and buying two at-the-money calls). These strategies all entail limited risk and have unlimited profit potential in one or both directions.

Previously, the fictional stock XYZ has been used in examples, but in this one an actual stock will be used, Nokia (NOK), just because it is sometimes easier to relate to a specific stock when a specific strategy is being examined in detail. These are actual prices that existed in October 1999, in reference to buying the April 105 straddle.

Example: Suppose you are investigating straddle purchases and find the following: Nokia (NOK): 103, Composite Implied Volatility: 36 percent

Criterion #1: The options must be cheap

Looking back at the previous 600 trading days for NOK, its composite implied volatility ranged from 34 to 82 percent. In fact, the current reading of 36 percent is determined to be in the 3rd percentile of implied volatility. Consequently, the first criterion for straddle buying—that the options are cheap (i.e., in the 10th percentile or lower of past implied volatility readings) is satisfied.

In general, a volatility buying strategy should use options with at least three months, and preferably, five or six months, until expiration. If you adhere to this period, the options can be held for quite some time without being ravaged by time decay. Conversely, if the straddle initially has too little time remaining, the time decay may be too difficult of an obstacle for the buyer to overcome.

Specifically, the following prices actually existed. First, notice that the two options have slightly different implied volatilities. In theory, they should have the same, but the offering (asked) price of the put is set at a slightly higher implied volatility than that of the call. Also, notice that both of these individual implied volatilities are slightly higher than the composite reading, but are near the composite figure.

OPTION	ASKED PRICE	IMPLIED VOLATILITY	DELTA
April 105 call:	11.75	37.3%	0.56
April 105 put:	10.63	38.8%	−0.44

Criterion #2: The probabilities of success must be high

To satisfy this criterion, you need a probability calculator, preferably one that gives not only the probability of the stock's being above a certain price at the end of a particular time period, but also the probability of its being above a certain price at any time during the time period. A neutral straddle would entail buying 56 puts and 44 calls, but for the purposes of this example, let's assume that a simple straddle—one put and one call—will be bought in order to make the analysis easier.

The straddle price is equal to the put price plus the call price, or 22 ⅜. That means that the stock needs to move that distance above or below the strike of 105 in order to guarantee a profit on expiration day:

April 105 straddle purchase price: 22.38 (11.75 + 10.63)
Upside break-even price, at expiration: 127.38 (105 + 22.38)
Downside break-even price, at expiration: 82.63 (105 − 22.38)

In essence, you need to know what the probability is that NOK can climb to 127 ⅜ or fall to 82 ⅝ at any time during the next six months until expiration. To determine this probability, any probability calculator requires you to input a volatility so that the calculator can use it for its projections. At this point, historical (statistical) volatility comes into play in the calculations.

The historical volatility is used in the probability calculations because you are now interested in knowing how fast the stock can move, and that is exactly what historical volatility measures. For the moment, implied volatility is not of concern. Of course, deciding which historical volatility to use is a matter of some opinion. In the case of NOK, on this day, the following information is known about the past movements of the underlying stock:

Historical Volatility Readings:
10-day: 50 percent
20-day: 43 percent
50-day: 37 percent
100-day: 40 percent
50th percentile over past 600 days: 44 percent

As you are evaluating a volatility purchase, you should use the lower of these volatility readings in the probability calculator projections, so as not to overstate the case for profitability. You should err on the side of caution rather than on the side of optimism. Hence, the projection used would be 37 percent. Note that this level of volatility is, coincidentally, about equal to the current implied volatility reading. It also points out how cheaply the marketplace is evaluating NOK options, for it is projecting volatility to be very low in light of where it has been in the past. That is very typical where cheap options are concerned, since the options are usually valued well below where history indicates they should be.

Returning to the example, you would use the following inputs:

Probability Calculation:
Stock price: 103
Straddle price: 22.38
Time to expiration: 6 months (132 trading days)
Volatility Projection: 37 percent

The probability calculator returns the projection that, given those inputs, there is a 92 percent chance that NOK will trade at one or the other of the breakeven points at some time during the life of the straddle.

As long as that probability is at least 80 percent, then the second criterion is satisfied. In this case, it is well satisfied.

Criterion #3: Actual past stock price movements must confirm the stock's ability to make such a move

The second criterion was based on past historical volatilities, which reflect stock price movements to a certain extent. However, this criterion is more specific. You want to look at actual price movements (for example, a chart) of NOK to see how often it has been able to move 22.38 points in six months, in either direction. If you have charts and a programming capability, you can find the answer to this question specifically. Otherwise, you can merely observe the price chart and attempt to estimate this probability. At the time of this analysis, the chart of NOK was as shown in **Figure 9.6**.

This chart has been specially sized, so that the height of the horizontal boxes

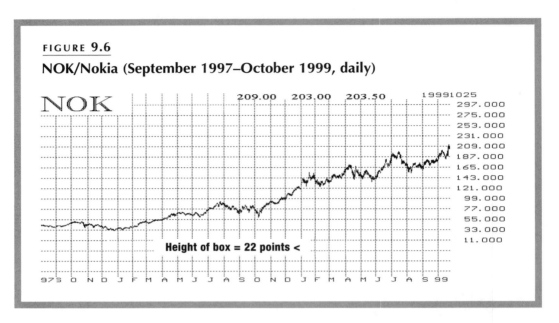

FIGURE 9.6

NOK/Nokia (September 1997–October 1999, daily)

is 22 points, about equal to the price of the straddle. This scale makes it easy to see whether the stock is able to move the required distance (22 points) in the allotted time frame (six months). As you can see, NOK often moved 22 points near the right side of the chart, but not two years earlier, when it was a $30 or $40 stock. A rigorous analysis showed, in fact, that it had moved 22 points only about 60 percent of the time on this chart. That is a nice percentage, but not the 80 percent that you should require to satisfy criterion number 3.

However, this analysis needs to be refined a little: you really should be looking at *percentage* moves, especially for a stock that has increased this much in price over the two-year period. In this case, the straddle costs 22.38, 22 percent of the current stock price (103). Hence, the question that needs to be answered to satisfy criterion number 3 is how often does NOK move 22 percent in a six-month time period? (When considering percentages, you could use a lognormal chart for observation.) A rigorous analysis of data shows that NOK moved 22 percent in six months nearly 98 percent of the time on this chart. That easily satisfies criterion number 3.

Criterion #4: There is no fundamental reason why volatility is low
Finally, you must check the fundamentals to determine if there is a valid reason why NOK's implied volatility is low. One reason might be a takeover via a cash bid or tender offer for all the shares of NOK. Obviously, if a cash bid were made,

and it was likely to be completed, there would be no further volatility in a stock, and the options would be cheap. That was not the case for Nokia. Another reason might be a pending merger between NOK and another company. The merged entity might have a totally different statistical volatility than the current NOK stock. Again, that was not the case for NOK. About the only other reason that a stock would lose its volatility is if the company had matured dramatically and its business, which once was considered highly speculative, had become more stable. This sort of thing has happened with some Internet companies (America Online, for example). However, that also was not pertinent to NOK.

Hence all four criteria were satisfied and this was an excellent candidate for a straddle purchase.

Following Up on a Straddle Purchase

Of course, selecting a position or a strategy is only half the battle. You need to manage the position once it is in place. A long discussion could ensue on this topic, but to keep it short, here are some suggestions regarding how much to risk and how to take profits, should they occur.

First, as far as risk goes, you *could* risk the entire straddle price since it is a fixed amount. That would not be an unreasonable tactic, as a lot of work went into selecting a high-probability position. Or you could limit risk to something like 60 percent of the initial straddle purchase price, prepared mentally to stop yourself out if the straddle bid dropped to that level. In either case, you have limited risk and very large profit potential, because a straddle can increase in value by several times its initial price. Using the 60 percent stop still allows you to hold a six-month straddle for nearly five months, because it takes that long for time decay to wear away the straddle price, even if the stock remains near the striking price of the straddle.

There are many ways to take profits, but you should attempt to let profits run as far as possible without being greedy. The risk of greed can be avoided by taking a partial profit as soon as the stock crosses through a break-even point, or if it breaks through a technically significant level (resistance on the upside or support on the downside): sell a third or a half of the option that is in-the-money and sell all of the losing options. (This turns you into an outright option trader, but you had already become that anyway.) As soon as the underlying stock begins to make a significant move, you are no longer a neutral trader. Rather, your position now has a delta (positive if the stock has moved up, or negative if it has moved down), and you must now manage the position more as you would a long option position than a neutral straddle. That is why this approach is recommended.

Finally, if the underlying stock should continue to move favorably, use a trailing moving stop. Perhaps the 20-day simple moving average of the stock price on a closing basis would be sufficient.

The chart of NOK after the straddle was purchased is shown in **Figure 9.7**. The simple 20-day moving average is marked on the chart, as is the upside break-even point (the line drawn at the 127 price level). Once NOK crossed above the upside break-even point—and it took only a couple of days for that to happen, as NOK traded up through 130 before the end of November—April 105 puts were sold to recapture whatever premium might be left in them, and half of the profitable April 105 calls were sold. Beginning with those adjustments, the remaining calls were held, using the 20-day moving average of the stock price as a mental closing stop. As you can see, NOK traded up into January of 2000 before finally having a bad few days and closing below the 20-day moving average. That day is marked as "stopped out" in Figure 9.7. The stock was above 155 at that time, so the remaining long calls would have been sold at a price of 50 or more (since their striking price was 105, they were 50 points in the money with the stock at 155).

Of course, there is another way that the volatility buyer can make money: if implied volatility increases while the position is being held. This method of profit does not even require that the underlying trade up to or through the break-even

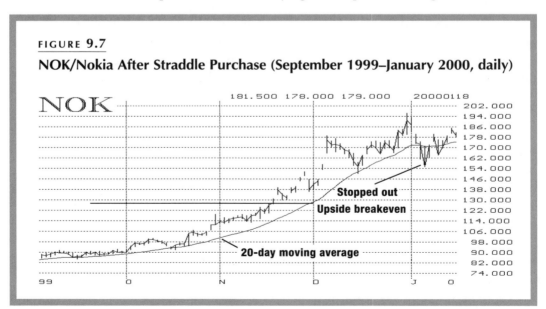

FIGURE **9.7**

NOK/Nokia After Straddle Purchase (September 1999–January 2000, daily)

points. If you see profits developing in this manner while you hold the position, you should take some partial profits—perhaps even closing down the entire position if implied volatility should return to its 50th percentile.

There are other methods that you could use with regard to the long straddle, including a method called *trading against the straddle,* which is somewhat similar to taking partial profits as suggested above. The point to remember is that you want to allow at least a portion of your position to make unlimited profits. Thus, the use of targets or other profit-limiting strategies is not recommended in conjunction with this approach.

Selling Volatility
Naked Option Selling

Simplistically, you could just reverse the process discussed above and use it for selling volatility. The simplest volatility selling strategy is to sell naked options unhedged. This is not necessarily the best or smartest approach, but it can be analyzed easily. For naked options, you would probably want to sell a strangle: out-of-the-money puts and out-of-the-money calls. In that case, you would want to satisfy the same criteria used for buying volatility and adjust them for volatility selling. When selling naked options, you are most concerned with the probability of the stock hitting the strike of any naked option, that is, with the probability of the naked option becoming an in-the-money option. This probability is particularly important, because a naked option seller should most likely close out or roll a naked option once it becomes perilous, that is, when it goes into-the-money.

The strangle should meet the following criteria before you sell:

- The options are expensive—trading in the 90th percentile of implied volatility or higher.
- The probability of making money is high. A probability calculator can once again determine the chances of the stocks hitting the break-even points. However, in the case of naked option selling, you want the probability of ever hitting either of the break-even points during the life of the position to be small, something on the order of 25 percent or less.
- Scrutiny of the stock's chart reveals the stock has not often made moves large enough to be able to place any of the options in-the-money during the life of the position.
- Fundamentals show no obvious reason why the options have gotten expensive. This might include a pending earnings announcement, or an announce-

ment of a new product, or a business combination, or a lawsuit verdict, or the recommendation of a government agency (the FDA, for example) regarding an important product. When options get expensive, though, there is always the possibility that someone has inside information which you will not be able to learn in advance. This might include takeover bids or perhaps earnings pre-announcements.

For these reasons, selling unhedged naked options is often an unwise strategy, unless the trader is highly experienced, well capitalized, and has a high tolerance for risk. Even such traders generally concentrate on selling index options and futures options, as opposed to stock options, for there is far less chance of a severe trading gap in those markets. However, there are some alternatives to outright naked option selling as a strategy for selling volatility.

Credit Spreading

One alternative is to sell credit spreads instead. That is, sell out-of-the-money options, but then simultaneously buy options that are even further out-of-the-money. It is a naked strangle protected by a long strangle. This strategy is called a *condor.* It is also sometimes known as *buying the wings.*

Example: With XYZ at 60, you determine that its options are very expensive. So you implement the following strategy because you want some protection; you do not want to have naked options:

Buy the July 75 call	Sell the July 50 put
Sell the July 70 call	Buy the July 45 put

Thus the position consists of a credit bull spread in the puts and a credit bear spread in the calls. The maximum risk is 5 points, less whatever credit is received when the position is initially established.

The margin required for this condor position is the risk—on both spreads, or 10 points less any initial credit received. This is considerably less than the margin requirement for a naked option, which is:

- Margin for selling a naked stock option: 20 percent of the value of the underlying stock, plus the option premium, less any out-of-the-money amount. Notwithstanding this formula, the requirement cannot be less than 15 percent of the value of the underlying stock.
- Margin for selling a naked index option: 15 percent of the value of the underlying index, plus the option premium, less any out-of-the-money amount. Notwithstanding this formula, the requirement cannot be less than 10 percent of the value of the underlying index.

A lot of novice traders employ this credit spread strategy but soon find out that commission costs are huge relative to profits realized, and that profit potential is small in comparison to risk potential. Moreover, there is the risk of early assignment, which is substantial in the case of cash-based index options and which may change margin requirements dramatically, thereby forcing the strategist to exit the position prematurely at a loss.

However, if you are careful in establishing a position that satisfies the criteria as stated above, and you are careful about managing your positions, the sale of volatility through naked options or credit spreads can be profitable.

An Alternative Strategy for Selling Volatility

Most traders find both of these strategies, naked option selling and credit spreading, to be more trouble than they are worth. They wonder if there is not a volatility selling strategy that has limited risk with the potential of larger profits. There is one strategy that fits this description, although it is not a common one. This strategy benefits from a drop in option prices (that is, a decline in implied volatility). The most expensive options, pricewise (but not in terms of implied volatility), are the longer-term ones. Selling options such as these and hedging them can be a good strategy.

The simplest strategy that has the desired traits is selling a calendar spread, that is, selling a longer-term option and hedging it by buying a short-term option at the same strike. True, both are expensive (and the near-term option might even have a slightly higher implied volatility than the longer-term one); but the longer-term option trades with a far greater absolute price so that if both become cheaper, the longer-term one can decline quite a bit further in points than the near-term one. An example should help to illustrate this situation.

Example: Suppose that the following prices exist sometime in August. Assume that they are expensive options and satisfy the first criterion for volatility selling, options in the 90th percentile or higher.

XYZ: 119

October 120 call: 6.75

January 120 call: 11.25

The strategy entails selling one January 120 call and buying one October 120 call. At the above prices, such a spread would bring a credit of 4 1/2 points (the difference in the option prices) into the account. Since this is a spread strategy, it should be closed out at October expiration. The spread would profit if it can subsequently be bought back for a price less than 4 1/2. Such a strategy can be evaluated with the same criteria as stated above when volatility selling was discussed.

Consider several scenarios. First, if XYZ collapses in price, the October 120 call will expire worthless, and if XYZ is below 105 at October expiration, the January 120 call would sell for less than 4½ and the spread will profit. Second, if XYZ rises dramatically in price, the time value of the January 120 call will drop, allowing the spread to be repurchased for less than 4½ if XYZ is above 138 or so at October expiration. Where is the risk? It occurs if XYZ is near the 120 strike at October expiration. In that case, the October call will expire worthless, but the January 120 call will most assuredly sell for more than 4½ points, so there will be a loss in that case when the position is closed. **Figure 9.8** depicts how the profitability of this spread would look at October expiration.

None of these scenarios factor in any drop in implied volatility. But, if XYZ options return to the more normal pricing structure, the strategy would benefit. For example, at the current time this spread would normally sell for about 3½ points, not 4½. It is the current high level of implied volatility that is producing the increased spread price. Figure 9.8 also shows where profits might lie if implied volatility drops to the 50th percentile of past XYZ readings.

The above strategy is technically known as a *reverse calendar spread*. A modification to this spread strategy can create a potentially even more desirable position: to buy a call with a higher strike (while still selling the same call as in the reverse calendar spread). To keep things neutral, you would buy more options than you are selling. For example, sell one XYZ January 120 call as before, but

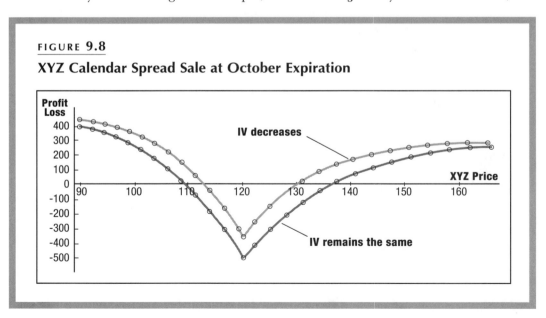

FIGURE **9.8**

XYZ Calendar Spread Sale at October Expiration

now buy two XYZ October 130 calls (note the strike is 130). Two against one is approximately a neutral position.

Again, the spread brings an initial credit into the account, and you will remove the spread at October expiration. As before, if XYZ drops sharply in price, the spread will profit because there is some point at which the January 120 call can be bought back at a price less than the initial credit received from the spread. If XYZ were to skyrocket to the upside, however, this spread could make unlimited profits because there are two long calls and only one short call. A decline in implied volatility while the spread is in place would be a benefit as well. This position has limited risk until October expiration because the long October calls protect the short January calls. The greatest risk in this spread occurs only when XYZ is exactly at 130—the strike of the long calls—at October expiration. This ratio spread's risk is greater than that of the reverse calendar spread described above, but that is to be expected since it has far greater upside profit potential.

There is a caveat to these strategies when they are used for stock or index options: due to the stock option exchanges' antiquated margin rules, the sale of the longer-term option must be margined as a naked option (even though it is clearly protected by the short-term option until October expiration). Hence these strategies are most suitable for traders who have excess equity available from their stocks or bonds. That equity can be used for the margin requirement for the option position, without necessitating the sale of the stocks or bonds. For futures options, these types of spreads are considered hedged, a far more logical approach.

In summary, these reverse strategies are applicable whenever options have become very expensive. They entail limited risk and can make money if the underlying is volatile, (it rises or falls far enough)—or if implied volatility declines (the options become less expensive). The maximum risk arises if the stock or index is right at the striking price of the long options when those options expire.

Key Benefits of Volatility Trading

Volatility trading is a predictable way to approach the market, because volatility almost invariably trades in a range and therefore its value can be estimated with a great deal more precision than can the actual prices of the underlying instrument. Even so, you must be careful in your approach to volatility trading because diligent research is needed to determine if, in fact, volatility is cheap or expensive. As with any systematic approach to the market, if your research is sloppy, you cannot expect to achieve superior results.

Volatility buying is useful for many traders, novice and professional alike, and should be added to their arsenal of strategies. However, volatility selling is a more professional strategy, and you should carefully evaluate whether that strategy is suitable for your investment philosophy before attempting to use it. However, with a rigorous approach based on probability analysis, you should be able to profit from volatility trading. The true advantage is that, with proper construction of positions—ones with unlimited profit potential and limited risk—you can approach the market in a manner that is relatively stress-free. Moreover, you can make money from either stock price movement or from a return of volatility to its previously normal levels. These factors make the strategy of volatility trading one in which the practitioner should be able to get a good night's sleep, regardless of the movements of the overall stock market.

CHAPTER 10

Enhancing Technical Analysis by Incorporating Sentiment

BERNIE SCHAEFFER

"It's all in the charts," say the technicians. "Nonsense," say the "random walkers." "One cannot predict future prices from charts because stock price movement is random and the current stock price reflects all available knowledge and expectations about a company's business prospects and is thus the best estimate of that stock's future price."

As a practicing technician and Market Technicians Association member, I naturally disagree with the random-walk argument. But I also take issue with the technicians' argument. I agree wholeheartedly with my fellow technicians that it is ludicrous to argue that there is no way to predict future stock prices based on the study of past price and volume patterns. But at the same time, I strongly believe that the chart does not "tell all," as pure chart analysis will not reveal the sentiment component that is so vital to successfully predicting future stock prices.

The basis of sentiment analysis is contrarianism. According to Wall Street analyst and author William O'Neil, "The stock market is neither efficient nor random. It is not efficient because there are too many poorly conceived opinions; it is not random because strong investor emotions can create (price) trends." (See *Market Wizards* by Jack D. Schwager, New York Institute of Finance, 1989.)

"Poorly conceived opinions" come in many flavors on Wall Street, and these opinions very often fly in the face of the "known facts" for many years. For example, the *Business Week* annual December poll of economists has underestimated the rate of economic growth for the following year by $1\frac{1}{2}$ to 2 percentage points for each of the past four years. Such an error is huge in magnitude relative to the average annual growth rate over this period of about 4 percent. Moreover, it is the result of the near-universal belief among economists and Wall Street's "opinion leaders" that the powerful economic growth of the second half of the 1990s was aberrant and would revert to the mean. In the field of behavioral finance, such behavior is know as "cognitive dissonance," or the holding of a belief plainly at odds with the evidence, usually because the belief has been held and cherished for a long time. As was noted in the December 18, 1999 issue of *The Economist,* "psychiatrists sometimes call this 'denial.'" So much for "efficient markets" and the ability of their "sophisticated participants" to correctly assess "all the known facts."

"But," you might ask, "are there exploitable inefficiencies in the financial markets that result from this cognitive dissonance on Wall Street?" The answer is a resounding "yes!" In the second half of 1998, the yield on 30-year Treasury bonds plunged to a record low 4.70 percent, even as the economic crises in Asia and Russia convinced economists and Wall Street that the world economy was headed for deflation, recession, and quite possibly an economic depression. Treasury bond yields as low as 4 percent were forecast for 1999 and a bear market in stocks was declared by numerous widely quoted pundits in August, September, and October 1998.

In other words, the Wall Street "experts" were eagerly anticipating being rewarded at long last in 1999 for years of underestimating the resilience of the U.S. economy and the U.S. stock market. The reward would be in the form of a bear market in stocks combined with low interest rates. In fact, the real economic world in 1999 proved to be little changed from its recent past—cognitive dissonance-based fear on Wall Street had simply reached a new peak in late 1998. Economic growth accelerated to new heights in 1999. By the fourth quarter, annualized real gross domestic product (GDP) growth had soared above 6 percent.

How was this strong economic backdrop reflected in the financial markets? From a low of about 1,500 in October 1998, the Nasdaq Composite Index (COMP) rallied to 2,000 by year-end to post a solid 40 percent gain for the year. Nevertheless, the December 1998 *Business Week* Market Forecast Survey, published amid talk of recession and potential depression for 1999, pegged the COMP at 2,081 for year-end 1999, little changed from its 1998 close. The COMP in fact closed out 1999 above 4,000, nearly *double* this consensus forecast. Moreover, bonds in 1999 experienced their second worst total return year since 1927, with yields rising as high as 6.50 percent.

Proper Application of Contrary Thinking

Illustrating how horribly wrong the opinion leaders on Wall Street can be over the course of years (and sometimes decades) serves as a warning against an uncritical acceptance of conventional investment wisdom and as a demonstration of the folly of the "efficient market hypothesis." To use sentiment analysis to profitably exploit the opportunities created by the sloppy thinking on Wall Street and the fear and greed that such sloppy thinking begets you must employ *contrary thinking*.

Humphrey Neill was perhaps the most lucid and intelligent contrarian of modern times. Neill was an author, investment adviser, and analyst who published an investment newsletter from the 1940s through the 1960s. He wrote a number of valuable books on investing, including *The Art of Contrary Thinking* (Caldwell, Idaho: Claxton Printers, Ltd., 1992) which was first published in 1954. Neill described contrary theory as "a way of thinking" and "a thinking tool...not a crystal ball. It is plainly nothing more than developing the habit of doing what every textbook on learning advises, namely, to look at both sides of all questions."

Although Neill had much to say about the habits of the "crowd" and its implications for investors, he was very careful not to define the theory of contrary opinion in terms of the still-popular belief that it entails always going against the crowd. In fact, Neill believed that it was most important for investors to develop their ability to think critically and independently and to develop a healthy, though not all-consuming, skepticism. If the result of such a process was an opinion consistent with that of the crowd, so be it, according to Neill.

Given that the crowd tends to think emotionally rather than critically and that "no trait is stronger...than that of defending one's own opinion and of being unwilling to admit error in judgment," it is likely that those who apply a true contrarian approach will often reach conclusions that differ widely from those of the consensus. But Neill took great pains to describe the contrarian thought process as a *synthesis* of the components of the prevailing opinion and the components of a *contrary* view of the prevailing opinion. This is because "not every element of a generalized opinion may be wrong, or ill-timed...in this way, we avoid denying *facts* which are elements in the generalized opinions we are analyzing contrarily." In other words, it is foolish to dismiss all elements of the consensus opinion *a priori,* and in fact there are times when the consensus should not be disputed. This is quite far afield from the popular belief that contrarians reject the consensus belief out of hand.

Regarding the more specific process of analyzing investor sentiment, Neill had much to say about the "crowd" as represented by the "investing public." The following quotes from *The Art of Contrary Thinking* contain the basic concepts behind sentiment analysis.

- "Because a crowd does not think, but acts on impulses, public opinions are frequently wrong."

- "Is the public wrong *all the time?* The answer is, decidedly, 'No.' The public is perhaps right more of the time than not. In stock market parlance, the public is right *during* the trends but wrong at both ends!"
- "The crowd is most enthusiastic and optimistic when it should be cautious and prudent; and is most fearful when it should be bold."
- "The crowd has always been found to be wrong when it counted most to be right... the crowd is wrong at the *terminals* of trends, but is right, on the average, *during* the trends."
- "One finds that over- and underestimates of the *generality* of crowd opinions ... are not uncommon."
- "No problem connected with the Theory of Contrary Opinion is more difficult to solve than... (a) how to know what prevailing general opinions are; and (b) how to measure their prevalence and intensity."

The fact that the crowd is frequently wrong is beyond dispute even in the context of conventional investment wisdom. But the fact that *the crowd is right more frequently than it is wrong and is consistently wrong only at critical turning points* in the market is not at all accepted or understood on Wall Street. In fact, one of the major mistakes the legion of bears made throughout the bull market of the 1990s was to assume that the increasing public participation in and enthusiasm for the market was a clear signal of the bull market's imminent demise. The public will be caught flatfooted and way overinvested at the ultimate top of the bull market that began in the early 1980s, just as it has been caught at every ultimate market top in history. In the meantime, the successful investor needs the tools to recognize whether investor sentiment is consistent with the trend period in which the public is right, or whether sentiment is warning of an impending end at which the public will be disastrously wrong.

The final two quotes above from Neill relate to the critical issue of developing a workable methodology for sentiment analysis—the objective measurement of investor sentiment. Time and again in the 1990s, the opinion leaders on Wall Street and in the financial media portrayed themselves as a "bold minority," flying in the face of conventional bullish wisdom to save investors from the inevitable disaster of a "bursting market bubble." Yet their belief that the market is way overvalued and is headed for a sharp fall, if not a crash, has *actually comprised the conventional wisdom about the stock market throughout the 1990s.* The disastrous investment consequence of this sloppy thinking was the failure to recognize the pervasiveness of the skepticism that has accompanied this bull market.

Interrelationships of Sentiment Indicators with Technicals

In my opinion, there is no way you can successfully trade the market without a solid foundation in technical analysis. The components of such a foundation must include an awareness of the traditional technical indicators, as well as the development of a package of technical indicators that work well for you as "trade drivers." You need to be aware of the traditional technical indicators simply because they are popular, and as such, they will define certain price levels and conditions that will drive others to act. In other words, you should make these indicators part of your core awareness level, and while they may also play some role in driving your trades, it is best if it is not a primary role.

Your primary technical trade drivers should include indicators that, while not necessarily unique or proprietary to your work, are at the very least not found in "Technical Analysis 101" discussions. To the extent you can develop an array of such indicators without rendering your approach too complex, your chances of achieving success in trading will increase. (Of course, a trader's personality, risk tolerance, and money management skills are also vital to one's ultimate trading success.)

Unfortunately, there are critical periods in the market when technical analysis is silent, or worse yet, gets caught up in the very emotions in the market that the technical approach is supposed to avoid. A recent example of such a period was in the fall of 1998, when a huge preponderance of my technical brethren had moved into the bearish camp. To illustrate how sentiment analysis can add major value to technical analysis, consider the following Bernie Schaeffer market commentary from the September 1998 Special Bulletin of The *Option Advisor* newsletter (italics are those used at the time of publication):

Are we in a bear market? One would surely think so if one exercised the intestinal fortitude required to pay attention to the daily panicky cacophony from the financial media. The problem is that while it may *feel* like a bear market, *it is not a bear market by any reasonable definition.* Take a look at the accompanying chart of the S&P 500 Index (SPX) from 1987 to date, along with its 20-month moving average [reproduced here as Figure 10.3 on page 236]. The bear market periods are very clearly defined by the areas circled on this chart in 1987–1988, 1990–1991, and 1994 in which the SPX dipped below this key long-term moving average. Going back a bit further in time, dips by the

SPX below its 20-month moving average occurred during the bear markets of 1973-1974, 1977, and 1981-1982. Fast-forwarding to today, we find the SPX has thus far *successfully tested support at its 20-month moving average* and now stands 5% above this key level. Bear markets have also been defined as beginning upon corrections of 20% or more from a bull market high. And once again we find the "bear label" does not fit, as the lowest close by the SPX on this correction was 19.6% from its highs. Why am I going to such great lengths to "prove" that we have not yet moved into a bear market? Because investor sentiment right now is so abjectly negative that it can only be remotely considered "normal" within the context of a bear market. And if, as I argue, we are still in a bull market by objective standards, then the implications of this extremely negative sentiment are unambiguously bullish! By what standards do I qualify sentiment as "abjectly negative?" (1) Record high equity put/call ratios. (2) Readings on the CBOE Volatility Index (VIX), a measure of the fear level of option speculators, that have not been seen since the October 1987 crash. (3) Equity mutual fund outflows in August and billions of dollars flowing into low-yielding money market funds, with a record level of assets in the Fidelity Select Money Market Fund. (4) The IPO market is legally dead. (5) Over the past month, we've seen an array of "the world is coming to an end" magazine covers that compares favorably with the mountain of doom and gloom that was cranked out after the October 1987 crash. And what of the "valuation" concerns about which the bears have been complaining since Dow 5000? Over the past year, we've experienced a two-percentage point decline in the yield on 10-year Treasury notes. With the stock market just slightly higher over that same period, the earnings yield on stocks compared to the yield on 10-year notes is now at levels comparable to those at the 1987 and 1994 market bottoms. If you are currently fully invested, you should not disturb your positions; if you are currently out of the market, I strongly advise you to move to a fully invested position in the large-cap end of the market.

Note first that the fact the market had not yet moved into the logical definition of a bear market in October 1998 became irrelevant, not only to the "crowd" of the investing public, but also to Wall Street strategists and many market technicians. All were swept up in the emotions of that period, which were rife with fears about a potential global depression and a market collapse. Technicians concerned themselves heavily with such indicators of "negative breadth" as the advance/decline line, despite the fact that such indicators in the past had been no better than a coin flip at forecasting bear markets.

Another important point made in this market commentary relates to the interrelationship and symbiosis of sentiment indicators with the technicals of the market. My hypothesis in October 1998 was that we were not yet in a bear market by objective standards, yet investor sentiment as measured by my sentiment indicators was "off the charts negative" and thus had bullish implications. When such negative sentiment manifests itself during a *bear market,* it can be described as "dog bites man" and thus is not terribly significant. Bear markets by definition engender bearish sentiment, and evidence of bearish sentiment in a bear market is by no means in and of itself a reason to expect a market bottom. But negative sentiment in the context of a *bull market,* particularly if the sentiment is at a negative extreme, is more like "man bites dog." It is a relatively rare occurrence and is powerfully bullish in its implications.

Investors are normally quite bullish during bull markets and quite complacent and relatively lacking in fear on pullbacks in bull markets. It then becomes an art for the sentiment analyst to determine when this bullish sentiment has reached an extreme, at which point buying power will have become dissipated to such an extent that the market will top out. But when *negative* sentiment accompanies a bull market, the task of the "sentimentician" becomes much easier, as it is thus clear that buying power has not yet been dissipated and that the bull market has further to run before a top.

There are two major lessons to be learned from this October 1998 market commentary. First, emotional thinking and sloppy investment analysis are not limited to the "public," as professionals often fall prey to these pitfalls. This is why the disciplined and objective thought process recommended by Neill is so important to your investment success. Second, objective sentiment indicators can add very substantial value to traditional technical analysis, because sentiment extremes are *not* visible on the charts and can be viewed and measured only by a separate class of sentiment indicators. A trend that is about to end cannot be distinguished on a chart from a trend that has a long way to go in price and time. In fact, there is an old saying in technical analysis to the effect that "the chart looks prettiest just ahead of a top." But sentiment indicators can help you distinguish the pretty chart that is going to remain pretty from the pretty chart that is about to turn ugly.

Sentiment Measures

Approaches to sentiment analysis can be categorized as qualitative or quantitative. Each approach can be powerful, and this power can be enhanced exponentially by using them in tandem. Qualitative approaches do not derive their conclusions from an analysis of actual money flows. A qualitative approach involves gleaning the expectations of the market through an intensive review of newspaper and magazine articles, comments on radio and television, commentary on the Internet and in newsletters, and surveys of various market players, including advisers, futures traders, strategists, economists, and individual investors. These are very important sources of information in attempting to gauge the expectations of the market.

Reviewing all these information sources can be a time-consuming process that can become open-ended unless you focus on the most useful sources of information. In addition, not everyone "puts their money where their mouth is," so relying strictly on qualitative measures of sentiment may be less than accurate in assessing potential buying power or selling pressure. Consider, for example, the sometimes startling differences between pre-election polls and actual voting results. Finally, it can be extremely easy to trick yourself into believing that your qualitative indicators are concluding what you want them to conclude.

Quantitative sentiment measures, on the other hand, put the microscope on what individuals and money managers are actually doing with the money at their disposal by collecting transaction data on specific market instruments. For example, Schaeffer's Investment Research (Schaeffer's) collects and analyzes data in such areas as option activity, mutual fund inflows and outflows, and short interest on stocks in an attempt to objectively measure (using Neill's words) "the prevalence and intensity" of investor sentiment.

Qualitative Measures

Surveys

Neill had the following to say with regard to the forecasts of the "experts:" "Countless forecasts ... are made largely upon projecting into the future what is happening in the present." This was true back in the 1950s and it remains true today, despite the increase in the depth and breadth of the various forecasting tools. The economists surveyed by *Business Week* at year-end 1993 expected 1994 to be another good year for the bond market. But in 1994, bonds experienced their worst year since 1927. So at year-end 1994, these experts were dutifully expecting another poor year for bonds in 1995. Instead, 1995 proved to be a very strong year for bonds.

But what are the implications when forecasters *don't* extrapolate from recent trends? *Business Week* publishes a survey near the end of each calendar year in which market strategists and advisers project where the market, interest rates, and certain stocks are headed in the upcoming year. Over the past four years, this survey has proven to be a reliable contrarian indicator, as shown in the table below.

Business Week Annual Survey for the Dow Jones Industrial Average, 1996–2000

FORECAST YEAR	AVERAGE FORECAST (PERCENT CHANGE)	YEAR-END CLOSE (PERCENT CHANGE)	CLOSE/FORECAST PERCENT DIFFERENCE
1996	5,430 (+6.1%)*	6,448 (+26.0%)*	18.7
1997	6,587 (+2.2%)	7,908 (+22.6%)	20.0
1998	8,464 (+7.0%)	9,181 (+16.1%)	8.5
1999	9,567 (+4.2%)	11,497 (+25.2%)	20.2
2000	12,154 (+5.7%)	†	†

* Dow closed 1995 at 5,117, a 33.5 percent gain for the year.   † Data unavailable at press time.

Note how this group of professionals forecast *below-average* historical market returns following blistering returns in the Dow Jones Industrial Average, beginning with 1995's 33.5 percent gain. Note also how these forecasts consistently underestimated the Dow's returns as shown in the final column of the above table. The lesson in this example is that the experts have been betting *against* the underlying trend of consistent, well-above-average historical returns. As long as this "antiextrapolation" sentiment persists, these strong returns are likely to continue. Why? Because bull markets top out only when there is near-universal belief in their sustainability, as evidenced by an extrapolation (and often a magnification) by "opinion leaders" of recent returns into future expectations. Once such a strong belief level prevails, most of the money that can be committed to the market has been invested, and the path of least resistance becomes "down."

Even though annual forecasts can provide a good perspective for the upcoming year, these predictions may not be as useful in navigating the broader market on a shorter-term basis. There are, however, publications that survey traders and advisers on a weekly basis. For example, *Investors Intelligence* (www.chartcraft.com), edited by Michael Burke, surveys various investment advisers on a weekly basis and posts the results in terms of percentage bulls, percentage bears, and percentage of those looking for a correction. Note in **Figure 10.1** (see arrows) that in the few instances since 1996 when the percentage of bears equaled or exceeded the percentage of bulls, outstanding short-term buying opportunities occurred within the context of the market's longer-term uptrend.

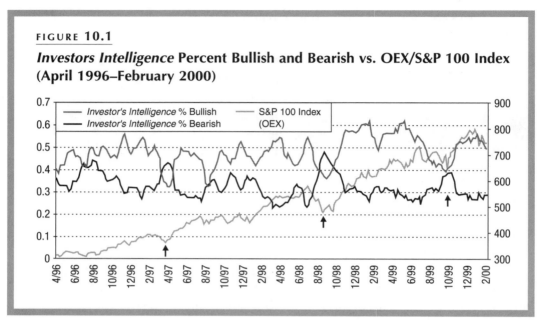

Source: Schaeffer's Daily Sentiment. See SchaeffersResearch.com.

FIGURE 10.1

Investors Intelligence **Percent Bullish and Bearish vs. OEX/S&P 100 Index (April 1996–February 2000)**

At the same time, when the bullish percentage became relatively high, short-term corrections or trading ranges soon followed.

Consensus (www.consensus-inc.com) is a weekly periodical that also publishes surveys. Its weekly poll of futures traders, "*Consensus*® Index of Bullish Market Opinion," summarizes the percentage of bulls on several futures instruments, including stocks, bonds, and gold. Similar to *Investors Intelligence,* this information can be useful for contrarians. As illustrated in **Figure 10.2**, when the percentage of bulls is relatively high (April 1998, January 1999, January 2000), the stock market tends to languish. But when the percentage of bulls is low (August 1998, October 1999), buying opportunities abound.

Why does bearish sentiment, as measured by these surveys, have bullish implications within the context of a bull market? As indicated above, this is the "man bites dog" situation. Bull markets usually beget bullish sentiment as well as complacency on pullbacks. When pullbacks in a bull market result in high levels of fear and bearishness, it is an indication that sideline cash is available to support the market and then drive it higher.

Cover Stories

Another excellent qualitative source used to gauge sentiment on a particular stock, sector, or the broader market is magazine cover stories. Why is this so? It

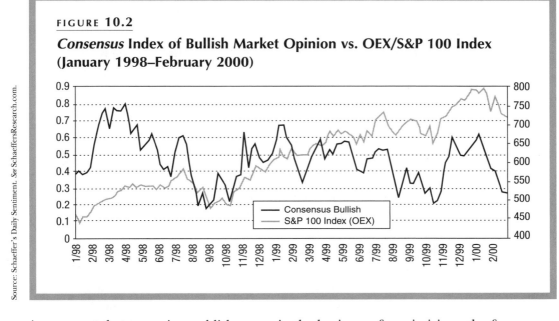

FIGURE **10.2**

***Consensus* Index of Bullish Market Opinion vs. OEX/S&P 100 Index (January 1998–February 2000)**

is no secret that magazine publishers are in the business of maximizing sales for each issue. To achieve such goals, magazines often grace their covers with the "hot" topic of the day. The crucial thing to remember is that by the time a story has become so mainstream that it graces the cover of a major news publication, most who would normally have acted on the news have probably done so. In other words, there is a good chance that the trend being portrayed in the cover story has already been fully discounted (or very nearly so) into the stock's current price *before* the story hits the newsstands. Cover stories are most effective as contrarian indicators when several publications have a similar theme with similar concluding remarks.

One of the best examples of the dramatic contrarian aftermaths of cover stories is found in the slew of bearish-themed covers that appeared in August and September 1998. A number of major publications featured covers highlighting the poor price action of the stock market and the "global economic meltdown." Taken chronologically, these included:

- *The Economist* (August 8): "Grin and Bear It" with a picture of a grinning bear wearing sunglasses reflecting a plunging chartline.
- *Barron's* (August 31): "Can the Bull Bounce Back?" The cover shows a bear steamrolling a bull.

- *Fortune* (September 6): "Has This Market Gone to the Pigs?"
- *Barron's* (September 7): "Knockout Punch?" with a bear working over a bull speed bag.
- *Fortune* (September 20): "The Crash of '98: Can the U.S. Economy Hold Up?" Cover text announced that "a troubled world may finally halt America's miracle expansion."
- *Forbes* (September 21): "Is it Armageddon … or October 1987 Revisited?"
- *Time* (September 24): "Is the Boom Over?" The cover emphasized its point by showing people tumbling down a steeply descending chartline.

These cover stories hit the street at a time when the S&P 500 Index (SPX) was testing strong technical support at its 20-month moving average (see arrow in **Figure 10.3**). This media skepticism was an excellent indication that the technical support levels would hold. In fact, the SPX went on to rally by 25 percent over the three months following the early-October 1998 bottom.

National news magazines often provide even stronger contrarian cover stories than do business publications. For example, *Time* magazine's November 15, 1999 issue, entitled "Busting Bill," depicted Bill Gates on a balloon with needles about to prick the balloon. There was definitely a great deal of doom and gloom surrounding Microsoft (MSFT) at the time with the Justice Department investiga-

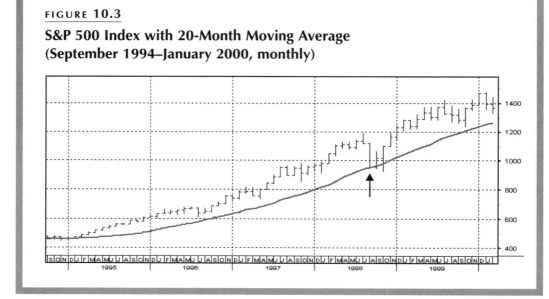

FIGURE 10.3

**S&P 500 Index with 20-Month Moving Average
(September 1994–January 2000, monthly)**

Source: Schaeffer's Daily Sentiment. *See* SchaeffersResearch.com.

tion hogging the news. A similar cover was published by *The Economist* entitled, "Now Bust Microsoft's Trust." Fortunately for MSFT bulls, the market took the November 18, 1999 Justice Department ruling in stride, and the stock went on to appreciate by 13 percent over the subsequent month while rebounding off significant support at its 10-month moving average.

Of course, cover stories do not always work as contrarian indicators. For example, Sun Microsystems (SUNW) was bullishly featured on various magazine covers (October 13, 1997 *Fortune* and January 18, 1999 *Business Week*), but the stock continued to post new highs. In taking a contrarian stance to a cover story, a trader must carefully scrutinize fundamental and technical factors to determine whether or not to "fade" the story. Note again that you must recognize when sentiment *agrees* with the trend or is a warning of an impending reversal. In SUNW's case, the company's fundamentals remained strong, while the technical price action was very powerful. In this instance, as in others, it proved wise to wait for a change in the fundamental outlook, or spot a technical deterioration in the charts before looking to bet against the crowd.

Quantitative Measures

While qualitative sentiment measures do have their limitations, they still have their place in assessing the sentiment of market participants. They also enjoy the advantage of being available in the public domain. However, these measures cannot accurately depict how cash is actually being allocated and to what degree (Neill's "prevalence and intensity" concerns). This is where the quantitative analysis of sentiment plays a vital role. In quantitative sentiment analysis, you collect specific data that can accurately measure the direction and quantity of how cash is being allocated. The historical data is then analyzed and tested to accurately compute the underlying sentiment and assess the implications. Thus, extremes in optimism and pessimism are identified by the actual actions of investment constituencies rather than through general feelings or attitudes as reflected in polls or news stories.

For example, the various options exchanges provide daily statistics that allow for this kind of research and analysis. An option is a contract that entitles the holder to buy or sell a number of shares (usually 100) of a particular stock at a predetermined price on or before a fixed date (the expiration date). A call option is a contract that gives the buyer the right, not the obligation, to buy a stock or index (called the underlying) at a particular price before a specific time. Buyers of call options expect the underlying to move higher before the expiration date. Conversely, the buyer of a put option has the right, not the obligation, to sell the shares at a particular price on or before the expiration of the put. The put buyer expects the underlying to move lower over the defined time period. Thus, at the most basic level, disproportionate demand for calls is reflective of optimism, while excessive put demand is indicative of pessimism.

There are several ways to analyze option activity. One is to break down the volume of puts versus calls on a day-to-day basis. Option volume is simply the number of contracts that trade on a particular option (given a specific underlying stock, expiration month, and strike level) each day. By combining the volume on all of the different series and strikes of options available on a particular stock or index, it is possible to determine its relative call and put activity. This, in turn, provides a glimpse into the market's sentiment on that stock, independent of its price action.

Another manner in which options can be used to measure sentiment is through the open interest statistic. Stock shares represent actual physical ownership of a part of a company. Options are merely standardized contracts, each of which has a buyer (holder) and a seller (writer). While option volume is an indication of trading activity or turnover, open interest represents the number of contracts that are held "open" at the end of each trading day, comparable to the "float" on a stock. How an option transaction affects open interest depends on whether the participants are opening a new position or closing out an existing one. If both parties are trading to open a new position (one to buy long the option and the other to sell short the option), then open interest will increase by the number of contracts traded. If both parties are trading to close out old positions, then open interest will decrease by the number of contracts traded.

The goal of sentiment analysis is to uncover the presence of pessimism and optimism in the form of put demand and call demand, respectively. Simply stated, higher volume and open interest numbers generally indicate demand. While it is possible for a given amount of volume or open interest to be driven by selling rather than buying, options purchasing remains more common than option selling or spread strategies on a per contract basis. This is particularly the case for the most actively traded options, which are concentrated in the nearest expiration months and in the more speculative "out-of-the-money" strike prices. Thus, in the majority of cases, high option volume or open interest indicates high option demand by speculators. Note that futures market analysts must *guess* whether changes in open interest are due to bulls or bears, while options market analysts enjoy the benefit of the breakdown of open interest between puts and calls. Let's now see how options and other market measures can be applied to sentiment quantification for the market, stocks, and sectors.

Quantified Market Timing Indicators

Put/Call Ratios

As previously mentioned, overall market sentiment can be quantified through the use of option volume measures. Two of the most commonly used indicators for market sentiment are the Chicago Board Options Exchange (CBOE) equity put/call ratio and the S&P 100 Index (OEX) put/call ratio. When used correctly, these sentiment gauges can effectively help an investor time significant market moves.

The CBOE equity put/call ratio has proven to be a highly reliable sentiment measure for overall market timing. The indicator is a ratio that is formed by dividing the daily volume of equity put options by call options traded on the CBOE. Since 1990, a range between 0.31 and 0.67 has bound about 90 percent of the daily readings of this ratio.

What can this simple indicator tell us about market sentiment? Put/call ratio analysis is simply a way to gauge whether the market is poised for a rally based on large amounts of potential buying strength, or poised to stall out due to a lack of cash available to push it higher. High put/call ratios are often indicative of excessive pessimism and thus of large amounts of money on the "sidelines." Conversely, low put/call ratios indicate a point at which there is so much optimism that there is very little money left to push the market higher.

To smooth the data to get more reliable signals, Schaeffer's Investment Research has focused on the 21-day moving average of the CBOE equity put/call ratio. Using this moving average, Schaeffer's is able to define ranges at which this indicator is signaling bullish and bearish conditions. Since 1990, the 21-day moving average of this ratio has been primarily bound between 0.33 and 0.55. Typically, when the ratio's moving average reaches levels above 0.47, Schaeffer's stands ready for bullish market conditions due to the oversold implications of this high reading. Conversely, when the ratio reaches levels that are lower than 0.37, it is a sign that short-term traders are near or fully invested, and the market becomes vulnerable to a trading-range environment or even a significant decline if negative news dominates the headlines.

These ratios simply indicate that the market is ripe for a reversal—it is not until the ratio ultimately peaks and reverses direction before you should take any kind of action. A peak in this ratio indicates investors are becoming more optimistic after moving to the sidelines or selling short the market. The market then rallies, as previous short positions are covered and cash moves in from the sidelines. In contrast, a trough in this indicator means investors are becoming more pessimistic after a period of optimism. The market will then begin to decline as previous long positions are sold and cash moves out of the market.

Figure 10.4 illustrates these relationships. Note that peaks (arrows in the chart) in the put/call ratio in April 1997, September 1998, and October 1999 were followed by major upside moves. Conversely, troughs (circles in the chart) in October 1997, July 1998, and December 1999 preceded market weakness. You should make sure that a peak or trough in this ratio is firmly in place when it reaches high or low absolute numbers, as the ratio can always go even higher or lower. The fact that extreme bullish sentiment can become even more extreme (ditto for bearish sentiment) has proved to be a big trap for those analysts in the 1990s who have arbitrarily and repeatedly decreed that bullish sentiment had climaxed and that the market had therefore topped. They simply did not understand, at their great peril, that "the public is right during the trends."

While the equity put/call ratio remains an effective tool, the S&P 100 Index (OEX) put/call volume ratio was a very reliable market sentiment gauge up until the early part of 2000. Nevertheless, this indicator is included in this sec-

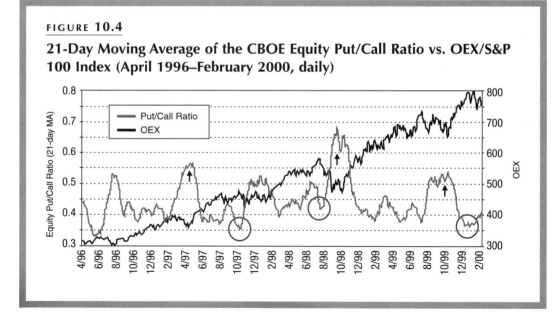

FIGURE 10.4

21-Day Moving Average of the CBOE Equity Put/Call Ratio vs. OEX/S&P 100 Index (April 1996–February 2000, daily)

tion not only to demonstrate an approach to using index put/call ratios, but also to drive home the point that it is necessary to constantly stay on top of your indicators and always be open to fresh indicators, as the market's makeup can quickly change.

From 1990 through early 2000, OEX options averaged over 15 percent of the total daily option volume traded on the CBOE. No individual stock was able to make such a staggering claim in the equity market. Although no single equity can represent the entire stock market, the OEX, which contains 100 of the larger-cap stocks, can act as a reasonable surrogate. When OEX options were widely traded, they could be used to gauge investor sentiment in the broad market. In this case, Schaeffer's used daily OEX option volume information to construct the OEX put/call ratio. This ratio measured investor sentiment by dividing the daily volume of OEX puts by OEX calls. When the ratio reached extremely high levels due to excessive put volume relative to call volume, bullish conditions existed, as potential buying power had increased. The reverse was also true. When call volume was high compared to put volume, the ratio reached low extremes, signifying excess market optimism, which often served as a warning sign.

In general, the OEX put/call ratio was an effective indicator. However, there

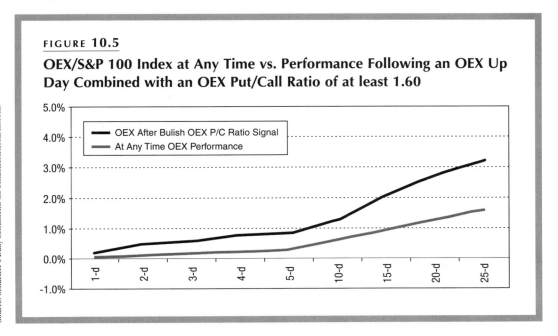

FIGURE **10.5**

OEX/S&P 100 Index at Any Time vs. Performance Following an OEX Up Day Combined with an OEX Put/Call Ratio of at least 1.60

Source: Schaeffer's Daily Sentiment. *See* SchaeffersResearch.com.

were times when the bullish implications of this indicator would become even more powerful. One such circumstance was when a single-day ratio reading of 1.60 or higher was coupled with an OEX advance that same day. **Figure 10.5** shows that the OEX would typically outperform following such a signal. In fact, the chart reveals that the OEX would nearly *double* its typical "at-any-time" performance twenty-five days after this bullish combination.

Why would this be? On days when the OEX is up, the natural reaction of investors should be to buy calls so that they can profit from the rising index. When investors choose instead to buy *puts* heavily on an up day, they are fighting an underlying trend ("man bites dog") and run the risk of short positions being stopped out. If that happens, the covering of these positions only adds fuel to the market's momentum. As such, stocks are apt to outperform, as this pessimism quickly unwinds and shorts begin covering.

As of the writing of this chapter, OEX volume has dropped off significantly, partly due to the emerging popularity of Nasdaq-100 Trust (QQQ) options (discussed in the section that follows). For example, the average daily volume of OEX options in the second half of 1999 totaled 90,036 contracts, compared to 71,856 in the first half of 2000. This decreasing volume means that fewer participants are trading OEX options, which makes this ratio a less reliable tool to measure investor sentiment. On the other hand, QQQ options are gaining in popularity. For instance, daily QQQ option volume averaged 13,001 contracts in the latter half of 1999, compared to 72,438 contracts in the first six months of 2000. Schaeffer's is adapting to this trend by studying the directional implications of high and low put/call volume ratios on QQQ options. The market can transform quickly, and what was once reliable may no longer be dependable given changing market conditions, an important point that can apply to other indicators as well.

SPY and QQQ Volume

An additional market indicator that is effective in predicting major market bottoms is the volume of AMEX-traded S&P 500 Depositary Receipts (SPY) and Nasdaq-100 Trust Shares (QQQ). Both of these securities represent portfolios that are invested to match the performance of the S&P 500 Index (SPX) and Nasdaq 100 Index (NDX), respectively. While these securities provide individual investors with an easy way to invest in these major market indices, they also provide an effective vehicle to measure market sentiment. Why? SPY and QQQ share the rare distinction of being able to be shorted on downticks. Most equities can only be shorted following upticks to prevent aggressive short selling

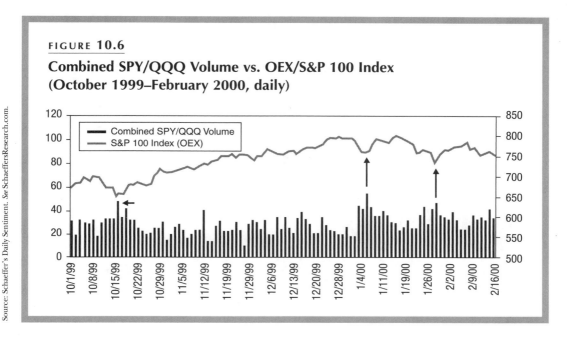

Source: Schaeffer's Daily Sentiment. *See* SchaeffersResearch.com.

FIGURE 10.6

**Combined SPY/QQQ Volume vs. OEX/S&P 100 Index
(October 1999–February 2000, daily)**

from collapsing the price of an illiquid stock. Since the price of SPY and QQQ are derived from the value of their parent indices rather than directly from temporary excesses in supply and demand, their prices cannot be affected by a rush of shorting activity. Because these index trusts can be shorted at any time, pessimistic activity is drawn to these instruments on days when the market is declining. Due to this trait, Schaeffer's monitors SPY and QQQ volume, both individually and on a combined basis, focusing on the activity when the market is declining to determine when there might be an excess of pessimistic shorting activity.

Of particular interest is a down market day that is accompanied by a climactic amount of SPY and QQQ volume. Such occurrences indicate that sentiment has become exceptionally negative, as investors scramble to short these securities to hedge portfolios on fears of further declines. This degree of investor negativity is generally bullish for the market, as the crowd is not just defensively closing out long positions but even aggressively establishing short positions at precise market lows. At the same time, if volume in these instruments does *not* spike on significant declines, investors may be too complacent, which is a sign that the market is vulnerable to further selling. **Figure 10.6** shows OEX price action in relation to SPY/QQQ volume. Note that QQQ had a 2-for-1 split on

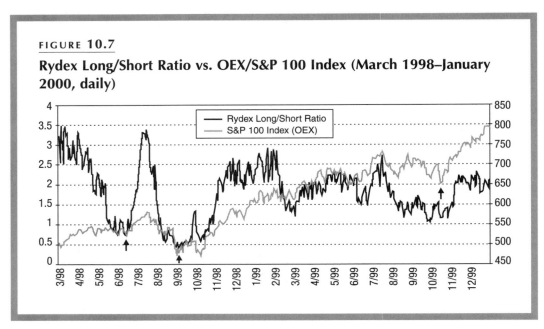

FIGURE 10.7

Rydex Long/Short Ratio vs. OEX/S&P 100 Index (March 1998–January 2000, daily)

March 17, 2000. The volume spikes in October 1999 and twice in January 2000 marked short-term bottoms for the index.

Mutual Fund Asset Flows

Market sentiment can also be quantified by monitoring the flow of funds between bullishly and bearishly oriented mutual funds. Schaeffer's follows money flows within the Rydex fund family, which has several funds that enable investors to cheaply and conveniently switch their asset allocations based on how bullish or bearish they are on the market. The Rydex Nova fund is designed to return 150 percent of the performance of the SPX, while the Ursa fund seeks returns that are *inversely* correlated to the movement of the SPX. Although the Ursa fund has certainly not fared well throughout the current bull market as a long-term investment, it can be very effective when trying to "time" corrections or pullbacks in the market.

Initially, Schaeffer's used the ratio of Nova to Ursa assets as a rough gauge of investor sentiment. As the technology sector gained in popularity in late 1998 and throughout 1999, mutual fund investors increasingly turned to the Rydex funds that were bullishly (OTC fund) and bearishly (Arktos fund) positioned on Nasdaq stocks. Similar to the Nova Fund, the OTC fund is managed to mirror the movement of the tech-laden NDX, and the Arktos fund is allocated to provide a return *opposite* that of the NDX. Schaeffer's added the Rydex OTC/Arktos ratio to its arsenal of quantified sentiment indicators as a result. Moving a step beyond that, Schaeffer's Rydex Long/Short ratio is calculated by dividing the total assets in both of the bullish funds (Nova + OTC) by the total assets in both of the bearish funds (Ursa + Arktos). This combined ratio is a measure of the complete mutual fund sentiment picture, not just that of the SPX or NDX. Due to the long-term growth of the stock market, there is a great disparity between the performances of the bullish funds and the bearish funds over time. Schaeffer's Rydex ratios adjust for this factor by dividing out the net asset value (NAV) of each component fund. The resulting NAV-adjusted ratios are thus only influenced by actual fund flow into and out of each fund.

A move by the NAV-adjusted Long/Short ratio to extreme lows represents extreme pessimism. This indicates a potentially bullish environment for the market, as cash has been removed from the "long" funds and has been built up in the "short" funds. On the other hand, extreme highs of this ratio indicate excess optimism. This often precedes or runs concurrent with poor market conditions, as cash has been fully committed to the market and the buying power provided by the covering of short positions has dissipated. **Figure 10.7** shows the NAV-adjusted Rydex Long/Short ratio along with the OEX. Note that bullish conditions tend to exist when the ratio drops below the 1.50 level (arrows in the chart), while readings above 3.00 are consistent with market weakness.

Quantified Stock and Sector Timing Indicators

Open Interest Put/Call Ratios

To this point, the discussion has focused on various volume ratios as measures of sentiment for market timing. Now let's turn to using open interest to gauge sentiment on individual stocks and sectors. For individual stocks, daily option volume can vary to such a large degree that it is often difficult to distinguish bullish and bearish signals from the noise created by these large fluctuations. This point is illustrated in the following table, which shows the option activity for Motorola (MOT) over a five-day period. It would be impossible to derive any meaningful sentiment conclusions from a put/call ratio that ranged from 0.09 to 0.62 within such a short time frame. Although a few stocks have larger and somewhat more consistent daily volume figures, let's consider another method to gauge investor sentiment via option activity for particular stocks—open interest.

Option Volume Activity for Motorola over a Five-Day Period

Source: Schaeffer's Research Review

DATE	CALL VOLUME	PUT VOLUME	VOLUME PUT/CALL RATIO
9/2/99	856	499	0.58
9/3/99	8,137	748	0.09
9/7/99	10,530	1,489	0.14
9/8/99	4,248	1,419	0.33
9/9/99	2,595	1,621	0.62

There are a number of ways in which open interest can be used to evaluate the current sentiment on individual stocks. The simplest form of analysis involves put/call ratios. Put open interest divided by call open interest can provide a snapshot of the sentiment on a stock. Because a stock's open interest numbers do not start at zero each day, the "daily" readings are much smoother over time. The table below shows the effect of using Motorola option open interest rather than volume over the same time period. Note that these open interest numbers are far less volatile than their volume counterparts, which gives the analyst a better reading on sentiment. Another advantage of focusing on open interest is that volume that is both initiated and closed out during the course of the same trading day does not appear in the open interest figures. Such volume can represent a significant portion of the data included in traditional put/call ratios, yet it has no directional implications beyond the day it occurred.

Option Volume Activity for Motorola over a Five-Day Period

Source: Schaeffer's Research Review

DATE	CALL OPEN INTEREST	PUT OPEN INTEREST	OPEN INTEREST PUT/CALL RATIO
9/2/99	25,979	14,071	0.54
9/3/99	26,432	13,942	0.53
9/7/99	29,793	14,112	0.47
9/8/99	31,547	14,699	0.47
9/9/99	30,931	14,801	0.48

When gauging sentiment, you should be primarily interested in the convictions displayed by the speculative public. A contrarian view of public (rather than institutional) sentiment often proves to be a more reliable predictor of market

Source: Schaeffer's Daily Sentiment. *See* SchaeffersResearch.com.

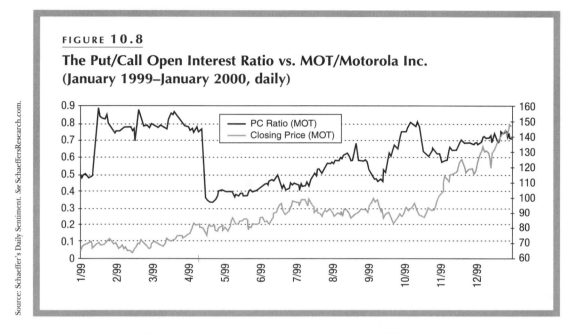

FIGURE **10.8**

**The Put/Call Open Interest Ratio vs. MOT/Motorola Inc.
(January 1999–January 2000, daily)**

movement. To collect options information that is more likely attributable to these speculators, focus on the front three months of options data, which is where the small speculators tend to gravitate. By comparing the current put/call open interest ratio to previous readings for that stock, you can accurately gauge relative levels of investor optimism and pessimism. This is extremely important because the absolute ratio readings can vary substantially from stock to stock. Thus, comparing a stock's ratio to previous ratios sets up an "apples to apples" comparison that provides a truer picture of relative sentiment.

Figure 10.8 shows Motorola's put/call open interest ratio for a one-year period. Note that relatively high levels of the ratio either precede or are concurrent with bottoms in the stock price. These high ratios reflect growing or peaking pessimism for the shares, which can signal an approaching or already formed intermediate bottom. Low ratio levels can act as a warning of a stock's being potentially overextended prior to forming an intermediate top. More important, a low put/call ratio indicates that a stock already in the midst of a decline may be far from a bottom, as selling potential could still be substantial with investors continuing to perceive "value" in the stock. However, these value players may capitulate as the stock further depreciates or the opportunity cost becomes too great to hold the shares any longer.

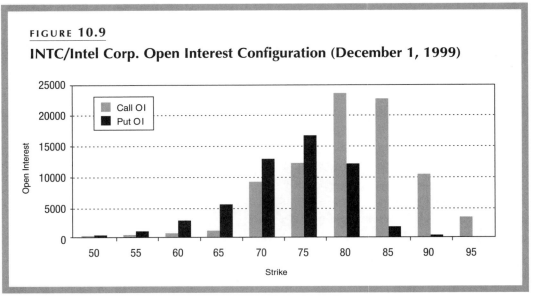

FIGURE **10.9**

INTC/Intel Corp. Open Interest Configuration (December 1, 1999)

Source: Schaeffer's Daily Sentiment. *See* SchaeffersResearch.com.

Open Interest Configuration

Another way to use open interest to analyze sentiment on individual stocks is to examine the "open interest configuration." The open interest configuration of a stock is simply the number of open puts or calls at the various strike prices. This approach has proven effective in determining possible resistance and support levels. This process is most effective when front-month option data is used. The open interest configuration can be constructed by plotting a chart with adjacent call and put bars representing the open interest at every strike price.

Figure 10.9 displays the open interest configuration for Intel (INTC) on December 1, 1999. Note that the 80 strike contains the peak open interest for calls, while the 75 strike is the peak put open interest strike. Not so coincidentally, Intel spent much of the previous month in a trading range, bouncing between the 75 and 80 levels. How do these levels act as potential support or resistance points? First, round-number price levels have always tended to serve as support and resistance. Buyers tend to view pullbacks to round-number levels such as 75 as potential entry points for long positions or closeout levels for short positions; sellers look to rallies to round numbers such as 80 as opportunities to exit long positions or to establish short positions. The fact that there may be significant option open interest at strike prices corresponding to these round number price levels serves to accentuate their significance as support and resistance.

In the Intel example in Figure 10.9, bullish speculators were heavy buyers of 80-strike call options in anticipation of a breakout above this level. So in addition to the "usual suspect" sellers at 80, those who had *sold* the 80-strike calls (and who are thus exposed to substantial losses should the stock rally above 80) had a big stake in the stock remaining range-bound. These call sellers can become a very significant factor as the options approach expiration, as they generally own stock that they can sell to create overhead resistance. Of course, this game is far from a sure thing, and when buying demand becomes sufficient to rally the stock well above the strike price, this rally accelerates due to call option sellers scrambling to properly hedge their positions by buying the stock.

From a sentiment perspective, heavy out-of-the-money calls are a sign of an

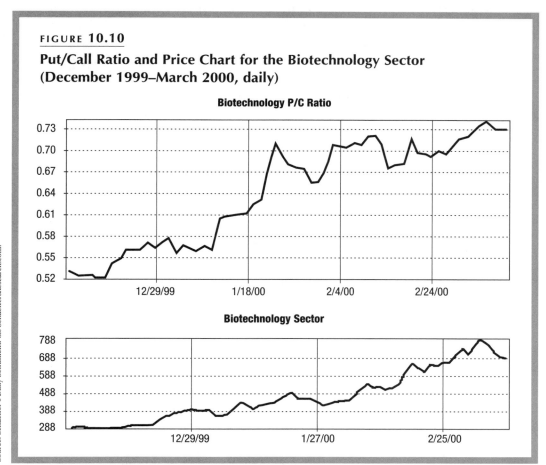

FIGURE **10.10**

Put/Call Ratio and Price Chart for the Biotechnology Sector (December 1999–March 2000, daily)

Source: Schaeffer's Daily Sentiment. *See* SchaeffersResearch.com.

optimistic options crowd. On the other hand, heavy out-of-the-money put open interest is a sign of skepticism among option speculators.

Sector Put/Call Open Interest Ratios

To take this method one step further, you can monitor investor sentiment for various sectors by compiling a composite put/call open interest ratio of the major stocks within that sector. This is a fairly simple task once the individual stock data has been collected. Because you want to gauge speculative sentiment for sectors, use the same front-three-month open-interest data collected for individual stocks. The composite ratio is calculated using a process to weigh each individual ratio equally. An effective way of monitoring these sector put/call ratios is by ranking the current reading against the past year's worth of readings. Readings higher than at least 70 percent (the 70th percentile) of all other readings indicate excessive pessimism toward the group, which is viewed as bullish if the fundamental and technical backdrop for the sector is bullish as well. Conversely, a put/call ratio at or below the 30th percentile indicates substantial optimism, which can have bearish implications if the sector fundamentals are poor and components of the index are deteriorating from a technical standpoint. Therefore, you should be very bullish on relative-strength leaders within an uptrending sector that had a high relative composite put/call ratio.

An example of this analysis can be found in the biotechnology sector in late 1999 and early 2000. As the sector heated up in mid-December 1999, so did put buying on individual components of the AMEX Biotechnology Index (BTK). As shown in **Figure 10.10**, the sector advanced over 150 percent in less than three months, while its put/call ratio rose to its highest point in over a year. This is another illustration of increasing pessimism adding fuel to strong price action.

Short Interest

Monitoring short interest is another method for deriving valuable sentiment data for individual stocks. Short interest is created when an investor sells stock that has been borrowed. A basic short-selling strategy is profitable when the price of the shorted stock declines, allowing the short seller to buy the stock back at a lower price to replace the borrowed shares. Once a month, brokerage firms are required to report the number of shares that have been shorted in their client accounts. This information is compiled for each security and then released to the public. By monitoring a stock's monthly short-interest figures, you can get an idea of the public's level of pessimism toward the stock. In most instances, large amounts of short interest indicate that the general outlook for the company is negative (sometimes, heavy short interest is created out of arbitrage situations,

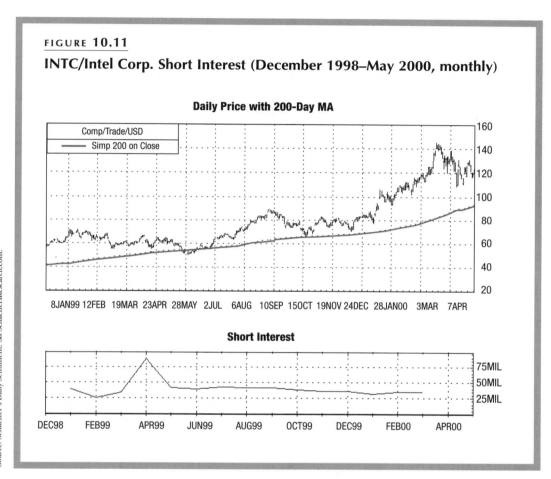

FIGURE **10.11**

INTC/Intel Corp. Short Interest (December 1998–May 2000, monthly)

Daily Price with 200-Day MA

Comp/Trade/USD
Simp 200 on Close

8JAN99 12FEB 19MAR 23APR 28MAY 2JUL 6AUG 10SEP 15OCT 19NOV 24DEC 28JAN00 3MAR 7APR

Short Interest

DEC98 FEB99 APR99 JUN99 AUG99 OCT99 DEC99 FEB00 APR00

such as mergers). From a contrarian viewpoint, this pessimism is bullish for the stock if it is in an uptrend. As previously noted, negative sentiment (in this case, heavy short interest) in the context of strong price action often has powerful bullish implications.

Figure 10.11 illustrates the amount of short interest for Intel during 1999. Notice the dramatic increase in short interest that took place in April. This occurred as the stock was pulling back to the support of its 200-day moving average in April and May 1999. This increase is indicative of overwhelming investor pessimism for the stock. Heavy short interest on a stock displaying strong price action with pullbacks contained at key support levels is a place where you will potentially see quick, significant rallies, caused by the shorts rushing to buy back shares to limit their losses as the stock moves higher from support. This adds fuel to an already powerful uptrend, as seen in INTC's rise from June through September 1999.

The notion that short interest is no longer an accurate gauge of sentiment because much of this activity now relates to hedging can be dismissed. There is no hard data to support this argument. In fact, the argument that short positions are now hedged with long call positions is not at all evident in the listed options market. Moreover, short-covering buying panics regularly occur in heavily shorted stocks, which is later confirmed by substantial declines in short interest.

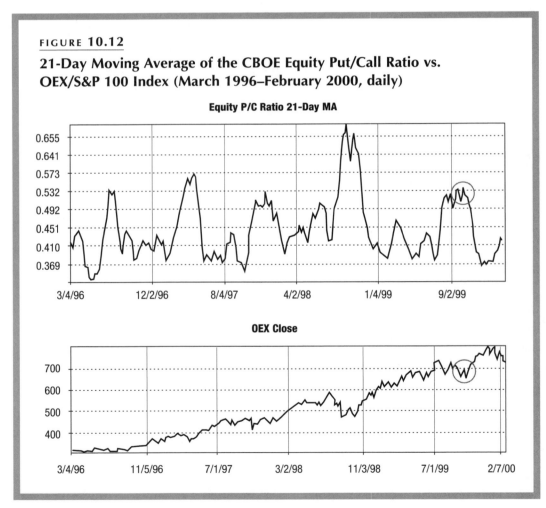

FIGURE 10.12

21-Day Moving Average of the CBOE Equity Put/Call Ratio vs. OEX/S&P 100 Index (March 1996–February 2000, daily)

Source: Schaeffer's Daily Sentiment. *See* SchaeffersResearch.com.

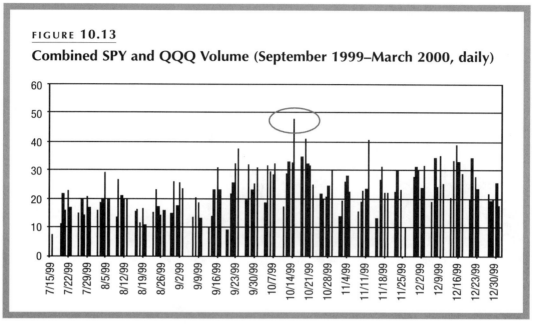

FIGURE **10.13**

Combined SPY and QQQ Volume (September 1999–March 2000, daily)

Source: Schaeffer's Daily Sentiment. *See* SchaeffersResearch.com.

Monitored regularly, these methods and techniques can offer investors many profitable opportunities that do not appear on the "radar screen" of traditional technical and fundamental analysis.

Sentiment at Work: A Case Study

Here is an example demonstrating how to apply Expectational Analysis[SM] (Schaeffer's unique approach that combines sentiment analysis with technical and fundamental tools) and how you can use this methodology to improve your own trading results.

One approach to Expectational Analysis[SM] is the "top-down" method, which is applied by determining (1) the stock market direction, (2) those sectors that are expected to outperform or underperform, and (3) the stocks that will benefit from or become vulnerable to relevant stock market and sector environments.

Stock Market Backdrop

As discussed above, key quantifiable measures you can use to determine the sentiment backdrop surrounding the equity market are the equity put/call ratio, SPY and QQQ volume, and Rydex mutual fund flows. In October 1999, these

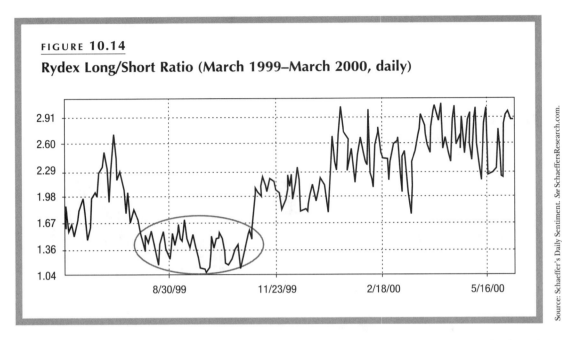

FIGURE **10.14**

Rydex Long/Short Ratio (March 1999–March 2000, daily)

Source: Schaeffer's Daily Sentiment. *See* SchaeffersResearch.com.

broad-market sentiment indicators were bullishly aligned, creating an ideal environment for the bulls.

For example, the 21-day equity put/call ratio (see **Figure 10.12**) reached a reading of 0.54 in October 1999 and began to roll over, creating a powerfully bullish omen for stocks. Confirming the skepticism displayed by options players was the combined volume on the SPY and QQQ, which was reaching extreme levels as investors speculated on a further drop in the equity market. As seen in **Figure 10.13**, the combined volume of SPY/QQQ hit the 47.9 million mark in mid-October when pessimism was reaching a fever pitch. That figure was so excessive at the time that it shattered the previous record of 39.3 million. Finally, from August through November 1999, the Rydex Long/Short ratio was producing readings well below the key 1.50 level (see **Figure 10.14**). Mutual fund players were wagering on a negative move from the equity market, as there was a marked increase of assets flowing into the bearish Rydex funds relative to the bullishly oriented funds.

Sector Timing

After determining that the market is preparing for a major bottom, the next step is to focus on those sectors that have the optimal chance to outperform in a bull market. You should check the component put/call open interest ratio for twenty

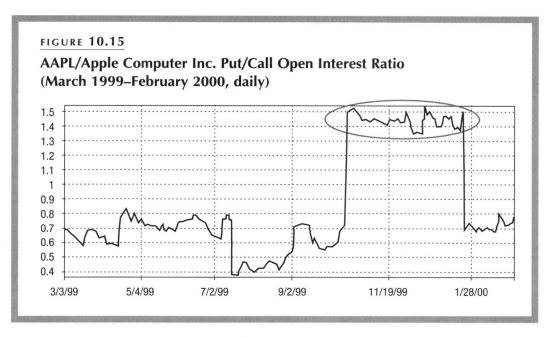

FIGURE 10.15

AAPL/Apple Computer Inc. Put/Call Open Interest Ratio (March 1999–February 2000, daily)

Source: Schaeffer's Daily Sentiment. *See* SchaeffersResearch.com.

major industry sectors. In October 1999, one of the sectors showing strong bullish potential over the subsequent one to three months was the computer hardware index. The Philadelphia Box Maker Index (BMX) had a Schaeffer's Put/Call Open Interest Ratio (SOIR) reading of approximately 0.80. What made this ratio significant was that it was the highest reading for the sector over the past year, a sign of peak speculator pessimism on a pullback within a strong uptrend (the BMX had pulled back to its 10-month moving average).

Stock Selection

With ten stocks comprising the BMX, the next decision is to select the stock that has the best chance to outperform its peers. Among the equities that comprise the index, Apple Computer (AAPL) was the potential relative-strength leader among the group. Why? First, AAPL's put/call open interest ratio was well above the pivotal 1.0 level. This means that there were actually more put contracts open than call contracts, an unusually pessimistic configuration, particularly in a bull market. As seen in **Figure 10.15**, AAPL's SOIR reading was achieving extreme heights of pessimism. In fact, the SOIR reading on AAPL was in the 92nd percentile when SIR recommended this stock to subscribers on October 15, 1999.

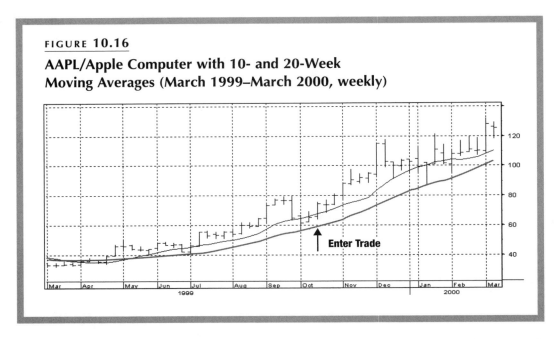

FIGURE **10.16**

AAPL/Apple Computer with 10- and 20-Week Moving Averages (March 1999–March 2000, weekly)

As shown in AAPL's price chart (see **Figure 10.16**), the stock had been trending along its 10- and 20-week moving average for months, and these trendlines were providing flawless support. This supported the notion that the intermediate trend in AAPL was in the favor of the bulls.

Not only were the technicals and sentiment backdrops bullishly aligned on AAPL, but also fundamentals were just as strong. AAPL's interim CEO, Steve Jobs, was once again breathing life into the company, a change reflected in AAPL's newfound earnings growth, which exceeded Wall Street expectations by a wide margin.

Results

The application of Expectational Analysis℠ in this case yielded dramatic results, as every piece of the three-part analysis worked out as projected. First, the SPX rallied 6.2 percent in October and maintained its strength through the rest of the year, finishing 14.5 percent higher over 1999's final quarter. Although the BMX did not fare as well as expected in October, it rallied more than 25 percent over the final two months of 1999. Finally, AAPL's uptrend accelerated as expected, as the shares appreciated 26 percent in October and totaled gains of 62 percent for the final three months of 1999.

Caveats in Using Contrarian Analysis

Humphrey Neill was very modest about the potential for his contrarian analysis as a stand-alone trading approach. In *The Art of Contrary Thinking* he wrote:

> The contrary theory is a way of thinking, but let's not overweigh it. It is more of an *antidote* to general forecasting than a system *for* forecasting. In a word, it is a thinking tool, not a crystal ball. It forces one to think through a given subject. As has been said: If you don't think things through, you're through thinking." He went on to say, "I believe it is correct to say that the theory is more valuable in *avoiding* errors in forecasting than in employing it for definitive forecasting.

Neill had two major concerns about the use of his approach as a direct forecasting tool. The first related to the difficulty in developing objective and accurate measures of "prevailing opinion" or sentiment. This should always be a guiding concern, and I have devoted myself for nearly two decades to developing and refining the quantitative sentiment tools discussed in this chapter so that they can meet the test of objectivity and accuracy. Throughout the course of these endeavors, I have had a singular advantage that was unavailable to Neill when he was formulating his theory—a robust listed options market that has provided a treasure trove of objective information about the collective opinions of investors and speculators.

The second concern of Neill's regarding the use of the contrarian approach as a direct forecasting tool related to the crucial element of timing. As Neill stated, "a contrary opinion is usually ahead of (its) time." Nevertheless, he wrote, "Your watch is still useful, although it may run fast; you allow for the error and recognize that you may be early for appointments, but you do not miss the train."

A problem from a trading standpoint is that a contrarian analysis will often identify that conditions are in place for a market top or a market bottom well ahead of the actual top or bottom. This is very much a first cousin to the "dog bites man" concept discussed previously in this chapter. In a bull market, bullish sentiment is to be expected and excesses of bullish sentiment can continue well beyond "expected" levels. Bullish sentiment in the context of a bull market, therefore, is *not* a timing tool, nor is bearish sentiment in the context of a bear market.

You can tackle this timing issue by using objective technical tools to define the current market environment so you can evaluate your sentiment indicators in the context of that environment. If you see objective evidence of pessimistic sentiment in the context of a bull market, or optimistic sentiment in the context of a bear market, your timing task becomes significantly easier. As previously stated, the "man bites dog" condition of pessimistic sentiment in a bull market strongly supports the continuation of that bull market, just as optimistic sentiment in the context of a bear market supports the continuation of that bear market.

But what if you are in the more common "dog bites man" situation of sentiment being congruent with market direction? Bull markets top out when bullish sentiment reaches an extreme and bear markets bottom at extremes of bearish sentiment. But this is a very difficult principle to apply to the real world of trading because of the impossibility of determining just how far an extreme in sentiment will go before it reaches its peak. In the Schaeffer's database, the CBOE equity put/call ratio 21-day moving average has never recorded a reading below 30 percent, and a future move below this level would certainly indicate a historically unprecedented level of investor bullishness. But to call for a market top the day such a reading is reached would be the height of folly, for as long as investors remain bullish and their buying power is not seriously depleted, the market can continue to rise. And if the put/call ratio can move below 30 percent, who is to say that it cannot move below 25 percent before the ultimate market top?

For a trader incorporating sentiment into technical analysis, it is critical to distinguish the ideal trade setup situation (as was discussed in the Apple Computer case study above) from situations in which sentiment analysis is relatively silent. To short a stock that has very bullish technicals because sentiment on that stock is "too bullish" and because it is "expensive" on a valuation basis would be just plain foolish. And it would be just as foolish to buy a stock whose chart is abominable because of "bearish sentiment" and "cheap valuation." Contrarianism is not about buying "cheap stocks" and "low prices;" it is about buying "low expectations." And as in the Apple Computer case study, low expectations can often occur within the context of strong technicals and strong fundamentals.

CHAPTER 11

Measuring Investor Sentiment in Individual Stocks

LARRY WILLIAMS

Ninety percent of short-term traders lose money. That means that the majority of traders are wrong most the time. So how do you make sure you usually do the opposite of what they do?

Trading against the majority is far from a new idea. Writing in the 1930s, Garfield Drew was most likely the first analyst not only to espouse this view but also to present a workable solution to the problem. Drew divided public investor activity into two categories: customers' equity (or balance at their brokers) and odd-lot short sales. The most enduring of these indicators has been odd-lot short sales. Because an odd lot, Drew reasoned, was fewer than 100 shares, such activity most likely represented the small investor, someone without enough money to buy in the traditional 100-share increment.

For more than seventy years this indicator has proven the following: abnormally high levels of odd-lot short sales occur at market lows, whereas a decline in odd-lot short sales, which signals public bullishness, usually heralds market declines. It is a truism, but a sad one, that the majority of investors just can't seem to get it right.

The happy truth is that we can fade the majority.

Other analysts such as Wally Heiby, Richard Dysart, Marty Zweig, and Ned Davis have done additional work along this line. Their work has concentrated on overall stock market timing. Perhaps the most notable indicator in this field has been the *Investors Intelligence* Service, which measures the sentiment of folks who write investment advisory newsletters. For more than thirty-five years the record of the hotshot newsletter writers has paralleled the public's inability to correctly forecast future activity.

Jim Sibbett, a commodity analyst and the original publisher of *Market Vane*, began recording the bullishness of newsletter writers on individual commodities in the late 1960s. His work showed that sentiment data can be used not only for overall market timing but also for individual commodity timing.

His data is quite clear: all of the major commodity markets respond to too much adviser bullishness by declining and to too little bullishness by rallying.

Sibbett based his work on weekly data. Market analyst Jake Bernstein, however, began measuring fifty traders' bullishness/bearishness on a daily basis. His work on daily sentiment, on a list of widely followed commodities, drives home the same point: even on an individual and daily basis, investor sentiment can provide real insight into the next move in the marketplace.

How Investor Sentiment Affects Individual Stocks

Thanks to the Internet, it is now possible to track many advisers on a daily as well as a weekly basis to determine the majority opinion. Heretofore, this would have been almost impossible to do in a timely fashion. Now, however, with instant communication to traders' and investors' opinions all over the world, it is possible to collect the views of the majority.

Although the specific index discussed and illustrated in this chapter is proprietary, the general components are not. You could do this yourself if you had the resources and time. The index is arrived at by visiting Web sites and scanning print media to determine how many of the analysts surveyed are bullish. This number is then expressed as a percentage of all votes cast, thus giving a base or raw number of percent bullishness.

There is some smoothing of the data, but only after a technical measure of public bullishness has been tossed into the concoction. Instead of interviewing individual members of the trading public each day, we at Commodity Timing, Inc. measure their most likely activity in the market as a percent of all market activity. (This is a slightly different view from my written work on accumulation and distribution, which I began in the 1960s.) These measures from daily market activity are blended with the weekly readings.

The resulting index confirms what you would expect: intermediate-term market highs are marked by high levels of investor optimism, whereas market lows are almost always revealed by low levels of optimism.

René Descartes, the seventeenth-century French mathematical genius credited with the dictum, "I think, therefore I am," is perhaps the founding father of this philosophy based on methods of systematic doubt. He apparently made his living gambling and, in addition to his philosophical works, coined quotations for speculators such as "it is more likely the truth will have been discovered by the few rather than by the many."

In trader talk that means, "Just when the many have discovered the trend is up, it is most likely to change."

So, whether it is through Descartes's words, or the work of Garfield Drew, Marty Zweig, or this author, a truth of market activity has been uncovered or at least confirmed: you can fade the uninformed investor or majority view, most of the time.

The figures in this chapter depict the sentiment on weekly charts. The sentiment index appears below each chart. Excessive bullish levels occur over 75 percent while market lows are most likely to take place when 25 percent or less of the survey sample is looking to be buyers.

The Basic Rule

The first rule in using the sentiment index is that zones of excessive bullishness and bearishness are where prices usually reverse themselves. As Heraclitus said in 500 BC, "Every trend must go too far and evoke its own reversal."

As proof of this phenomenon, look at **Figure 11.1**, a chart of the activity of J.P. Morgan from 1996 through the spring of 2000. The excessive bullish and bearish areas are marked. The vast majority of these areas indicate opportunities for setting up profitable trades. This is, indeed, the rule rather than the exception.

The chart of Minnesota Mining and Manufacturing (MMM) in **Figure 11.2**

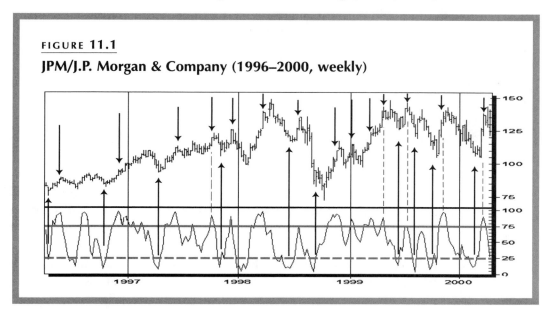

FIGURE 11.1

JPM/J.P. Morgan & Company (1996–2000, weekly)

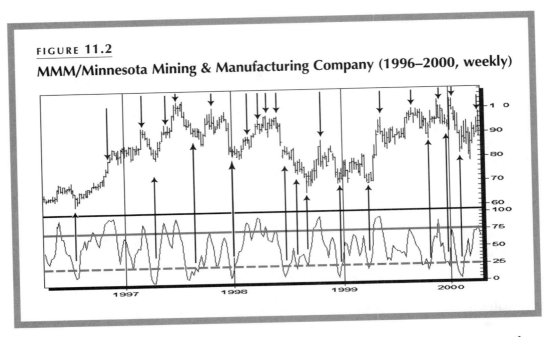

FIGURE **11.2**

MMM/Minnesota Mining & Manufacturing Company (1996–2000, weekly)

shows the same general observation to be true. When the majority—more than 75 percent—of advisers are too bullish, prices are more likely to decline than rally over the ensuing weeks.

By the same token, when the number of bullish advisers is less than 25 percent the odds of a market rally are greatly enhanced. Indeed, the most profitable rallies in the past four years were all indicated by sentiment readings in the lower quartile. In physics, the second law of thermodynamics states that all things tend to go from an ordered state to a less ordered state. Disorder, or entropy, always increases. That is pretty much what happens in the market—the order embodied in the trend, which represents a decrease in the entropy of the common outlook, actually increases the entropy in another area, namely, trend reversal.

It does not matter what the company does; it can be a bank like J.P.Morgan, a conglomerate like MMM, or a drug company like Merck (see **Figure 11.3**). The rule of the jungle still prevails. Virtually all the ideal buy and sell times in Merck from 1997 forward have coincided with the sentiment index being in the correct zone.

The index calls just about all major highs and lows. That's the good news. The bad news: it does give a few signals that are not accurate. There is at least one technique to avoid some inaccurate signals, which is discussed below.

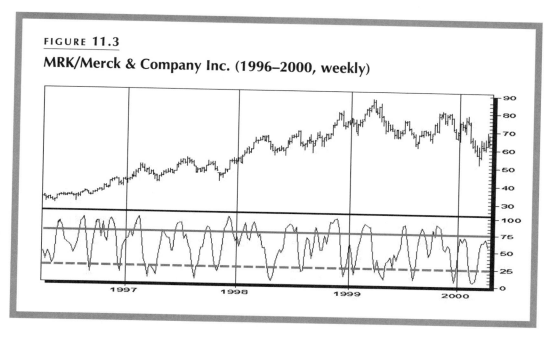

FIGURE **11.3**

MRK/Merck & Company Inc. (1996–2000, weekly)

Using the Index

Say you are a long-term player in Merck. You own the stock but want to earn some extra income by writing puts and calls. The sentiment index can be of great value: simply write puts when less than 25 percent of the advisers are bullish and sell calls against your position when over 75 percent are bullish.

Perhaps you are following a stock you want to add to your portfolio. The only question in your mind is when the best time to buy will be. Why buy stock when the majority is bullish, given its record of most often doing the wrong thing? Simply wait until the weekly index dips below the 25 percent line or lower, then make your investment. Considering the mechanical simplicity of the technique, the results are truly remarkable.

Figure 11.4 shows buy arrows for Merck from 1993 into 2000. Although the technique is not perfect, it is awesome to see how many of the arrows denoted ideal entry points for the long-term acquisition of Merck (or, if you owned the stock, precise points to write puts so you get the income without the stock being taken away).

No longer do you need to throw darts—instead you can track the dart throwers!

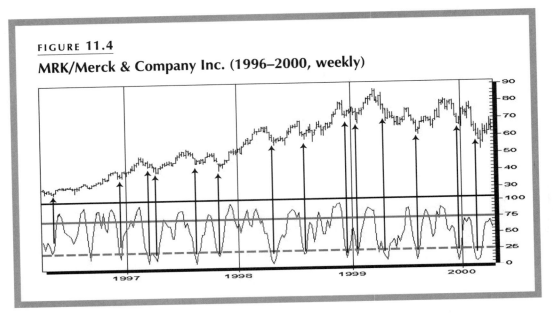

FIGURE **11.4**

MRK/Merck & Company Inc. (1996–2000, weekly)

America's love affair with Microsoft cooled off in the year 2000, largely due to government interaction. Countless families lost millions of dollars thanks to the judicial and bureaucratic attitude of "The government is here to help you

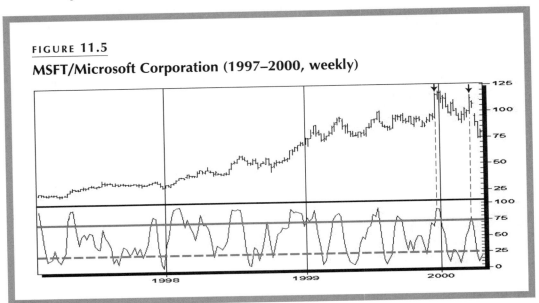

FIGURE **11.5**

MSFT/Microsoft Corporation (1997–2000, weekly)

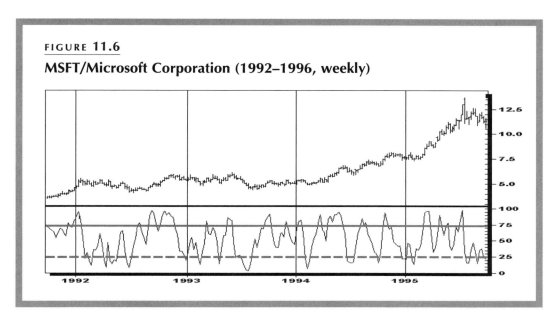

FIGURE **11.6**

MSFT/Microsoft Corporation (1992–1996, weekly)

and has decided that the most successful entrepreneur in the country's history must have cheated—how else could he have succeeded?" Interestingly enough, however, our "fade the crowd" rule was alive and working. The sentiment index stood at 77 percent the week prior to the largest decline in that company's history (see **Figure 11.5**). Indeed, most of the major moves have been clearly indicated by the excessive bullishness and bearishness of a group of popular advisers.

This is not a new phenomenon. Consider the chart of Microsoft from 1992 to 1995 in **Figure 11.6**. Again, the same pattern of excess was at work. It shows the natural cycle of a pendulum swinging from the point when everyone believes the trend will last to the point when no one believes it.

Speculation is largely the art of doing what others are not, when they think they are doing what they ought to be doing.

What Makes the Advisers Too Bullish and Too Bearish?

The driving force of the index is the course of the market at any given time. The stronger and longer a rally is, the more bullish advisers become. Only one thing makes these folks bullish: a strong market rally. Only one thing makes them turn bearish: a decline. True, the trend is your friend; but it is exactly that, trend strength, that gets these advisers to a bullish or bearish extreme.

Yet isn't the first rule of trading not to buck the trend? The sentiment index helps you understand the old adage that "The trend is your friend until the end."

The end of a trend, a money-making opportunity, comes when too many of these players have climbed aboard the bandwagon. In short, the data on sentiment has been as good a record of indicating when a market is close to the end of the trend as anything I have seen in my thirty-eight years of tracking stock prices.

Trend strength (that is, a strong rally) apparently has a hypnotic effect on market prognosticators. The greater the rally, the deeper their somnambulistic trance. Nothing gets these people more bullish than a rally. It is almost as though they stop thinking, in lemminglike fashion. The closer it is to the end of a trend, the more of them want to jump off the cliff!

If you take the time to study the index you will see that near the end of the trend this camp is on the wrong side of the trade. The advisers begin getting in phase with the trend around the midpoint, then become excessive in their view as the trend nears completion. In other words, the crowd can catch a trend and be correct, for a while. The stronger the trend, the more committed to it these folks become.

Rallies reach their peak when everyone is bullish, so who is left to buy? As my

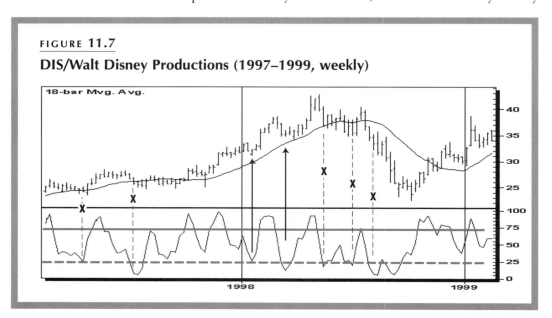

FIGURE 11.7

DIS/Walt Disney Productions (1997–1999, weekly)

colleague and fellow contributor to this volume Tom DeMark points out, "Markets don't bottom because buyers rush in; they bottom because there are no more sellers and top out when there are no more buyers." The sentiment index simply indicates this in an unemotional and mathematical format.

Keep in mind that this group of advisers can and will be correct in its market outlook at the midpoint. When the crowd becomes extraordinarily one-sided, however, and the index gives readings above 75 percent as potential sells or below 25 percent as potential buys, opportunity knocks.

Americans are brought up to believe that the majority is right—heck, they get to rule. This is a dangerous belief. If there are three of us and two of us decide to kill you, should we have that right? The majority, or mob rule, says yes.

The majority is not a priori wrong in its view; it is not a given it will be incorrect. But the evidence shows, and rather markedly so, the majority is more likely to be wrong than right at its extremes. Thus, sentiment traders have an advantage, a window of opportunity when their odds for success are increased. What more could a speculator want?

Even then, you should recognize that you may still be early. You most likely will need additional confirmation or a short-term entry technique to enter the trade. There are many entry techniques, but without the proper setup, such as the one the sentiment index provides, most are doomed to fail.

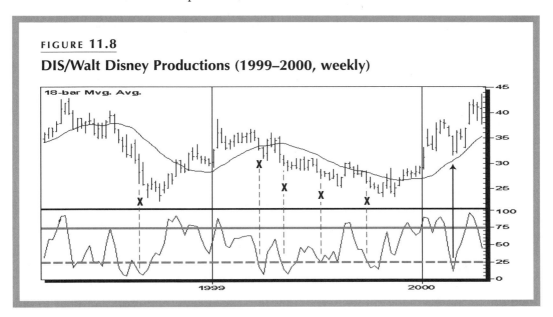

FIGURE 11.8

DIS/Walt Disney Productions (1999–2000, weekly)

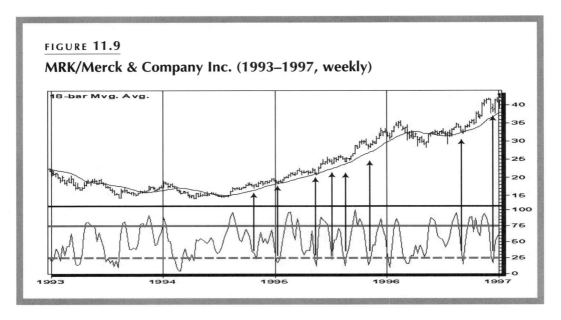

FIGURE **11.9**

MRK/Merck & Company Inc. (1993–1997, weekly)

Avoiding Pitfalls

How can you filter out some of the less desirable calls that the sentiment index makes?

As a long-term buyer of a stock I have noticed that the very best 25 percent buy signals come when the overall market trend is up. You can measure this in a most elementary way, by simply saying if the weekly closing price is above the eighteen-week moving average, the longer-term trend is up. If at the same time a sentiment index buy zone is reached, it will be a better bet to buy than if price is below the eighteen-week average of closing prices.

Let's begin the analysis with a weekly chart of Disney from 1997 into 1999. **Figures 11.7** and **11.8** mark off the instances when both conditions were met: The long-term trend was positive as the weekly close was above the eighteen-week average while the sentiment index was below 25 percent. The Xs indicate all the other signals. Notice how many of them there are! Some were good, some not so good, but pay particular attention to the signals when the two indicators were in sync. (Notice there were only three such signals from 1997 into 2000—the fewer trades the better.)

Keeping the above in mind, let's revisit Merck with a study of some charts that show only the buying indications when both indicators coincided. What a differ-

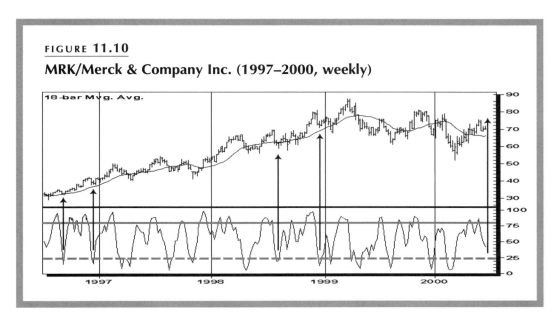

FIGURE 11.10

MRK/Merck & Company Inc. (1997–2000, weekly)

ence from Figure 11.3. **Figures 11.9** and **11.10** indicate far fewer trades, with virtually all of them making money if you exited the first time the index went above 75 percent!

Figures 11.11 and **11.12**, charts of Philip Morris, present plenty of opportunities to buy using the sentiment index. Many of these opportunities made money until 1999, when class action lawsuits brought prices tumbling. Note how none of the buy points would have been acted upon because the weekly close was below the eighteen-week average.

There are certainly other approaches an investor might choose to filter out the less than ideal points, but this one is not bad.

Short selling would be instigated with just the opposite rules, watching for the sentiment index to be above 75 percent while weekly closing prices are below the 18-bar average.

Doing What the Majority Is Not Doing

In the long run, stocks move up and down for "real" reasons, reasons linked to debt, earnings, insider buying, and the like. Those reasons really matter, as any long-term student of stock market history realizes. In fact, these fundamentals are among the best ways of isolating long-term position plays in equities.

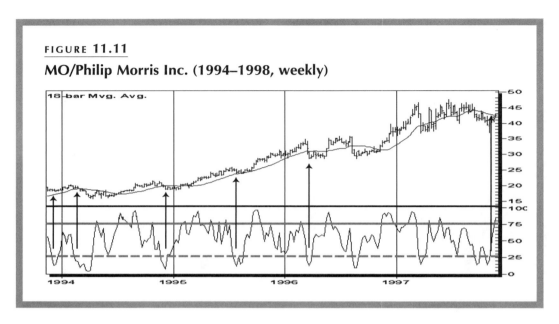

FIGURE 11.11

MO/Philip Morris Inc. (1994–1998, weekly)

On a short- or intermediate-term basis, however, prices fluctuate, sometimes wildly. Many of these gyrations are undoubtedly random and defy prediction. Yet the vast majority of these intermediate-term highs occur at the precise moment

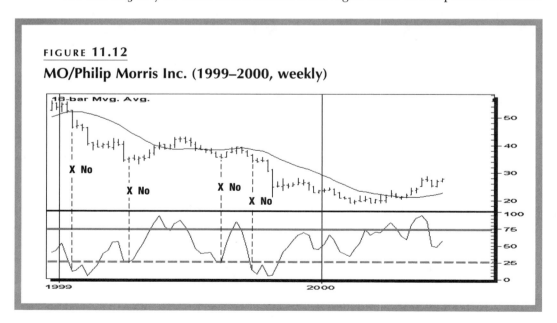

FIGURE 11.12

MO/Philip Morris Inc. (1999–2000, weekly)

the sentiment index indicates there are too many buyers.

Market lows are just the reverse. The majority of them are formed when there are too many people selling or advising others to sell, clear evidence that the market seems destined to prove the majority of people wrong the majority of the time.

An equally interesting point is that it does not seem to matter what a particular company does or does not do. What matters is that when too many of the crew get on one side of the boat, it is going to tip over. Just when the majority thinks it has figured out that the trend is up, it is destined to change.

Studying the fundamental underpinnings of companies to select long-term investments pays big dividends. But when it comes to timing your entry into these issues, you certainly want to be doing what the majority is not doing. Thanks to today's communications and Internet sites, it is possible to track and tabulate the mind-set of the many players in this game so that you do not get caught up in the peer pressures that make for market turning points.

CHAPTER 12

Controlling Risk with Money Management Techniques

COURTNEY SMITH

The most critical aspect of trading success is the mental state of the trader. Money and risk management, the subject of this chapter, is a close second. Actual entry and exit techniques, the subject of all the previous chapters, are a distant third.

It is almost impossible to make money trading without proper risk management. It does not matter how amazing your technical method or system is. The World's Most Amazing Trading System will fail without proper money management techniques.

Here is an absurd example to make the point. Let's say that you have a system that wins 75 percent of the time and that when you are wrong, you lose $1,000 and when you are right, you make a billion dollars. You start trading with a bankroll of $1,000. You make your first trade, and it is a loser—you're wiped out! You have completely blown the chance to make a billion dollars. You did not have a large enough bankroll to handle even a single loss and still have the ammunition to keep trading.

Of course, this is an absurd example, but it is not too far from the reality of most traders. Here is a more realistic example. Assume that you are going to bet on the flip of a coin and you will win $1 for every win and lose $1 for every loss. (In the real world, most profitable trading systems would win only 35 to 40 percent of the time but make roughly $2 for every $1 they lose.) You start out with $100. Further assume that you are going to flip the coin 1,000 times and then be finished with the game. What are the chances that you will be wiped out if you bet $25 per flip? Almost 100 percent! What if you bet only $10? Still almost 100 percent!

The problem is that you will have a string of losing trades at some time during the 1,000 flips. If you risk 25 percent of your bankroll on each bet, then all it takes is a net string of losers of only four to be wiped out. For example, assume that you lost, won, lost, lost, won, lost, lost, and lost. That's it! You are wiped out in only eight flips!

You are better off if you bet $10 each time instead of $25, but not by much. Now, you need a net loss of ten flips before you are bankrupt. The chances of having ten net losers sometime within 1,000 flips is almost 100 percent.

But what if you were to bet only $1? Now you need a net string of losers of 100 before you are wiped out. The chances of 100 net losers within 1,000 flips is less than 1 percent. In other words, the chances of being wiped out drop to less than 1 percent when you shift your bet size down to $1. The lesson of this example is critical: you can basically eliminate the chances of being wiped out by simply dropping the bet size.

Experts agree that 90 percent of futures traders lose money, 5 percent break even, and only 5 percent make money. Thus, simply changing the bet size to a very small number can shift a futures trader from being among the 90 percent who are losers to being among the 10 percent who at least break even.

It is impossible to make millions trading if you are wiped out. You have to make sure that you can continue to play the game if you are ever going to win. Many traders, however, get wiped out before they even have a chance to succeed. A little bad luck and they are back to their day jobs. It is imperative to remain in the game. What if you have a system that needs only a little tweaking to make it turn the corner? You need to live another day and have the capital to live through the inevitable drawdown. You need to make sure that you can play the game long enough to master the skills and information needed to become a profitable trader.

The Fixed Fractional Bet

The system that can keep you trading is called a *fixed fractional bet*. That is, every bet or trade risks a set percentage of the total bankroll. For example, assume that you are willing to bet 1 percent of your bankroll on every trade. You would bet $1,000 on each trade if you had $100,000 in your account or $200 if you had $20,000. (I tend to risk only 0.5 percent on each trade and rarely go over 1 percent. This makes me very conservative.) It is almost impossible for you to get wiped out.

The reason can be illustrated by Zeno's Paradox. Zeno was a Greek philosopher who "invented" the following paradox: Assume that you shoot an arrow at a wall. At some point, the arrow will be halfway to the wall. From that halfway point lies another point that is halfway from the first halfway point to the wall. Now, there lies another point halfway from this second halfway point to the wall.

And so on. There is an "infinite" number of points that are halfway to the wall from any point. Zeno asked the obvious question: how can the arrow ever hit the wall if there is always another point that is halfway to the wall?

The answer is best left to philosophers, but traders can use the basic premise. If you always risk a fixed percentage of your account, you will risk fewer dollars on each trade as you lose money. For example, say you have $100,000 in your account and you decide to risk 1 percent on each trade. Assume you lose on the first three trades. On the first trade, you will lose $1,000, leaving $99,000 in your account. That means that you can risk only $990 on the next trade because 1 percent of $99,000 is $990. If you lose, you can risk only $980.10 on the next trade because that is 1 percent of the $98,010 left in your account. You will be risking only $500 by the time there is only $50,000 in your account. Just like Zeno's Paradox, there appears to be an "infinite" number of times that you can risk 1 percent of your account.

Of course, the real world doesn't quite work that way. You will eventually run your account to a level that does not allow trading. Still, the fixed fractional system can keep you in the game for a very long time even with a monster losing streak. This means that you will be able to stay in the game, giving you a greater than fighting chance to win the game.

Place Your Stops, Then Apply the Rules

Suppose that you have $100,000 in your trading account and that you are willing to risk 1 percent on each trade. You spot a potential head-and-shoulders top in the bond market. You see that a breakdown below the neckline would catch you short, so you identify the ideal place to stop yourself out if you are wrong. It turns out that the ideal stop out point means risking $750 per contract. How many contracts should you put on?

The rule is that you are allowed to risk only 1 percent of your $100,000 on each trade. Thus, you are allowed to risk $1,000. That means that you can put on only one contract because you would be risking $1,500 if you entered into two short contracts.

No, you are not allowed to change the stop point so that you risk only $500 per contract. Identify the *ideal* stop point and then apply the money management rules, not the other way around. The money management rules are there to create self-discipline to prevent overtrading and to ensure trading longevity.

You are also not allowed to short another contract of the 10-year note, the

5-year, the 2-year, and some German bunds for good measure. The 1 percent risk applies to every position that would be highly correlated with the core position. You can short the bonds but not any other interest-rate futures contract. The total risk for the bonds plus everything else highly correlated can be no more than 1 percent of the account value.

Notice that means trading very few contracts, because so many contracts are correlated with other contracts. You must pick the best opportunity in each futures group. You must decide whether to buy the S&P 500, the Dow Jones Industrial Average, or Nasdaq futures—the rules do not allow you to buy all of them.

Start with Sufficient Capital

One of the potential problems with restricting your risk so much is that you need to have a large bankroll. It is hard to trade futures without risking at least $750 on each contract. That means that you must have $75,000 in your account to stick to the 1 percent rule. Many traders do not have that much money in their accounts. If you are one of them, get another job and save the money until you have at least $100,000 in your account. (Of course, nobody listens to this suggestion, but, frankly, it is the best solution to the problem.)

Otherwise, you must try other solutions. For example, start trading oats and hogs. These are small contracts whose risk can usually be reduced to less than $500 per contract. Another possible solution is to trade options or spreads. Both of these add another level of complexity to the analysis.

Money management rules can control the level of risk in the total portfolio. For example, while limiting the risk on any one position to 1 percent of the total account value, limit the risk on the whole portfolio to less than 5 percent, or perhaps even 3 percent. Therefore, you would lose 5 percent if every position was stopped out simultaneously. This means that you would be out only 5 percent of your total account value if every position were wiped out. Big deal.

Stay Cool

Discretionary traders (as opposed to systematic traders) should take off a few days when they have a particularly poor trading period. For example, suppose you get hit on the 5 percent rule mentioned above. Take a couple of days off work. Clear your head. Get back to being calm, cool, and collected. People are tremendously attracted to doing stupid things after losing a good chunk of money. You may be tempted to "double up to catch up" or to punish the market. Alternately, you may lose your confidence and flinch on the next trade. In either case, it is better to take off a couple of days and come back to the markets with your head screwed on straight. Your mental state is the most influential factor in creating investment profits. Do not take it lightly.

Here's another related rule. Make sure that you do not lose more than 10 percent in one month. If you do, simply shut down trading and take a longer vacation. You need to make sure that you do not have a catastrophic month. The 10 percent rule ensures that you will never have a disaster even if you are bleeding somewhat.

In fact, one of the key benefits of money management is that it prevents catastrophes. Most traders can handle the usual string of losses, but nobody can stand a catastrophe. You are out of business as a money manager if you lose 50 percent in one month. This author knows several professional traders who had exactly that happen to them. They were lucky that none of their investors sued them. They are all doing something else with their lives now.

You might be able to handle that kind of loss as a private investor, but it is unlikely. Besides, why put yourself in the situation where you have to find out?

Maintain Your Discipline

Notice how many risk management rules are really ways of dealing with the psychology of trading. This chapter began with the idea that the psychology of trading is the most important aspect of trading. Read any book or interview with a successful trader and they all highlight that the most important factor in trading success is to have the right psychology. Specifically, discipline is the key psychological trait that the trader needs to make money. Risk management rules are an effort at trying to enforce the necessary discipline.

Another interesting aspect of examining risk management is that it can turn poor systems into good systems! Consider, for example, the fact that there are many reasons that trading systems look bad during testing. One common problem is that a system has shown a few huge losses during the testing period. Here is how money management concepts can help.

Make a histogram of all of the losses with the left axis the size of the loss and the bottom axis the number of times that loss occurred. What you will often find is that most of the losses are rather moderate but that there are several whopping losses. Simply look at the histogram to see where you could put a dollar-based stop that would cut out most of the major losers but only account for a few trades.

For example, assume that you have 100 losses in your test. Assume that 95 of the losses are less than $1,000, which you can handle. However, there are five losses that are greater than $1,000, including a couple that are greater than $5,000.

Change the rules for exiting positions to either the signal of the system or $1,000, whichever shows the least loss. What you will find is that you will reduce the total losses by typically 20 to 40 percent. Once in a blue moon, a trade will show a big open loss only to turn around and move to a profit position. However, that outcome is so rare that this simple technique can turn many losing systems into profitable systems. In addition, it will likely significantly enhance nearly all systems.

Now, what is the bad news about money management? Not much.

First, you have to be much more disciplined in your trading. You have to do a little more work to figure out your risk on each position and the total portfolio risk. Frankly, this is no big task.

Second, your returns will likely go down, though this is not a given. Generally, traders with powerful risk management rules will not have years that put them in the top 10 percentile of traders in a given year. It is difficult to make 100 percent per year using the kinds of risk management rules outlined here. It takes a lot of risk to make a ton of money.

However, the risk-adjusted return (the return in a portfolio divided by the standard deviation of the monthly returns) will skyrocket. You will likely be producing lower returns but will dramatically lower risk.

Sharply controlling the risk in your portfolio can keep you in the game for a long time. Use the 1 Percent Rule to calculate how large your positions should be, use the 5 Percent Rule to control the total risk in your portfolio, and make sure that you have the right attitude to keep trading. If you follow these rules you will find a sharp increase in both your profits and your confidence.

Index

About Bloomberg

Bloomberg L.P., founded in 1981, is a global information services, news, and media company. Headquartered in New York, the company has nine sales offices, two data centers, and 85 news bureaus worldwide.

Bloomberg, serving customers in 126 countries around the world, holds a unique position within the financial services industry by providing an unparalleled range of features in a single package known as the BLOOMBERG PROFESSIONAL™ service. By addressing the demand for investment performance and efficiency through an exceptional combination of information, analytic, electronic trading, and Straight Through Processing tools, Bloomberg has built a worldwide customer base of corporations, issuers, financial intermediaries, and institutional investors.

BLOOMBERG NEWS℠, founded in 1990, provides stories and columns on business, general news, politics, and sports to leading newspapers and magazines throughout the world. BLOOMBERG TELEVISION®, a 24-hour business and financial news network, is produced and distributed globally in seven different languages. BLOOMBERG RADIO™ is an international radio network anchored by flagship station BLOOMBERG® WBBR 1130AM in New York.

In addition to the BLOOMBERG PRESS® line of books, Bloomberg publishes *BLOOMBERG® MARKETS, BLOOMBERG PERSONAL FINANCE*™, and *BLOOMBERG® WEALTH MANAGER.* To learn more about Bloomberg, call a sales representative at:

Frankfurt: 49-69-92041-200	São Paulo:.....................5511-3048-4500
Hong Kong: 85-2-2977-6600	Singapore: 65-212-1200
London: 44-20-7330-7500	Sydney: 61-2-9777-8601
New York: 1-212-318-2200	Tokyo:...........................81-3-3201-8950
San Francisco: 1-415-912-2980	

For in-depth market information and news, visit the Bloomberg website at **www.bloomberg.com,** which draws from the news and power of the BLOOMBERG PROFESSIONAL™ service and Bloomberg's host of media products to provide high-quality news and information in multiple languages on stocks, bonds, currencies, and commodities.